Study Guide

to accompany

LIPSEY ◆ PURVIS ◆ COURANT

MICROECONOMICS

Eighth Canadian Edition

E. Kenneth Grant
University of Guelph

William J. Furlong
University of Guelph

Richard G. Lipsey
Simon Fraser University

Study Guide to accompany Lipsey/Purvis/Courant MICROECONOMICS, Eighth Canadian Edition

Copyright © 1994   HarperCollins College Publishers

ISBN: 0-673-46982-4

94   95   96   97   98   9   8   7   6   5   4   3   2   1

Contents

To the Student

The content of this book tests and reinforces the student's understanding of the concepts and analytical techniques stressed in each chapter of *Microeconomics*, eighth Canadian edition, by Professors Lipsey, Purvis, and Courant. Our own teaching experience has led us to believe that students have the most trouble understanding technical information and applying theoretical concepts to particular situations. Consequently, most multiple-choice questions and exercises are technical and numerical in nature. We feel that policy issues and specific applications of theory to real-world examples are primarily the responsibility of the textbook. You will find excellent discussions of issues and applications in the body of the text, especially in the policy "boxes" that appear in each chapter.

Each chapter in this *Study Guide* corresponds to a text chapter and is divided into four basic sections. The *Learning Objectives* briefly summarize the important concepts and analysis covered in the textbook and Study Guide. It might be useful for you to compare this section with the summary section appearing at the end of each text chapter.

The *Hints and Tips* section lists some of the most common errors that our students make on mid-term and final examinations. Other instructors will undoubtedly have their own lists. It will be interesting for you to compare our list with yours after you have received your examination results. Good luck!

The *Multiple-Choice Questions* test your comprehension of definitions, analytical concepts, and numercial techniques. When you answer these, avoid the temptation to leap at the first answer that seems plausible. There is one best answer for each question. You should be able to explain why any other answer is not as satisfactory as the one you have chosen.

In some ways the greatest reinforcement to learning economics comes from doing the questions in the *Exercises* section. Some of our colleagues have indicated that students rarely attempt the questions in this section, since the format of many introductory economics examinations consists primarily of multiple-choice questions. We urge you *not* to make this mistake. These questions often require you to demonstrate numerically and/or graphically the sense of what has been expressed verbally. You may wish to review the mathematical exercises in Chapter 2 before attempting the questions in subsequent chapters. In addition, you are often asked to explain your method of analysis and your results. The ability to solve problems and to communicate and interpret results are important goals in an introductory economics course. We believe that the exercises will enhance your ability to do well on multiple-choice questions! Do not be discouraged if you have difficulties with certain questions. Those marked with an asterisk (*) are quite challenging for the beginner, and a full appreciation of the points involved can be achieved only after you have participated in lectures and have carefully read the text.

Unlike other study guides, answers are provided for all questions in this one. However, we caution that our answers are brief. Your instructors often require much fuller explanations on midterm and final examinations.

Acknowledgments

In revising this edition of the *Study Guide*, we have benefitted from comments of reviewers of previous editions: Peter Burrell (University of Windsor), Beverly Cook (University of New Brunswick), Geoffrey Hainsworth (University of British Columbia), Sunil Kaplash (University of Victoria), Susan Kamp (University of Alberta), K.T. MacKinnon (York University), Jamshid Shahidi (Kwantlen College), Larry Smith (University of Waterloo), Leon Sydor (University of Windsor), C.M. Waddell (University of New Brunswick), and Bruce Wilkinson (University of Alberta).

We also thank those individuals who assisted in preparing this revision: John Greenman of Harper Collins for editorial assistance; Don Irvine and Rob Froese for the artwork, Monique Roch for her computing and typing assistance, and Anastasia Lintner for her capable research assistance.

Finally, we dedicate this edition of the *Study Guide* to the memory of our former teacher and colleague, Douglas D. Purvis, who died suddenly in early 1993. We extend our deepest sympathy to his family and his colleagues at Queen's University.

E. Kenneth Grant

William J. Furlong

PART ONE

THE NATURE OF ECONOMICS

Chapter 1

Economics and Society

◆ LEARNING OBJECTIVES

After studying this chapter, you should be able to:

✔   understand the problem of scarcity and the need for choice;

✔   illustrate the relationship between scarcity, choice, and opportunity costs with a production possibility boundary;

✔   explain why growth in a country's productive capacity can be represented by an outward shift in its production possibility boundary and why unemployment of resources can be represented by points inside its production possibility boundary;

✔   contrast how economic decisions are coordinated and who owns productive resources in traditional, command, and market systems;

✔   appreciate that people's living standards are affected by the availability of jobs, the productivity of labor in those jobs, and the distribution of income produced by those jobs;

✔   summarize how the economic structure of the Canadian economy has changed over the past century and what role the growing globalization of the world economy has played in this evolution.

◆ HINTS AND TIPS

You might be guided by the fact that some of the most common errors on examinations are:

✔   forgetting that opportunity cost measures the cost of obtaining more units of one good by the loss of another;

1

✔ failing to recognize that all points on the production possibility boundary represent the full employment of existing resources and that its slope measures the opportunity cost of reallocating the existing supply of resources;

✔ confusing the underlying factors the cause movements along the boundary as contrasted with those that cause shifts in the boundary.

◆ MULTIPLE-CHOICE QUESTIONS

1. The fundamental problem of economics is, in short,
    (a) too many poor people.
    (b) finding jobs for all.
    (c) the scarcity of resources relative to wants.
    (d) constantly rising prices.
    (e) None of the above.

2. Scarcity is a problem that
    (a) more efficient production would eliminate.
    (b) is nonexistent in wealthy economies.
    (c) exists due to finite amounts of resources and unlimited human wants.
    (d) arises when productivity growth slows down.
    (e) exists in command economies but not market economies.

3. Which of the following is not an example of a factor of production?
    (a) a bulldozer.   (b) a mechanic.
    (c) a farm hand.   (d) a tractor.
    (e) a haircut.

4. If the factors of production available to an economy were unlimited
    (a) the opportunity cost of producing more cars would be zero.
    (b) the price of cars would be infinitely high.
    (c) there would be no unemployment.
    (d) scarcity would become the most serious economic problem.
    (e) all of the above.

5. Opportunity cost measures the
    (a) different opportunities for spending money.
    (b) the monetary cost of purchasing a commodity.
    (c) alternative means of producing output.
    (d) amount of one good forfeited to obtain a unit of another good.
    (e) market price of a good.

6. If a compact disc costs $10 and a cassette costs $5, then the opportunity cost of five CDs is
    (a) 50 cassettes.   (b) 10 cassettes.
    (c) 5 cassettes.   (d) 2 cassettes.
    (e) $25.

7.   Assuming the alternative is employment, the opportunity cost of a university education is
        (a)   tuition costs only.
        (b)   tuition and book costs only.
        (c)   the forgone salary only.
        (d)   tuition costs plus book costs plus the forgone salary.
        (e)   the direct costs of university such residence fees and books.

8.   If a 12-month membership in a fitness club costs as much as tickets for 24 Montreal
        Expos baseball games, the opportunity cost of a one-month membership in the fitness
        club is
        (a) $^1/_2$ baseball game.   (b)   1 baseball game.
        (c)   2 baseball games.   (d)   12 baseball games.
        (e)   24 baseball games.

9.   A downward-sloping production possibility boundary that is also a straight line implies
        (a)   constant opportunity costs.   (b)   zero opportunity costs.
        (c)   only one good is produced.   (d)   rising opportunity costs.
        (e)   None of the above.

Questions 10 to 13 refer to the following graph:

Figure 1-1

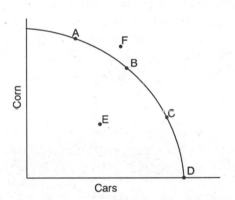

10.   If a market economy is operating at point A,
        (a)   resources are fully employed.
        (b)   there is considerable unemployment.
        (c)   the central planner values corn more than cars.
        (d)   car producers are losing money due to low sales.
        (e)   the opportunity cost of producing cars is zero.

11.   Point E represents a situation that
        (a)   is currently unattainable and can be expected to remain so.
        (b)   will be attainable only if there is economic growth.
        (c)   results from inefficient use of resources or failure to use all available resources.
        (d)   has a higher opportunity cost than points on the boundary itself.
        (e)   can never occur in a market economy.

3

12. With currently available resources, point *F* represents a situation that
    (a) results if resources are not fully employed.
    (b) can be achieved if consumers demand fewer cars than at point *C*.
    (c) is currently attainable.
    (d) can be achieved if all resources were allocated to the production of cars.
    (e) None of the above.

13. Assuming the initial situation is point *B*, which one of the following represents a reallocation of resources away from car production to corn production?
    (a) point *A*.   (b) point *C*.
    (c) point *E*.   (d) point *D*.
    (e) point *F*.

14. Which of the following causes an outward shift in the production possibility boundary?
    (a) A decrease in unemployment.
    (b) A loss in the productive capacity of agricultural acreage caused by a prolonged drought.
    (c) An increase in the productivity of all factors of production.
    (d) Shifting resources away from the production of corn to cars.
    (e) Any or all of the above.

15. Putting currently unemployed resources to work can be illustrated by
    (a) shifting the production possibility boundary outward.
    (b) a movement along a given production possibility boundary.
    (c) moving from a point on the boundary to a point outside it.
    (d) moving from a point inside the boundary to a point on it.
    (e) moving from a point on the boundary to a point inside it.

Questions 16 through 23 refer to the following production possibilities for combinations of corn and beef using a land tract of a given acreage.

Corn (bushels)	Beef (kilograms)
10,000	0
8,000	900
6,000	1,200
4,000	1,400
2,000	1,745
0	1,500

16. What would be the opportunity cost of producing 400 additional kilograms of beef if the current acreage were producing 8,000 bushels of corn and 500 kilograms of beef?
    (a) 500 bushels of corn.   (b) 400 kilograms of beef.
    (c) Zero.   (d) 900 kilograms of beef.
    (e) None of the above.

17. What would be the opportunity cost of producing 2,000 additional bushels of corn if the current acreage were producing 6,000 bushels of corn and 1,200 kilograms of beef?
    (a)   900 kilograms of beef.   (b)   1,200 kilograms of beef.
    (c)   300 kilograms of beef.   (d)   Zero.
    (e)   None of the above.

18. Which of the following combinations represent unattainable production levels with the current acreage?
    (a)   8,000 bushels of corn and 500 kilograms of beef.
    (b)   8,000 bushels of corn and 1,200 kilograms of beef.
    (c)   2,000 bushels of corn and 1,745 kilograms of beef.
    (d)   6,000 bushels of corn and 1,300 kilograms of beef.
    (e)   Both (b) and (d).

19. What is the opportunity cost of increasing beef from 1,475 kilograms to 1,500 kilograms?
    (a)   2,000 bushels of corn.   (b)   50 bushels of corn.
    (c)   25 kilograms of beef.   (d)   800 bushels of corn.
    (e)   None of the above.

20. The opportunity cost of increasing corn production from 4,000 to 6,000 is
    (a)   the same as the opportunity cost of increasing corn production from 8,000 to 10,000.
    (b)   the same as the opportunity cost of increasing corn production from 2,000 to 4,000.
    (c)   approximately equal to 0.1 kilograms of beef per additional bushel of corn.
    (d)   1,200 kilograms of beef.
    (e)   None of the above.

21. Which of the following events is likely to lead to an outward shift of the production possibility boundary?
    (a)   A reallocation of acreage such that corn production increases from 6,000 bushels to 8,000 bushels while beef production decreases from 1,200 kilograms to 900 kilograms.
    (b)   Some of the land is lost due to a flood.
    (c)   Twenty of the existing acres are not used for either beef or corn production.
    (d)   Corn prices fall relative to beef prices.
    (e)   None of the above.

22. The opportunity cost per additional bushel of corn is 3/20 kilograms of beef when
    (a)   corn production is increased from 8,000 to 10,000.
    (b)   corn production is increased from 6,000 to 8,000.
    (c)   corn production is increased from 4,000 to 6,000.
    (d)   beef production is decreased from 1,500 to 1,475 kilograms.
    (e)   All of the above.

23. Assuming that land is fully utilized and that corn production continually increases by 2,000 bushels, the opportunity costs in terms of beef production losses
    (a)   increase.   (b)   decrease.
    (c)   are zero.   (d)   remain constant.
    (e)   are undefined.

24. In a command economy, where to produce on the production possibility boundary is determined by
    (a)   the preferences of consumers, who spend their income accordingly.
    (b)   a central plan established by the government.
    (c)   traditional patterns of spending that change little from year to year.
    (d)   the preferences of workers, who vote to indicate their preferences.
    (e)   relative prices of goods.

25. Decisions on resource allocation are
    (a)   necessary only in centrally planned economies.
    (b)   made by central planners in traditional economies.
    (c)   necessary only in economies that are not industrialized.
    (d)   decentralized, but coordinated by the price system, in market economies.
    (e)   primarily determined by traditional customs in market economies.

26. A rising standard of living is most likely to occur in an economy
    (a)   that does not allow imports.
    (b)   that produces goods requiring skilled labor inputs.
    (c)   where output per worker is rising.
    (d)   that does not produce agricultural goods.
    (e)   where the labor-output ratio is rising.

27. The pattern of employment and production in the Canadian economy has changed considerably over the past century. As part of this evolution,
    (a)   the relative importance of agriculture has risen, due to a growing demand for food in foreign countries.
    (b)   the relative importance of services has risen, due to greater demand by consumers and by firms.
    (c)   less jobs were available in the early 1990s than in the early 1900s.
    (d)   the trend of labor productivity over the past century has been downward.
    (e)   Any or all of the above.

28. Using the *rule of 72*, which one of the following annual productivity rates will double output per worker in 12 years?
    (a)   8.6 percent.   (b)   6.0 percent.
    (c)   60 percent.   (d)   16.5 percent.
    (e)   84 percent.

29. Which of the following would *not* be a source of differences among alternative types of economic systems?
    (a)   Ownership of resources (private and public).
    (b)   The process for making economic decisions.

(c)   The need to determine what is to be produced and how to produce it.
(d)   The role that tradition plays in determining production and employment.
(e)   Both (a) and (c).

30.   Which of the following has *not* been an aspect of the globalization process?
(a)   The amount of international trade has decreased.
(b)   Increased international capital flows.
(c)   Corporations, called *transnationals*, now produce in many countries.
(d)   Domestic economies are more reliant on foreign markets.
(e)   Advances in communication networks and systems around the world.

◆ EXERCISES

1.   Four key economic problems are identified in Chapter 1:
(1)   What is produced and how? (resource allocation)
(2)   What is consumed and by whom? (distribution)
(3)   How much unemployment and inflation are there? (total employment and the price level)
(4)   How is productive capacity changing? (economic growth)

After each of the topics listed next, place the appropriate number indicating which type of problem applies. Use each classification only once.

(a)   Rises in oil prices during the 1970s induced a switch to alternative energy sources.
(b)   The standard of living in Canada, measured by real output per capita, has risen steadily over the past century.
(c)   Large harvests cause worldwide lower grain prices, helping consumers but hurting farmers.
(d)   The unemployment rate increased in the early 1990s.

2.   A certain economy produces only two consumer goods, X and Y. Only labor is required to produce both goods, and the economy's labor force is fixed at 100 workers. The table below indicates the amount of X and Y that can be produced daily with various quantities of labor.

Number of workers	Daily X production	Number of workers	Daily Y production
0	0	0	0
20	10.0	20	150
40	20.0	40	250
60	25.0	60	325
80	27.5	80	375
100	30.0	100	400

(a)   Draw the production possibility curve for this economy, using the grid on the next page. (*Hint*: The labor force must always be fully employed along the production possibility boundary.)

Figure 1-2

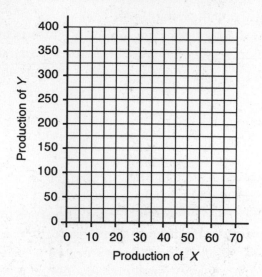

(b)   What is the opportunity cost of producing the first 10 units of good X? What is the opportunity cost of producing the next 10 units of X (i.e., from 10 to 20)? What happens to the opportunity cost of X as its production is continuously increased?

(c)   Suppose that actual production for a given period was 20 units of X and 250 units of Y. What can you infer from this information?

(d)   Suppose that a central planner in this economy were to call for an output combination of $X = 35$ and $Y = 150$. Is this plan attainable? Explain.

(e)   New technology is developed in X production, so that each worker can now produce double the daily amount of X indicated in the schedule. What happens to the production possibility curve? Draw the new curve on the graph. Can the planner's output combination in (d) now be met?

3. Junior gets a weekly allowance of $10. He spends all of his allowance on only two commodities: video games at the arcade and chocolate bars. Assume that the price of a video game is 50 cents and the price of a chocolate bar is $1.

    (a)   Plot Junior's weekly consumption possibilities.

Figure 1-3

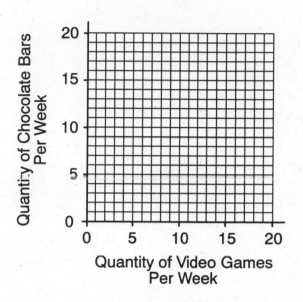

    (b)   Can Junior attain the following consumption combinations?
          (i)   15 video games and 2 chocolate bars
          (ii)   4 video games and 8 chocolate bars
          (iii)   7 video games and 7 chocolate bars
    (c)   What is the opportunity cost of Junior's first chocolate bar? his second? his third?

    (d)   By visual inspection of Junior's consumption possibility boundary, what could you say about his opportunity cost of consuming each of these commodities?

*4. An economy's production possibility boundary is given by the mathematical expression $20 = 4A + B$, where A is the quantity of good A and B is the quantity of good B.

    (a)   If all resources in the economy were allocated to producing good A, what is the maximum level of production for this good? What is the maximum level of production for good B?

    (b)   Suppose that the production of B is increased from 12 to 16 units and that the economy is producing at a point on the production possibility boundary. What is the opportunity cost per unit of good B? What is the opportunity cost per unit of good B if the production of this good was increased from 16 to 20?

9

(c)   In what way is this production possibility boundary different from that in exercise 2 in terms of opportunity costs?

(d)   In what way does the combination of four units of good *A* and five units of good *B* represent the problem of scarcity?

*5.   Consider the production possibilities for two totally dissimilar goods, such as apples and machine tools. Some resources are suitable for apple production and some for the production of machine tools. However, there is no possibility of shifting resources from one product to another. In this case, what does the production possibility boundary look like? Explain and show graphically.

◆ ANSWERS

Multiple-Choice Questions

1. (c) 2. (c) 3. (e) 4. (a) 5. (d) 6. (b) 7. (d) 8. (c) 9. (a) 10. (a) 11. (c) 12. (e) 13. (a) 14. (c)
15. (d) 16. (c) 17. (c) 18. (e) 19. (a) 20. (c) 21. (e) 22. (b) 23. (a) 24. (b) 25. (d) 26. (c)
27. (b) 28. (b) 29. (c) 30. (a)

Exercises

1.   (a) 1   (b) 4   (c) 2   (d) 3

2.   (a)

Figure 1-4

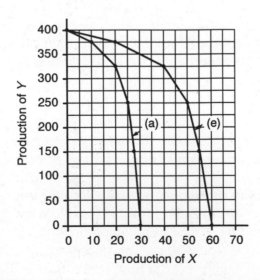

(b)   25 units of good *Y* (i.e., *Y* decreases from 400 to 375). 50 units of good *Y*. The opportunity cost of producing *X* is increasing—increasing *X* production by yet another 10 units from 20 to 30 would imply forgoing an additional 325 units of *Y*.

(c) This production combination lies inside the production possibility boundary, so some resources are unemployed or inefficiently used.

(d) This combination is outside the production possibility boundary and is therefore unattainable with current resources and technology.

(e) The production possibility boundary shifts to the right as graphed in (a). The planner's output combination is now attainable but is inside the new boundary, implying that if it were indeed achieved, the economy would be inefficiently using its resources.

3. (a)

Figure 1-5

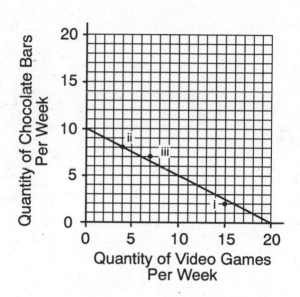

(b) (i) Yes, this combination lies inside his consumption possibility and is therefore affordable with $10.

(ii) Yes, this combination is on his consumption possibility boundary and therefore costs exactly $10.

(iii) No, this combination lies outside his consumption possibility boundary and therefore costs more than a $10 allowance permits.

(c) To purchase the first chocolate bar, Junior must pay $1, which could have been used to purchase two video games. Thus the opportunity cost of the first chocolate bar is two video games. The opportunity cost of the second and third bars is also two video games each.

(d) Since the consumption possibility boundary is linear (i.e., a straight line), the opportunity cost is constant.

*4. (a) If all resources were allocated to the production of good A, there is no production of good B. Hence, according to the mathematical expression, the maximum production of good A is five units. If all resources were used to produce good B, then $B = 20$ and the production of good A is zero.

(b) The increase from 12 to 16 requires a loss in production of good A of one (from two to one). An increase in B from 16 to 20 requires a loss in production of good A of one (from one to zero).

11

(c)   The opportunity cost is constant, whereas it was increasing for exercise 2.

(d)   According to the equation, four units of A and four units of B are possible. The combination of four units of A and five units of B is not feasible and indicates that more resources are required than are currently available.

*5.   When all resources suitable to apple production are employed, the resulting apple output is A'. When all resources suitable to machine tool production are employed, the resulting quantity of machine tools is M'. Since there is no possibility of shifting resources between these two outputs, the production possibility boundary is simply the point corresponding to the coordinates (A', M'). Any combination of apples and machine tools either inside or on the dashed lines implies unemployed or inefficiently used resources.

Figure 1-6

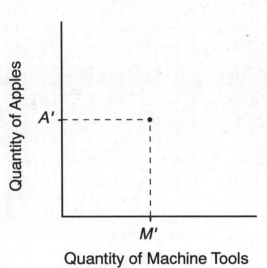

Quantity of Machine Tools

Chapter 2

Economics as a Social Science

◆ LEARNING OBJECTIVES

After studying this chapter, you should be able to:

✔ distinguish between positive and normative statements;

✔ explain how the "law" of large numbers allows successful predictions about group behavior;

✔ understand the roles of variables, assumptions, and predictions in developing and testing theories;

✔ distinguish between endogenous and exogenous variables;

✔ give an example of a functional relation;

✔ graph linear relationships and interpret graphs.

◆ HINTS AND TIPS

You might be guided by the fact that frequent errors on examinations are attributable to:

✔ confusion between endogenous (dependent) and exogenous (independent) variables, and;

✔ difficulty in reading graphs, and interpreting equations.

◆ MULTIPLE-CHOICE QUESTIONS

1. Normative statements
   (a) concern an individual's beliefs in what ought to be.
   (b) are based on value judgments.
   (c) cannot be subjected to empirical scrutiny.
   (d) cannot be deduced from positive statements.
   (e) All of the above.

2. "Capital punishment deters crime" is an example of a
   (a) positive statement.
   (b) value judgment.
   (c) normative statement.
   (d) analytic statement.
   (e) untestable statement.

3. "Capital punishment should be reintroduced in Canada" is an example of a
   (a) positive statement.
   (b) normative statement.
   (c) analytic statement.
   (d) testable hypothesis.
   (e) None of the above.

4. Which of the following is the best example of a positive statement?
   (a) Equal distribution of national income is a desirable goal for society.
   (b) Foreign ownership is undesirable for Canada and should therefore be eliminated.
   (c) Although free trade may cause some Canadians to lose their jobs, it will significantly increase the income of the average Canadian.
   (d) Taxes should be lowered.
   (e) Deficit reduction should be the government's priority.

5. Economic predictions are intended to
   (a) forecast the behavior of each consumer.
   (b) forecast the behavior of groups of individuals.
   (c) test normative statements.
   (d) anticipate the irrational behavior of certain odd individuals.
   (e) Both (b) and (c) are correct.

6. The "law" of large numbers basically says that
   (a) the greater the number of observations, the greater the sum of each variable.
   (b) measuring error increases with the number of observations.
   (c) a few observations are just as accurate as a large number of observations.
   (d) erratic behavior by individuals tends to offset itself in a large group.
   (e) the greater the number of observations, the greater is the potential for prediction errors.

7.	In measuring the area of a room, the "law" of large numbers implies that
	(a)	more people will make small errors than large ones.
	(b)	roughly the same number of people will understate the area as overstate it.
	(c)	the average error of all individuals is approximately zero.
	(d)	the more people taking the measurement, the smaller is the average error.
	(e)	All of the above.

8.	With respect to agriculture, weather is an example of
	(a)	an exogenous factor of production.
	(b)	an endogenous input.
	(c)	a dependent variable.
	(d)	an induced input variable.
	(e)	a positive statement.

9.	If the assumptions imposed in an economic theory are unrealistic, then the theory
	(a)	will always be refuted by the evidence.
	(b)	is incorrect and should be rejected.
	(c)	will not predict well and should be rejected.
	(d)	will require more complex statistical techniques for testing.
	(e)	may nonetheless predict better than any alternative theory.

10.	The role of assumptions in theory is to
	(a)	represent the world accurately.
	(b)	abstract from reality.
	(c)	avoid simplifications of the real world.
	(d)	ensure that the theory considers all features of reality, no matter how minor.
	(e)	None of the above.

11.	If annual per capita consumption expenditure decreases as average annual income decreases, these two variables are then said to be
	(a)	negatively related.
	(b)	positively related.
	(c)	randomly related.
	(d)	independent of each other.
	(e)	None of the above.

12.	Which of the following statements about economic theories is most appropriate?
	(a)	The most reliable test of a theory is the realism of its assumptions.
	(b)	The best kind of theory is worded so that it can pass any test to which it is applied.
	(c)	The most important thing about the scientific approach is that it uses mathematics and diagrams.
	(d)	We expect our theories to hold only with some margin of error.
	(e)	Economic theories are based upon normative statements, and can therefore never be refuted.

13. A theory may contain all *but* which of the following?
    (a) Predictions about behavior that are deduced from the assumptions.
    (b) A set of assumptions defining the conditions under which the theory is operative.
    (c) Hypotheses about how the world behaves.
    (d) One or more irrefutable normative statements.
    (e) Hypothesized relationships among variables.

14. A scientific prediction is a conditional statement because it
    (a) takes the form "if that occurs, then this will result."
    (b) is conditional on being correct.
    (c) is impossible to test.
    (d) is true in theory but not in practice.
    (e) is derived from normative statements.

15. Statistical analysis
    (a) is an exact science that eliminates all errors.
    (b) treats the errors in acceptance or rejection as exogenous.
    (c) can control the likelihood of making an erroneous decision.
    (d) cannot make predictions with data drawn at random.
    (e) All of the above.

16. Economic hypotheses are generally accepted only when
    (a) the evidence indicates that they are true with a high degree of probability.
    (b) they have been proved beyond a reasonable doubt.
    (c) they have been established with certainty.
    (d) the evidence supports the hypotheses in all cases.
    (e) Both (c) and (d) are correct.

Appendix Questions

The following multiple-choice questions are based on the material in the appendix to this chapter. Read the appendix before answering these questions.

17. The slope of a straight line is
    (a) always positive.
    (b) calculated by dividing the variable measured on the horizontal axis by that measured on the vertical axis.
    (c) zero.
    (d) constant.
    (e) increasing or decreasing, depending upon whether the slope is positive or negative, respectively.

18. The relationship between two variables on a scatter diagram
    (a) may be obscured by the movement of another variable.
    (b) cannot be significant because of errors of observation.
    (c) will show a wavelike pattern if the variables are related to time.
    (d) will usually be a straight line.
    (e) All of the above.

19. Suppose that a scatter diagram indicates that imports are, on average, positively related to national income over time. If in one year imports fall when national income increases, the observation
    (a) disproves the positive relationship between the two variables.
    (b) suggests that other factors also influence the quantity of imports.
    (c) proves a negative relationship between the two variables.
    (d) suggests that a measurement error has necessarily been made.
    (e) suggests that the two variables are independent of each other.

20. In statistical testing of a theory, choosing a random sample of observations is important because
    (a) it reduces the chance that the sample will be unrepresentative of the entire group.
    (b) it allows the calculation of the likelihood that the sample is unrepresentative of the whole group.
    (c) economic theories cannot be tested using scientific methods.
    (d) Both (a) and (b).
    (e) None of the above are correct.

21. The statement that the quantity produced of a commodity and its price are positively related is
    (a) an assumption economists usually make.
    (b) a testable hypothesis.
    (c) a normative statement.
    (d) not testable as currently worded.
    (e) a value judgement.

22. Which of the following equations is consistent with the hypothesis that federal income tax payments (T) are positively related to family income (Y) and negatively related to family size (F)?
    (a) $T = -733 + 0.19Y + 344F$.
    (b) $T = -733 - 0.19Y - 344F$.
    (c) $T = -733 + 0.19Y - 344F$.
    (d) $T = +733 - 0.19Y + 344F$.
    (e) None of the above.

23. Suppose that regression analysis estimates the following relationship between imports (IM) and national income (Y): $IM = 100 + 0.15Y$. This means that
    (a) imports are negatively related to national income.
    (b) when national income is zero, imports are zero.
    (c) imports are 15 percent of national income.
    (d) imports are 15 times greater than national income.
    (e) other things remaining constant, for every increase of $1 in national income, imports will rise by 15 cents.

Use the following graph to answer questions 24 to 26:

Figure 2-1

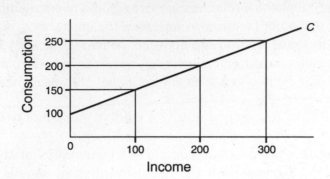

24. In the graph above, the slope of the line showing the relationship between consumption and income is
(a)   -2.   (b)   0.5.
(c)   2.   (d)   2.5.
(e)   150.

25. According to the graph above, when an individual has no income, consumption is
(a)   -200.   (b)   -100.
(c)   0.   (d)   100.
(e)   None of the above.

26. The line showing the relationship between consumption (C) and income (Y) can be represented mathematically as:
(a) $C = 0.5Y$.   (b) $C = 2Y$.
(c) $C = 100 + 0.5Y$.   (d) $C = 100 + 2Y$.
(e) $C = -100 + Y$.

◆ EXERCISES

1. After each phrase, write P or N to indicate whether a positive or a normative statement is being described.
(a)   A statement of fact that is actually wrong. _____
(b)   A value judgment. _____
(c)   A prediction that an event will happen. _____
(d)   A statement about what the author thinks ought to be. _____
(e)   A statement that can be tested by evidence. _____
(f)   A value judgment based on evidence known to be correct. _____
(g)   A hurricane forecast. _____

2. Are the italicized variables endogenous (N) or exogenous (X) in these statements?
(a)   *Market price and equilibrium quantity* of a commodity are determined by demand and supply. _____

18

(b)   The number of sailboats sold annually is a function of *national income*. _____

(c)   The *condition of forest ecosystems* can be affected by regional air pollutants. _____

(d)   The quantity of housing services purchased is determined by the *relative price of housing, income, and housing characteristics*. _____

(e)   Other things being equal, *consumer expenditures* are negatively related to interest rates. _____

Appendix Exercises

The following exercises are based on the material in the appendix to this chapter. Read the appendix before attempting these exercises.

3.   Given the relation between saving (*S*) and income (*Y*), $S = -100 + 0.10Y$, what is the amount of *S* for each of the indicated values of *Y*? Plot the relationship on the graph.

Figure 2-2

Y	S
0	___
500	___
1,000	___
1,500	___
2,000	___

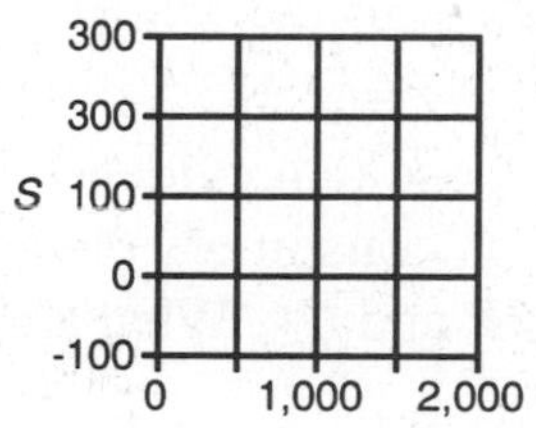

4.   Suppose that an economist hypothesizes that the annual quantity demanded of a specific manufacturer's personal computers (Q^D) is determined by the price of the computer (*P*) and the average income of consumers (*Y*). The specific functional relationship among these three variables is hypothesized to be the expression $Q^D = 1Y - 4P$.

(a)   Which of these variables are endogenous and which are exogenous?

(b)   What does the negative sign before the term 4*P* imply about the relationship between Q^D and *P*? What does the implicit positive sign before the term 1*Y* imply about the relationship between income and quantity demanded?

(c)   Suppose for the moment that average income equals $8,000. Write a simplified expression for the demand relationship.

(d)   Assuming that $Y = 8,000$, calculate the values of Q^D when $P = 0$, $P = \$500$, $P = \$1,000$, and $P = \$2,000$.

(e)   Plot the relationship between P and Q^D (assuming $Y = \$8,000$) on the graph. Indicate the intercept values on both axes.

Figure 2-3

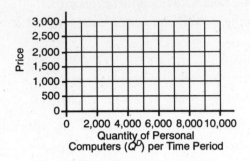

(f)   Assuming that $Y = \$8,000$, calculate the change in the quantity demanded when the price increases from $1,000 to $2,000. Do the same for a price increase from $500 to $2,000. Call the change in the quantity demanded ΔQ^D and the change in the price ΔP. Determine the ratio $\Delta Q^D/\Delta P$. Is this ratio constant?

(g)   Now suppose that evidence indicates that in subsequent time periods, the average income of consumers changes to $9,000 per month. Plot the new relationship between P and Q^D. What are the intercept values and the slope?

5.   The following exercise demonstrates how to obtain a solution to a system of equations diagrammatically. Suppose two variables are related by the following equations:

$$(1)\ N_1 = 5 + 0.5X$$

$$(2)\ N_2 = 55 - 0.5X$$

(a)   Complete the table using the N_1 column for equation 1 and the N_2 column for equation 2.

X	N_1	N_2	N_3
10			
20			
30			
40			
50			
60			

(b)   Plot the relationships between X and N_1 and N_2 in the graph provided below.

Figure 2-4

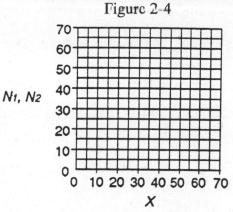

(i)   The linear curve relating variables X and N_1 has a (positive/negative) _____ slope of _____.

(ii)   The linear curve relating variables X and N_2 has a (positive/negative) _____ slope of _____.

(c)   These equations are said to be solved when $N_1 = N_2$— call this the solution value N. When does $N_1 = N_2$, and what are the corresponding values of N and X?

(d)   Assume that the constant term in equation 1 increases from 5 to 25. Complete column N_3 in (a), and plot the new relationship on the graph in (b). The curve in equation (1) has shifted _____. The slope is _____.

(e)   What is the new solution to this system of equations?

6.   The following exercise reviews the procedure for solving a system of simultaneous equations by algebraic methods. This approach is extremely useful in both micro and macro chapters of this Study Guide. It is an alternative to diagrammatic solutions that were reviewed above in question 5.

Consider two equations describing the relationships between two variables x and y

$$x_1 = a + by, \qquad (1)$$

$$x_2 = c - dy. \qquad (2)$$

where a, b, c and d are positive constants. The objective is to find values of x and y for which both equations are satisfied. First, note that there are two equations and three unknowns—the unknowns are the solution values to x_1, x_2 and y. Thus, if a unique solution exists, there is a missing equation. The missing equation to this system simply states that in the solution:

$$x_1 = x_2 \qquad (3)$$

The solution procedure requires elimination of unknowns and equations by means of substitution. Each substitution must reduce the system by both an unknown and an equation, until all that remains is a single unknown in a single equation.

(a)   Eliminate equation (1) and x_1 from the system. Count the remaining equations and unknowns.

(b)   Now eliminate equation (2) and x_2 from the system. Count the remaining equations and unknowns.

(c)   Solve for the solution value of y.

(d)   Use the solution value of y to obtain solution values for x_1 and x_2.

◆ ANSWERS

Multiple-Choice Questions

1. (e) 2. (a) 3. (b) 4. (c) 5. (b) 6. (d) 7. (e) 8. (a) 9. (e) 10. (b) 11. (b) 12. (d) 13. (d) 14. (a) 15. (c) 16. (a) 17. (d) 18. (a) 19. (b) 20. (d) 21. (b) 22. (c) 23. (e) 24. (b) 25. (d) 26. (c)

Exercises

1.   (a) P   (b) N   (c) P   (d) N   (e) P   (f) N   (g) P

2.   (a) N   (b) X   (c) N   (d) X   (e) N

3. S = -\$100; -\$50; 0; \$50; \$100

4.   (a) Q^D and P are determined in the market for personal computers; they are endogenous variables. Average income, which is determined in many other markets, is not influenced to any significant extent by the computer market; it is exogenous to the market for computers.

       (b) Q^D and P are negatively related; as P increases, Q^D falls. Q^D and Y are positively related; as Y increases, Q^D increases.

       (c)   The equation becomes $Q^D = 8,000 - 4P$.

       (d) Q^D = 8000; 6,000; 4,000; 0.

       (e)   The intercept on the P axis is 2,000, and the intercept on the Q^D axis is 8,000. Your plotting should also indicate that the demand curve is a straight line that slopes downward with a slope of -1/4.

       (f)   The change in quantity demanded is -4,000 when P increases from 1,000 to 2,000. When P increases from 500 to 2,000, quantity demanded falls by 6,000. In both cases the ratio $\Delta Q^D / \Delta P$ is equal to -4 (i.e., the inverse of the slope).

       (g)   The intercept on the P axis is \$2,250, and the intercept on the Q^D axis is 9,000. The slope remains -1/4.

5. (a)

X	N_1	N_2	N_3
10	10	50	30
20	15	45	35
30	20	40	40
40	25	35	45
50	30	30	50
60	35	25	55

(b)

Figure 2-5

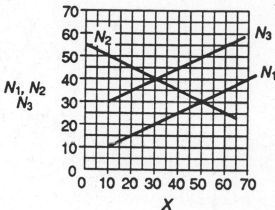

(i) positive; +1/2
(ii) negative; -1/2

(c) $N_1 = N_2$ when the two curves intersect. $N = 30$ and $X = 50$ solves this system of equations.

(d) leftward (or equivalently, upward); unchanged at +1/2.

(e) $N = 40$ and $X = 30$.

6. (a) Substitute equation (1) into equation (3) for x_1. This yields

$$a + by = x_2. \tag{3$'$}$$

There are two remaining equations, (2) and (3'), and two remaining unknowns, x_2 and y.

(b) Substitute equation (2) into (3') for x_2. This yields

$$a + by = c - dy. \tag{3$''$}$$

There is only one equation remaining (3') and only one unknown y.

(c) Rearranging terms in (3'') yields: $by + dy = c - a$, or equivalently, $(b + d)y = c - a$. Division by $(b + d)$ yields $y^* = (c - a)/(b + d)$ which is the solution value for y.

(d) Substitute y^* into equation (1), which yields

$$x_1^* = a + b(c - a)/(b + d)$$

which simplifies to $x_1 = (ad + bc)/(b + d)$. In view of equation (3), this is also the solution value to x_2^*.

23

Chapter 3

An Overview of the Market Economy

◆ LEARNING OBJECTIVES

After studying this chapter, you should be able to:

✔   understand how modern economies are based on the specialization and division of labor;

✔   explain how three kinds of economic decision-makers—households, firms, and government—interact in a market economy;

✔   explain the distinction between market and nonmarket sectors and between the private and public sectors;

✔   begin using economic reasoning to understand how the price system serves as a social control mechanism;

✔   explain the relationship between microeconomics and macroeconomics;

✔   understand the circular flow of income.

◆ HINTS AND TIPS

The following is a common source of confusion for many students:

✔   the distiction between injections and leakages in the circular flow of income.

◆ MULTIPLE-CHOICE QUESTIONS

1. In economics, the term market economy refers to
    (a) institutions such as the Toronto Stock Exchange.
    (b) a place where buyers and sellers gather on Saturday mornings.
    (c) a society where individuals specialize in productive activities and enter voluntary trades.
    (d) a society where most economic decisions are made by marketing analysts.
    (e) an economy in which advertising is central to the marketing of goods and services.

2. In a barter economy, individuals
    (a) haggle over the price of each and every commodity.
    (b) trade goods directly for other goods.
    (c) use money to lubricate the flow of trades.
    (d) must each be a "jack of all trades".
    (e) All of the above.

3. The introduction of production lines where individuals specialize in performing specific tasks is known as
    (a) the division of labor.
    (b) the specialization of labor.
    (c) the market economy.
    (d) the advent of labor as a factor of production.
    (e) lean production.

4. In a market economy, the allocation of resources is determined by
    (a) the government and its marketing boards.
    (b) the various stock exchanges in the country.
    (c) a central planning agency.
    (d) the millions of independent decisions made by individual consumers and firms.
    (e) the sobering discussions at the annual convention of the Canadian Economics Association.

5. The "invisible hand"
    (a) can only be seen by economists.
    (b) refers to excessive government taxation.
    (c) refers to a market economy's price system.
    (d) refers to the central planning agency of a command economy.
    (e) refers to hidden taxes.

6. Economic theory assumes that households
    (a) make consistent decisions as though each were comprised of a single individual.
    (b) seek to maximize profits.
    (c) are the principal buyers of the factors of production.
    (d) are comprised of a single individual.
    (e) are the sole buyers of goods and services in a market economy.

7. One reason for not assuming that governments behave in a consistent manner is that
   (a) different public officials have different objectives.
   (b) governments have become too big.
   (c) too many irresponsible policies have been introduced.
   (d) by offering higher salaries, the private sector has attracted most of the smart university graduates.
   (e) governments make too many separate decisions.

8. A central assumption in economic theory regarding firms is that they
   (a) are each owned by a single individual.
   (b) must be incorporated.
   (c) seek to maximize profits.
   (d) must all be making profits.
   (e) are the principal owners of the factors of production.

9. An example of a nonmarket activity is
   (a) volunteer coaching for Little League baseball.
   (b) government provision of weather reports.
   (c) police protection.
   (d) Big Sisters.
   (e) All of the above.

10. The distinction between the private sector and the public sector depends on whether the
    (a) product is sold or given away.
    (b) company is listed on a stock exchange.
    (c) organization is owned by individuals or the state.
    (d) financial statements of the organization are available for public scrutiny.
    (e) None of the above.

11. If households increase their desire to purchase fresh pasta, more resources will ultimately be allocated to the production of fresh pasta because
    (a) firms do not want dissatisfied consumers.
    (b) fresh pasta has good nutritional content.
    (c) the price of fresh pasta will be driven up and thereby permit profits to be made.
    (d) consumer organizations will inform pasta manufacturers of the change in demand.
    (e) regulatory agencies will inform pasta manufacturers of the change in demand.

12. If a hailstorm destroys a significant proportion of the Niagara Peninsula's peach crop, the average household in Ontario will desire to purchase fewer peaches because
    (a) of empathy for peach producers.
    (b) of altruistic concern that all households get their fair share of peaches.
    (c) the shortage will drive the price of peaches up.
    (d) peach purchases will be rationed by supermarkets.
    (e) the provincial government will ration consumption.

13. Macroeconomics is concerned with aggregate flows within the entire economy, whereas microeconomics might study how
    (a) price is determined in a single market.
    (b) resources are allocated across markets.
    (c) total employment in the automobile industry changes in response to government policies.
    (d) free trade affects production levels in the Canadian textile industry.
    (e) All of the above.

14. Macroeconomics involves the study of each of the following except:
    (a) total employment in the economy.
    (b) aggregate demand.
    (c) changes in the overall price level.
    (d) the national level of employment.
    (e) national consumption of oil.

15. Which of the following is a leakage from the circular flow of income?
    (a) Household savings.
    (b) Consumption expenditure.
    (c) Investment in plant and equipment.
    (d) National defense expenditure.
    (e) Export sales.

16. The two major types of markets in the circular flow of income are
    (a) public markets and private markets.
    (b) product markets and factor markets.
    (c) free markets and controlled markets.
    (d) markets for goods and markets for services.
    (e) regulated markets and "laissez faire" markets.

17. The circular flow of income refers to
    (a) the flow of goods and services from sellers to buyers.
    (b) the flow of money in and out of the banking system.
    (c) the flow of money incomes from buyers to sellers.
    (d) Both (a) and (c) are correct.
    (e) Both (b) and (c) are correct.

18. Which of the following is an injection into the circular flow of income:
    (a) government expenditure on highway construction.
    (b) government expenditures on recycling programs.
    (c) exports of goods produced in Canada.
    (d) investment expenditures on plant and equipment by firms.
    (e) All of the above are correct.

Questions 19 and 20 refer to the following data:

Purchases of goods and services by Canadian households   800
Savings   100

Government purchases	200
Investment	150
Imports	75
Taxes	225
Exports	50

19. According to the above data, total injections are
    (a) 1000.   (b) 1050.
    (c) 350   (d) 125.
    (e) 400.

20. According to the above, total leakages equal
    (a) 400.   (b) 300.
    (c) 125.   (d) 225.
    (e) 50.

21. The price system in a free market economy works in all but which of the following ways?
    (a) Price is a determinant of a firm's profits and therefore encourages or discourages production.
    (b) Prices signal to consumers how much they must sacrifice to obtain a commodity.
    (c) Prices indicate relative scarcities and costs of production.
    (d) Prices allocate resources equally among sectors of the economy.
    (e) Prices are a means of coordinating individual, decentralized decisions.

◆ EXERCISES

1. Indicate whether or not the following events would occur in a market economy with a shift in interest from snowmobiling to skiing. Explain each answer.

    (a) Initially, a shortage of ski equipment and a surplus of snowmobiles will develop.

    (b) Prices of snowmobiles will be increased to maintain profit levels.

    (c) Profits of ski equipment producers and retailers will rise; profits of snowmobile producers and dealers will tend to fall.

    (d) Central authorities will shift resources from production of snowmobiles to production of skis.

    (e) Production of skis will be expanded.

29

(f)   Resources will shift from production of snowmobiles to production of skis.

(g)   Resources particularly suited to producing snowmobiles will earn more, obtaining a greater relative share of national income.

2.   Indicate whether the following economic transactions are attributable (in Canada) to the market economy (M) or the nonmarket economy (NM) and to the private sector (PR) or the public sector (PU).
(a)   Provision of national defense. _____
(b)   Home repairs done by the homeowner. _____
(c)   The sale of fresh produce at the local farmers' market. _____
(d)   A government-operated toll bridge. _____
(e)   Tenants' rent payments to the landlord. _____
(f)   Albertan beef sales to the Soviet Union. _____
(g)   Municipal all-volunteer fire brigade. _____

3.   Classify the following transactions in the circular flow of income. Specifically, identify each as a household consumption expenditure, factor payment, injection, or leakage.
(a)   Government buys office equipment. _____
(b)   Households purchase automobiles. _____
(c)   Government receives business tax payments. _____
(d)   Firms borrow from banks for investment purposes. _____
(e)   Firms pay their workers. _____
(f)   Households deposit money with banks. _____
(g)   Governments purchase goods from firms. _____
(h)   Firms retain some profits and deposit these in banks. _____
(i)   Households pay butlers and maids. _____
(j)   Households pay income taxes. _____

4.   (a)   Through a biological quirk, the avocado, regardless of when or where the tree is planted, yields crops that are far greater in odd years of harvest than in even years. Under a market system, we would predict that the potential gluts in good crop years would result in _____ prices and that the potential shortages in poor crop years would lead to _____ prices.
(b)   In the period 1965-1977, the prices of avocados tended to increase more rapidly than the general price level. We would predict that this increase would result in _____ land and other resources being dedicated to avocado production.
(c)   In fact, avocado production more than doubled. The reasonable inference is that consumer demand had substantially _____.
(d)   Relative prices of avocados dropped significantly in 1978 and 1979 as compared with the previous poor and good crop years. What could this signal mean to growers and potential growers?

◆ ANSWERS

Multiple-Choice Questions

1. (c) 2. (b) 3. (a) 4. (d) 5. (c) 6. (a) 7. (a) 8. (c) 9. (e) 10. (c) 11. (c) 12. (c) 13. (e) 14. (e)
15. (a) 16. (b) 17. (d) 18. (e) 19. (e) 20. (a) 21. (d)

Exercises

1.   (a)   Likely to occur if shift takes place rapidly.

      (b)   No, lower prices are likely.
      (c)   Likely to occur.
      (d)   No, changing prices and profits will signal the shift automatically.
      (e)   Likely to occur as profits rise.
      (f)   Likely to occur as profits rise in skis and fall in snowmobiles.
      (g)   No, exactly the opposite will occur.

2.   (a)   NM, PU.   (b)   NM, PR.
      (c)   M, PR. (d)   M, PU.

      (e)   M, PR.   (f)   M, PR.
      (g)   NM, PU.

3.   (a)   injection.   (b)   consumption.
      (c)   leakage.   (d)   injection.
      (e)   factor payment.   (f)   leakage.
      (g)   injection.   (h)   leakage.
      (i)   factor payment.   (j)   leakage.

4.   (a)   Lower; higher.
      (b)   More.
      (c)   Increased (increased popularity in salads, in Mexican food, and greater familiarity with an unusual fruit could be reasons).
      (d)   To be wary of expanding output further; present and prospective profits have almost certainly been reduced.

PART TWO

A GENERAL VIEW OF THE PRICE SYSTEM

Chapter 4

Demand, Supply, and Price

◆ LEARNING OBJECTIVES

After studying this chapter, you should be able to:

✔ understand the concepts of quantity demanded, quantity supplied, and quantity exchanged;

✔ explain how demand schedules and demand curves show the relationship between quantity demanded and price;

✔ indicate what factors are most relevant in determining the demand for a good;

✔ explain how supply schedules and supply curves show the relationship between quantity supplied and price;

✔ indicate what factors are most relevant in determining the supply of a good;

✔ explain the difference between movements along a curve and shifts in the curve;

✔ use comparative static analysis to show how equilibrium price and quantity are affected by demand and supply shifts.

◆ HINTS AND TIPS

You might be guided by the fact that frequent errors on examinations are attributable to:

✔ a failure to distinguish changes in quantity demanded from changes in demand, and changes in quantity supplied from changes in supply;

✔ an incorrect determination of which curve (demand or supply) shifts in response to a change in an exogenous variable;

✔ confusion regarding response of the demand curve to changes in the price of substitutes and complements.

◆ MULTIPLE-CHOICE QUESTIONS

1. The term quantity demanded refers to the
    (a) amount of a good that consumers are willing to purchase at some price during some given time period.
    (b) amount of some good that consumers would purchase if they only had the income to afford it.
    (c) amount of a good that is actually purchased during a given time period.
    (d) minimum amount of a good that consumers require and demand for survival.
    (e) amount of a good that consumers are willing to purchase regardless of price.

2. An increase in quantity demanded refers to
    (a) rightward shifts in the demand curve only.
    (b) a movement up a demand curve.
    (c) a greater willingness to purchase at each price.
    (d) an increase in actual purchases.
    (e) a movement down a demand curve.

3. The demand curve and the demand schedule
    (a) each reflect the relationship between quantity demanded and price, *ceteris paribus*.
    (b) are both incomplete in that neither can incorporate the impact of changes in income or tastes.
    (c) are constructed on the assumption that price is held constant.
    (d) illustrate that in economic analysis, only two variables are taken into account at any one time.
    (e) characterize the relationship between price and actual purchases.

4. When the Multiple Listing Service (MLS) reports that in the month of April at an average selling price of $250,000, total sales of homes in Toronto were 2,000, they are referring to
    (a) quantity demanded.
    (b) quantity supplied.
    (c) equilibrium quantity.
    (d) actual purchases, which may or may not equal quantity demanded or quantity supplied.
    (e) Both (a) and (c) are correct.

5.   A decrease in the price of VCR's will result in
     (a)   an increase in demand for VCR's.
     (b)   a decrease in supply of VCR's.
     (c)   an increase in the quantity demanded of VCR's.
     (d)   a movement up along the demand curve for VCR's.
     (e)   a rightward shift in the demand curve for VCR's.

6.   An increase in demand means that
     (a)   consumers actually buy more of the good.
     (b)   at each price, consumers desire a greater quantity.
     (c)   consumers' tastes have necessarily changed.
     (d)   price has decreased.
     (e)   All of the above are correct.

7.   A decrease in the price of compact disc players will induce
     (a)   a leftward shift in the demand curve for record turntables (a substitute).
     (b)   an increase in demand for vinyl records.
     (c)   a rightward shift in the demand curve for compact discs (a complement).
     (d)   a rise in demand for compact disc players.
     (e)   Both (a) and (c) are correct.

8.   If goods A and B are complements, an increase in the price of good A will lead to
     (a)   an increase in the price of good B.
     (b)   a decrease in the quantity demanded of good B.
     (c)   a decrease in demand for good B.
     (d)   no change in demand for good B because A and B are not substitutes.
     (e)   a rightward shift in the demand for good B.

9.   Increased public awareness of the adverse health effects of smoking
     (a)   is a noneconomic event that cannot be incorporated into the demand and supply
           model.
     (b)   is characterized as a change in tastes that leads to a leftward shift in the demand
           curve for cigarettes.
     (c)   will lead to an eventual increase in the price of cigarettes due to shifts in the
           demand curve for cigarettes.
     (d)   induces a decrease in the supply of cigarettes.
     (e)   decreases the quantity demanded of cigarettes.

10. A change in demand could be caused by *all but which* one of the following?
     (a)   A decrease in average income.
     (b)   An increase in the price of a substitute good.
     (c)   A decrease in the cost of producing the good.
     (d)   An increase in population.
     (e)   A government program that redistributes income.

11. An increase in the supply of broccoli could be caused by *all but which* of the following?
    (a) An decrease in the price of broccoli.
    (b) A decrease in the price of labor employed in harvesting broccoli.
    (c) An improvement in pesticides, thereby decreasing the variability in broccoli output.
    (d) A change in the goals of producers.
    (e) An improvement in harvesting technology.

12. A movement along a supply curve could be caused by
    (a) an improvement in technology.
    (b) a change in the prices of inputs.
    (c) a shift in the demand curve.
    (d) a change in the objectives of producers.
    (e) an decrease in production costs.

13. Excess demand exists whenever
    (a) price exceeds the equilibrium price.
    (b) quantity supplied is greater than quantity demanded.
    (c) the equilibrium price is above the existing price.
    (d) there is downward pressure on price.
    (e) there is surplus production.

Questions 14 and 15 refer to the following diagram.

Figure 4-1

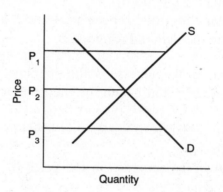

14. At a price of P_1,
    (a) there is upward pressure on price.
    (b) demand will rise to restore equilibrium.
    (c) quantity supplied is greater than quantity demanded.
    (d) the market has reached an equilibrium price.
    (e) a shortage exists.

15. When price equals P_3,
    (a) quantity exchanged equals quantity demanded.
    (b) there is excess supply.
    (c) there is a tendency for price to rise.
    (d) the market is in equilibrium.
    (e) a surplus exists.

16. The "laws of demand and supply" are
    (a) federal statutes and are therefore enforced by the RCMP.
    (b) enshrined in the Canadian Constitution.
    (c) irrefutable propositions concerning economic behavior.
    (d) basic assumptions in economic theory.
    (e) predictions of economic behavior that have tended to withstand much, but not all, empirical testing.

17. An increase in both equilibrium price and quantity is consistent with
    (a) an increase in supply.   (b) a decrease in supply.
    (c) a decrease in quantity supplied. (d) an increase in demand.
    (e) a decrease in demand.

18. Assuming a downward-sloping demand curve, an improvement in production technology for some good is predicted to lead to
    (a) a decrease in supply.
    (b) an increase in both equilibrium price and quantity.
    (c) a decrease in equilibrium price and an increase in equilibrium quantity.
    (d) a decrease in equilibrium price but no change in equilibrium quantity.
    (e) an increase in equilibrium price and a decrease in equilibrium quantity.

19. Should polyester leisure suits become fashionable, economic theory predicts
    (a) a decrease in the price of these suits but an increase in the quantity exchanged.
    (b) an increase in both equilibrium price and quantity.
    (c) a shift in the supply curve to the right.
    (d) an increase in equilibrium price and a decrease in equilibrium quantity.
    (e) a leftward shift of the demand curve.

20. Simultaneous increases in both demand and supply are predicted to result in
    (a) increases in both equilibrium price and quantity.
    (b) a higher equilibrium price but a smaller equilibrium quantity.
    (c) a lower equilibrium price but a larger equilibrium quantity.
    (d) a larger equilibrium quantity but no predictable change in price.
    (e) a higher price, but no predicable change in equilabrium quantity.

21. A decrease in input prices as well as a simultaneous decrease in the price of a good that is substitutable in consumption will lead to
    (a) a lower equilibrium price and a larger equilibrium quantity.
    (b) a lower equilibrium price but no change in equilibrium quantity.
    (c) a lower equilibrium price and an uncertain change in quantity.
    (d) a lower equilibrium price and a smaller equilibrium quantity.
    (e) an unpredictable change in both price and quantity.

22. Which of the following is *not* a potential cause of an increase in the price of housing?
    (a) Construction workers' wages increase with no offsetting increase in productivity.
    (b) Cheaper methods of prefabricating homes are developed.
    (c) An increase in population.
    (d) An increase in consumer incomes.
    (e) The price of land (an input) increases.

23. Comparative statics
    (a)   is the analysis of market equilibria under different sets of conditions.
    (b)   is the analysis of demand without reference to time.
    (c)   refers to constant equilibrium prices and quantities.
    (d)   describes the path by which equilibrium price changes.
    (e)   refers to disequilibrium prices and quantities.

24. Today the price of strawberries is 60 cents a quart, and raspberries are priced at 75 cents a quart. Yesterday strawberries were 80 cents and raspberries $1. Thus, for these two goods,
    (a)   the relative price of raspberries has fallen.
    (b)   the relative price of strawberries has fallen by 20 cents.
    (c)   the relative prices of both goods have fallen.
    (d)   relative prices have not changed.
    (e)   the relative price of strawberries has risen.

25. In price theory, which of the following represents a relative price increase for strawberries, assuming that the average price level rises by 10 percent?
    (a)   An increase in price from $1.00 to $1.05 per quart.
    (b)   An increase in price from $1.00 to $1.10 per quart.
    (c)   An increase in price from $1.00 to $1.15 per quart.
    (d)   Both (a) and (c) are correct.
    (e)   All of the above are correct.

Appendix Material

The following multiple choice questions are based upon the material in the appendix to this chapter. You should read the appendix before attempting these questions.

26. A single world price of oil is likely to exist if
    (a)   oil can be transported easily from one country to another.
    (b)   each country produces all of its domestic consumption.
    (c)   all governments restrict exports of oil.
    (d)   demand is the same in all countries.
    (e)   the cost of producing oil is the same in each country.

27. Canada is a major exporter of nickel because at the world price
    (a)   Canadian quantity demanded exceeds Canadian quantity supplied.
    (b)   Canadian quantity supplied exceeds Canadian quantity demanded.
    (c)   the quantity of nickel demanded by Canadians exceeds domestic production.
    (d)   Canada mines more nickel than any other country.
    (e)   domestic consumption and production are the same as they would be in the "no trade" equilibrium.

Use the following diagram to answer questions 28 and 29:

Figure 4-2

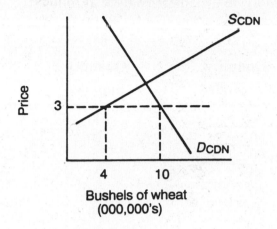

28. At a world price of $3, Canada will
    (a)   produce 4 million bushels of wheat.
    (b)   consume 10 million bushels of wheat.
    (c)   import 6 million bushels of wheat.
    (d)   consume more wheat than it produces.
    (e)   All of the above are correct.

29. If the world price remains at $3, while the Canadian demand for wheat increases, the primary result would be
    (a)   an increase in Canadian production of wheat.
    (b)   an increase in the price of wheat in Canada.
    (c)   a decrease in wheat exports.
    (d)   an increase in wheat imports.
    (e)   a decrease in quantity supplied by Canadian producers.

◆ EXERCISES

1. The demand and supply schedules for high-top, athletic pump shoes sold in the local mall (in pairs per month) are hypothesized to be as follows:

(1) Price	(2) Quantity Demanded	(3) Quantity Supplied	(4) Excess Demand (+) Excess Supply (-)
$120	40_____	130	_____
110	50_____	110	_____
100	60_____	90	_____
90	70_____	70	_____
80	80_____	50	_____
70	90_____	30	_____
60	100_____	10	_____

(a) Using the grid provided below, plot the demand and supply curves (approximately). Indicate the equilibrium levels of price and quantity.

Figure 4-3

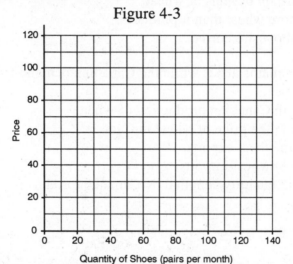

Quantity of Shoes (pairs per month)

(b) Fill in column 4 for values of excess demand and excess supply. What is the value of excess demand (supply) at equilibrium? _____

(c) Suppose there is a change in teenage fashion such that a substitute shoe, Doc Martens, becomes trendy. As a result, the quantity demanded of high-top, atheletic pump shoes at the local mall decreases by 30 units per month at each and every price. Fill-in the new quantity demanded in column (2) in the above schedule, and draw the new demand curve on the grid.

(d) Suppose that price initially remains at the level you reported in answer (b), explain the pressures that are exerted upon price by this change in tastes.

(e) After price has adjusted to the new equilibrium, what are the equilibrium price and quantity?

2. Read the description of certain events in the markets for selected commodities. Predict the economic impact of these events by drawing the appropriate shifts in the diagrams. Also, use + and - to indicate whether there will be an increase or decrease in demand (D), supply (S), equilibrium price (P), and equilibrium quantity (Q). If there is no change, use 0. If the change cannot be deduced with the information provided, use U for uncertain

Market	Event	Figure	D	S	P	Q
(a) Canadian wine	Early frost destroys a large percentage of the grape crop in British Columbia		—	—	—	—
(b) Wood-burning stoves	The price of heating oil and natural gas triples		—	—	—	—
(c) Videocassette recorders (VCR's)	Technological advances reduce the costs of producing VCR's		—	—	—	—
(d) Gold	Vast gold deposits are discovered in northern Ontario		—	—	—	—
(e) Fast foods	The public show greater concern over high sodium and cholesterol; also, there is an increase in the minimum wage		—	—	—	—
(f) Bicycles	There is increasing concern about physical fitness; also, the price of gasoline rises		—	—	—	—
(g) Beer	Population of drinking age increases: also, brewery unions negotiate a large increase in renumeration		—	—	—	—

43

3.   Suppose that student demand for on-campus concert tickets is as follows:

Price	Quantity Demanded
$6	8,000
8	5,000
10	2,500
12	1,500
14	1,000

Concert pricing policy is set by the Executive of the Students' Association which has decided that all seats will sell at the same price regardless of location or popularity of the performer (clearly, there are no economics majors on the Executive). Also, the only concert hall available on campus has a seating capacity of 5,000.

(a)   If the Executive sets a price of $10 per seat, is there an excess demand or supply of concert tickets?

(b)   What price would fill the concert hall without creating a shortage of seats?

(c)   Suppose the above demand schedule refers to an "average" concert, and when a particularly popular performer is booked the quantity of tickets demanded at each price doubles. What would be the equilibrium ticket price for a popular performer?

(d)   Do you think ticket scalping would be more profitable if price were set equal to, above or below equilibrium? Explain.

4.   The purpose of this question is to encourage you to obtain the market equilibrium by algebraically solving a system of simultaneous equations. You may refer to Chapter 2 of this Study Guide before attempting this exercise.

The demand and supply of widgets are given by

$$Q^D = 30 - 1.0P \text{, and}$$

$$Q^S = 1.0P \text{, respectively.}$$

(a)   Plot the demand and supply curves on the graph below, and label them D and S, respectively.

Figure 4-5

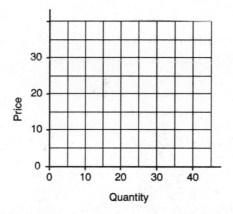

(b)   Determine the equilibrium price and the equilibrium quantity. Do this using two methods. First interpret the diagram. Then impose the equilibrium condition that

$$Q^D = Q^S$$

and solve algebraically.

(c)   Now suppose that the demand curve changes to

$$Q^D = 30 - 1.5P$$

but the supply curve is unchanged. Plot the new demand curve and label it D'. Before price adjusts from your answer in (b), is there excess demand or excess supply in the market? How much?

(d)   Once price responds to market pressures created by the change in demand, what will be the new levels of equilibrium price and quantity?

5.   The following question demonstrates how changes in exogenous variables impact upon market equilibrium.

The quantity demanded of gadgets (Q^D) depends on the price of gadgets (P) and average household income (Y) according to the following relationship:

$$Q^D = 30 - 10P + 0.001Y$$

The quantity of gadgets supplied (Q^S) is positively related to the price of gadgets and negatively related to W, the price of some input (e.g., labor) according to

$$Q^S = 5 + 5P - 2W$$

(a)   Assume initially that Y = $40,000 and W = $5. Substitute these values into the equations to obtain the demand and supply curves.

(b)   Now use the equilibrium condition $Q^D = Q^S$ to solve the demand and supply curves simultaneously for the equilibrium price.

(c)   Finally, substitute the equilibrium price into either the demand or supply curve to obtain the equilibrium quantity.

(d)   Graph the demand and supply curves for gadgets in (a), and label them D_0 and S_0, respectively. Confirm that your answers in (b) and (c) are correct.

Figure 4-6

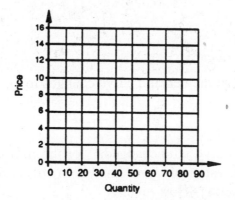

(e)   Suppose that average household income increases to $55,000 but W remains constant. What are the new levels of equilibrium price and quantity? Plot the new demand curve, label it D_1, and confirm your answer.

(f)   Now assume that the input price W increases to $12.50. Using the demand curve you derived in (e), determine the new levels of equilibrium price and quantity. Plot the new supply curve, label it S_1, and again confirm your answer.

*6.   The following diagram illustrates a hypothetical market for farm machinery in Canada.

Figure 4-7

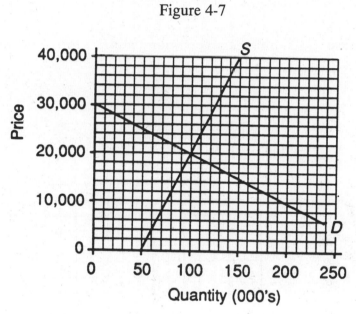

The federal government has decided that output in this industry should increase by 50 percent. Since current industry output is 100,000 units, it therefore plans to purchase 50,000 units of farm machinery *regardless of price*. The government intends to give away these units to third-world countries as part of Canada's foreign aid.

(a)   Draw the new demand curve for farm machinery that takes into account government demand. What are the new levels of equilibrium price and quantity?

(b)   By how much does industry output increase in percentage terms? Why does this increase fall short of the government's target of 50 percent?

47

(c) How many units would the government have to purchase in order to satisfy its objective of increasing industry output to 150,000 units? What is the associated quantity demanded by the private sector (i.e., by nongovernment consumers in Canada)?

◆ ANSWERS

Multiple-Choice Questions

1. (a) 2. (e) 3. (a) 4. (d) 5. (c) 6. (b) 7. (e) 8. (c) 9. (b) 10. (c) 11. (a) 12. (c) 13. (c) 14. (c) 15. (c) 16. (e) 17. (d) 18. (c) 19. (b) 20. (d) 21. (c) 22. (b) 23. (a) 24. (d) 25. (c) 26. (a) 27. (b) 28. (e) 29. (d)

Exercises

1.   (a)

Figure 4-8

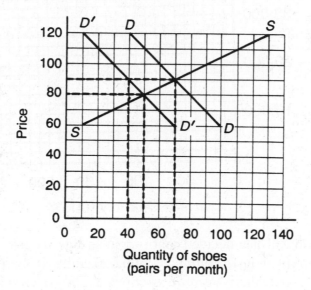

Equilibrium price and quantity are $90 and 70 pairs per month, respectively.

(b)

Price	Excess demand (+) or excess supply (−)
$120	−90
110	−60
100	−30
90	0
80	+30
70	+60
60	+90

48

There is no excess demand or supply.

(c)   See above diagram.

(d)   With the change in tastes (i.e., along D') quantity demanded at the original price of $90 is now 40 units per month while quantity supplied remains at 70 units. Thus, 30 units remain unsold each month; this accumulating inventory exerts downward pressure on price.

(e)   The new equilibrium obtains at a price of $80 and quantity of 50 units per month.

2.

	D	S	P	Q
(a)	0	-	+	-
(b)	+	0	+	+
(c)	0	+	-	+
(d)	0	+	-	+
(e)	-	-	U	-
(f)	+	0	+	+
(g)	+	-	+	U

3.   (a)   Excess supply of 2,500 seats.

(b)   At $8, quantity demanded and quantity supplied each equal 5,000 seats.

(c)   Since quantity demanded doubles at every price, 5,000 tickets would be demanded if price were $10.

(d)   Scalpers would do better if price were set below equilibrium which creates excess demand. For example, at a price of $6, the quantity demanded for an "average" concert is 8,000 but only 5,000 are sold. Thus, scalpers who are fortunate to purchase at $6 have a better chance of finding a buyer who is willing to pay more than $6.

4.   (a)

Figure 4-9

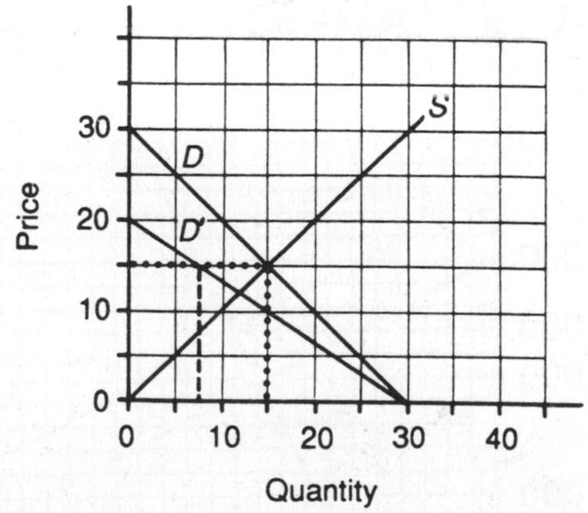

(b) $Q^D = Q^S$ is equivalent to: $30 - 1.0P = 1.0P$ which solves for $P = \$15$. Now substitute the equilibrium price into the equation for either Q^D or Q^S, and obtain the equilibrium quantity $Q = 15$. (e.g., $Q^S = 1.0(15) = 15$).

(c)   When price is $15, $Q^S = 15$ and $Q^D = 7.5$; thus there is excess supply of 7.5 units.

(d)   The new equilibrium obtains at the intersection of D' and S where $P = \$12$ (i.e., $30 - 1.5P = 1.0P$), and $Q = 12$.

5. (a) $Q^D = 30 - 10P + 0.001(40,000) = 70 - 10P$.
   $Q^S = 5 + 5P - 2(5) = -5 + 5P$.

   (b) For equilibrium, $Q^D = Q^S$, so that

   $$70 - 10P = -5 + 5P$$

   which solves for the equilibrium price of $5.

   (c) Substituting this value into either Q^D or Q^S, one obtains the equilibrium quantity of 20 units.

   (d)

Figure 4-10

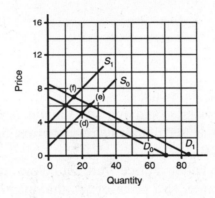

   (e) Now $Q^D = 85 - 10P$. Setting $Q^D = Q^S$, or $85 - 10P = -5 + 5P$ yields $P = \$6$ and $Q = 25$.

   (f) Now $Q^S = -20 + 5P$ and $Q^D = 85 - 10P$, so that $Q^D = Q^S$ solves for $P = \$7$ and $Q = 15$.

*6. (a)

Figure 4-11

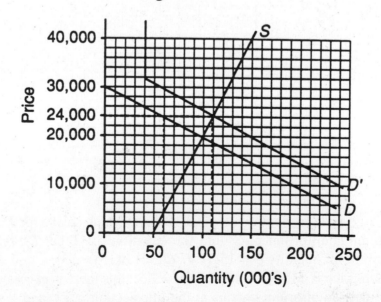

The equilibrium price is $24,000, and the equilibrium quantity is 110,000 units.

50

(b)   Industry output increases from 100,000 to 110,000 units, or by 10 percent. The additional demand of 50,000 units created by the government exerts upward pressure on the price of farm machinery and thereby decreases the quantity demanded by the private or nongovernment sector of the economy. These private-sector consumers reduce their purchases from 100,000 to 60,000 units.

(c)   The government would have to purchase all 150,000 units, which would be supplied only when the price reached $40,000. The quantity demanded by the private sector is reduced to zero when the price reaches $30,000.

Chapter 5

Elasticity and Market Adjustment

◆ LEARNING OBJECTIVES

After studying this chapter, you should be able to:

✔   understand elasticity of demand and elasticity of supply and how they are measured;

✔   explain the significance of elastic and inelastic demand and supply;

✔   identify what factors determine whether demand or supply is elastic or inelastic;

✔   understand the relationship between elasticity of demand and total expenditure (total revenue);

✔   explain the meanings of income and cross elasticities of demand;

✔   appreciate the distinction between arc and point elasticity.

◆ HINTS AND TIPS

You might be guided by the fact that frequent errors on examinations are attributable to:

✔   confusion among the several alternative ways of writing the same formula for elasticity;

✔   students' failure to understand that the relationship (positive or negative) between price and total revenue depends upon the strength of the elasticity of demand;

✔   students' lack of appreciation that although a linear demand curve has a constant slope, it does not have a constant elasticity, and;

✔   confusion between slope and elasticity.

◆ MULTIPLE-CHOICE QUESTIONS

1. The price elasticity of demand refers to a measure that shows the
    (a) responsiveness of quantity demanded of a good to changes in its price.
    (b) variation in prices due to a change in demand.
    (c) size of price changes caused by a shift in demand.
    (d) degree of substitutability across commodities.
    (e) magnitude of the shifts in a demand curve.

2. The price elasticity of demand is measured by the
    (a) change in quantity demanded divided by the change in price.
    (b) change in price divided by the change in quantity demanded.
    (c) slope of the demand curve.
    (d) percentage change in quantity demanded divided by the percentage change in price.
    (e) average quantity demanded divided by the average price.

3. If the price elasticity of demand for a good is 2 and price increases by 2 percent, the quantity demanded
    (a) decreases by 4 percent.   (b) decreases by 1 percent.
    (c) decreases by 2 percent.   (d) does not change.
    (e) is indeterminable with data provided.

4. If the percentage change in price is greater than the percentage change in quantity demanded, demand
    (a) is elastic.   (b) is inelastic.
    (c) is unit-elastic.   (d) shifts outward to the left.
    (e) shifts to the right.

Questions 5 through 8 refer to these figures.

Figure 5-1

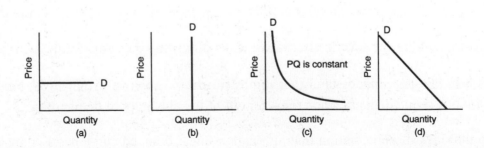

54

5. The demand curve with an elasticity of zero is
   (a)   a.   (b)   b.
   (c)   c.   (d)   d.
   (e)   None of the above.

6. The demand curve with an elasticity of unity is
   (a)   a.   (b)   b.
   (c)   c.   (d)   d.
   (e)   None of the above.

7. The demand curve with an elasticity of infinity is
   (a)   a.   (b)   b.
   (c)   c.   (d)   d.
   (e)   None of the above.

8. The demand curve with an elasticity that is variable is
   (a)   a.   (b)   b.
   (c)   c.   (d)   d.
   (e)   Both (c) and (d).

9. An increase in the price of a good and a decrease in total expenditure on this good are associated with
   (a)   inferior goods.   (b)   substitute goods.
   (c)   normal goods.   (d)   elastic demand.
   (e)   inelastic demand.

10. The price elasticity of demand for snowmobiles is estimated to be 1.2; thus an increase in price
   (a)   always decreases quantity demanded by 12 percent.
   (b)   always decreases quantity demanded by 1.2 percent.
   (c)   increases total expenditure.
   (d)   decreases total expenditure.
   (e)   decreases total expenditure by 1.2 percent.

11. If the demand for some commodity has an elasticity of unity, a decrease in price
   (a)   causes a 1 percent decrease in quantity demanded.
   (b)   induces no change in quantity demanded.
   (c)   results in no change in total expenditure.
   (d)   is matched by a unit increase in quantity demanded.
   (e)   Both (a) and (c) are correct.

12. The price elasticity of demand for a good will be greater
    (a)   the less available are suitable substitutes for this good.
    (b)   the longer the time period considered.
    (c)   for a group of related goods as opposed to an element of that group.
    (d)   the greater is income.
    (e)   All of the above are correct.

13. If a ten percent increase in the price of ski lift tickets causes a five percent decrease in total revenue of lift operations, then demand is
    (a)   elastic.   (b)   inelastic.
    (c)   perfectly inelastic.   (d)   normal.
    (e)   inferior.

Questions 14 to 16 refer to the following schedule. (Consult Box 5-1 in the text for the precise calculation of elasticity. Use average prices and quantities in your calculations.)

Price per Unit	Quantity Offered for Sale
$10	400
8	350
6	300
4	200
2	50

14. As price increases from $4 to $6, the elasticity of supply is
    (a)   1.0.   (b)   50.
    (c)   0.5.   (d)   5.0.
    (e)   2.0.

15. As price rises from $6 to $10 per unit, the supply response is
    (a)   elastic.   (b)   of unit elasticity.
    (c)   of zero elasticity.   (d)   inelastic.
    (e)   infinitely elastic.

16. The supply curve implied by the schedule is
    (a)   elastic for all price ranges.
    (b)   inelastic for all price ranges.
    (c)   of zero elasticity for all price ranges.
    (d)   of variable elasticity, depending on the initial price chosen.
    (e)   of constant elasticity.

17. Which of the following pairs of commodities is likely to have a cross-elasticity of demand that is positive?
    (a)   Hockey sticks and pucks.   (b)   Bread and cheese.
    (c)   Cassettes and compact discs.   (d)   Perfume and garden hoses.
    (e)   Hamburgers and French fries.

18. Margarine and butter are predicted to have
    (a)   the same income elasticities of demand.
    (b)   very low price elasticities of demand.
    (c)   negative cross-elasticities of demand with respect to each other.
    (d)   positive cross-elasticities of demand with respect to each other.
    (e)   elastic demands with respect to price.

19. Inferior commodities have
    (a)   zero income elasticities of demand.
    (b)   negative cross-elasticities of demand.
    (c)   negative elasticities of supply.
    (d)   highly elastic demands.
    (e)   negative income elasticities of demand.

20. Which of the following goods is more likely to have an income elasticity of demand that is less than one?
    (a)   Hamburger meat.   (b)   Microwave ovens.
    (c)   Perfume.   (d)   Winter vacations.
    (e)   Sailboats.

21. Which of the following commodities is more likely to have an elastic demand?
    (a)   Toothpicks.   (b)   Cigarettes.
    (c)   Heart pacemakers.   (d)   Broccoli.
    (e)   Vegetables.

22. A perfectly inelastic demand curve means that
    (a)   a percentage decrease in price exactly increases quantity demanded by the same percentage.
    (b)   an increase in price reduces quantity demanded.
    (c)   the price elasticity of demand is infinity.
    (d)   any change in price is perfectly matched by a change in quantity demanded.
    (e)   quantity demanded does not change in response to any price change.

23. A decrease in income by 10 percent leads to a decrease in quantity demanded by 5 percent; the income elasticity of demand is therefore
    (a)   -0.5.   (b)   2.0.
    (c)   0.5.   (d)   50.0.
    (e)   15.0.

24. A commodity is classified as a normal good if
    (a)   a decrease in consumer income results in a decrease in demand.
    (b)   it is consumed by a majority of the population.
    (c)   its price and quantity demanded are negatively related, *ceteris paribus*.
    (d)   an increase in its price leads to an increase in quantity supplied.
    (e)   a decrease in consumer income results in an increase in demand.

25. Suppose that the short-run demand for a good is relatively more inelastic than its long-run demand. A given rightward shift in the supply curve will lead to a
    (a)   smaller decrease in price in the long-run than in the short-run.
    (b)   smaller increase in quantity in the long-run than in the short-run.
    (c)   larger decrease in price in the long-run than in the short-run.
    (d)   smaller decrease in both price and quantity in the long-run than in the short-run.
    (e)   larger decreases in both price and quantity in the long-run than in the short-run.

26. If an individual allocates $200 for his monthly expenditure on compact discs and decides to spend no more and no less regardless of price, this individual's demand for compact discs is
    (a)   perfectly inelastic.   (b)   perfectly elastic.
    (c)   of unit elasticity.   (d)   less than one but greater than zero.
    (e)   of zero elasticity.

27. A shift in demand would not affect price when supply is
    (a)   perfectly inelastic.   (b)   perfectly elastic.
    (c)   of unit elasticity.   (d)   a straight line through the origin.
    (e)   of zero elasticity.

◆ EXERCISES

1. In each of the following scenarios, categorize the price elasticity of demand as *elastic*, *inelastic*, or *unit-elastic*. Where calculations are required, use average price and quantity. Note that categorization may not always be possible with the information provided.
    (a)   The price of personal computers falls from $2,750 to $2,250, and the quantity demanded increases from 40,000 units to 60,000 units.

    (b)   Canada Post increases the price of a stamp from 48 cents to 50 cents, but its total revenue remains the same.

    (c)   The price of matchbooks doubles from 1 cent to 2 cents, but the quantity purchased does not change.

(d)   An increase in the demand for blue jeans causes the price to increase from $45 to $55 and the amount purchased to increase from 1 million to 1.1 million.

(e)   A sudden decline in the supply of avocados leads to an increase in price by 10 percent and a concomitant reduction in quantity demanded by 20,000 units from the original level of 90,000 units.

(f)   A 5 percent decrease in the price of gasoline results in a decrease in total revenue of 5 percent.

(g)   An increase in consumer income results in a 15 percent decrease in price as well as a 15 percent drop in purchases.

2.   Two alternative demand curves are depicted in the upper panels of the following diagrams.

Figure 5-2

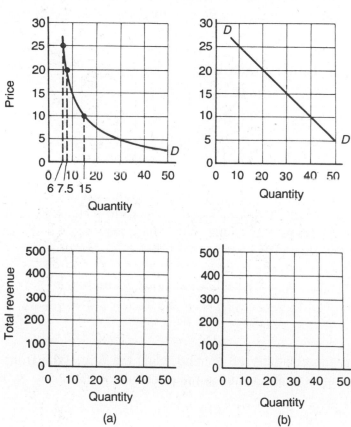

(a)   (b)

(a)   Calculate the total revenue associated with each demand curve at the following prices: $25, $20, $15, $10, and $5. Graph the respective total revenue curves on the lower panels.

(b)   By inspection of these total revenue curves, what can you say about the price elasticity of demand along each of the demand curves?

3.   Fill in the following table:

	Price elasticity	Change in price	Change in total revenue (up, down, none)
(a)	2.0	up	_____
(b)	1.0	down	_____
(c)	___	up	none
(d)	0.0	down	_____
(e)	0.6	_____	up

4.   Calculate the numerical values of price elasticity along the following demand curve. Use the four price-quantity segments indicated by the dots on the demand curve.

Figure 5-3

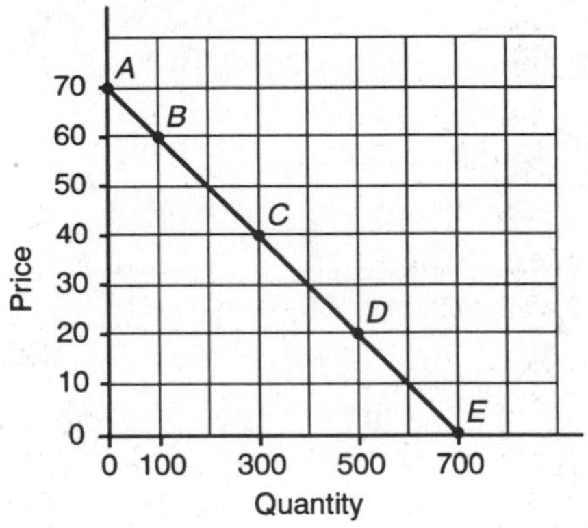

(a)   Confirm that elasticity declines as price decreases.

(b)   What is the elasticity of demand when the price falls from $40 to $30? What is happening to total revenue as the price falls further?

*5.   Suppose that you are hired as a consultant for the Guelph Transportation Commission. Its statisticians inform you that at the current fare of $1.30, the system carries 20,000 riders per day. They also indicate that for each $0.05 increase (decrease) in the fare, ridership decreases (increases) by 1,000 passengers.

(a)   What is the arc price elasticity of demand at the current fare? (*Hint:* Consider a change in fare from 5 cents below the current fare to 5 cents above.)

(b)   To consider raising total revenue for the transit system, the Guelph Transportation Commission has hired you to determine by how much it should increase the fare. What do you advise? Why?

(c)   What fare will maximize total revenue for the transit system? What is the associated ridership?

6.   The Honourable Mr. D. Runken, MP from the riding of Temperance, Ontario has introduced a private member's bill in Parliament that will increase taxes on all alchoholic beverages. He has argued this represents good social policy because it will reduce consumption of liquor, thereby increasing the amount of income families of alchoholics would have available to spend on items such as food and health care. Comment on Mr. Runken's reasoning using the concept of elasticity.

7.   (a)   If the price of wheat falls 10 percent and farmers produce 15 percent less, what is the elasticity of supply for wheat?

(b)   Suppose the government's goal is to raise wheat production by 30 percent to help fight famine. Based upon the elasticity calculated above, by what percentage must price increase to reach this goal?

(c)   If the price of wheat falls by 5 percent, by what percentage will wheat production decline, given the elasticity you calculated above?

*8. The table provides data on income and demand for goods x and y.

Period	Income	P_x	Q_{Dx}	P_y	Q_{Dy}
(1)	$10,000	$25	10	$10	42
(2)	10,000	28	9	10	40
(3)	10,000	28	8	15	35
(4)	11,000	28	9	15	36
(5)	11,500	34	7	20	32

(a) Why should no elasticities be calculated between periods 4 and 5?

(b) Calculate the following elasticities, selecting appropriate periods and using arc formulas:

price elasticity for x _____, based upon periods _____ and _____;

price elasticity for y _____, based upon periods _____ and _____;

income elasticity for x _____, based upon periods _____ and

_____;

income elasticity for y _____, based upon periods _____ and

_____;

cross-elasticity of demand for y with respect to the price of x _____, based upon periods _____ and _____;

cross-elasticity of demand for x with respect to the price of y _____, based upon the periods _____ and _____.

9. (a) Given the supply curves shown, demonstrate that the elasticity of supply equals 1 along S_1 but falls as price increases along S_2. (Compute arc elasticities between the points indicated.)

Figure 5-4

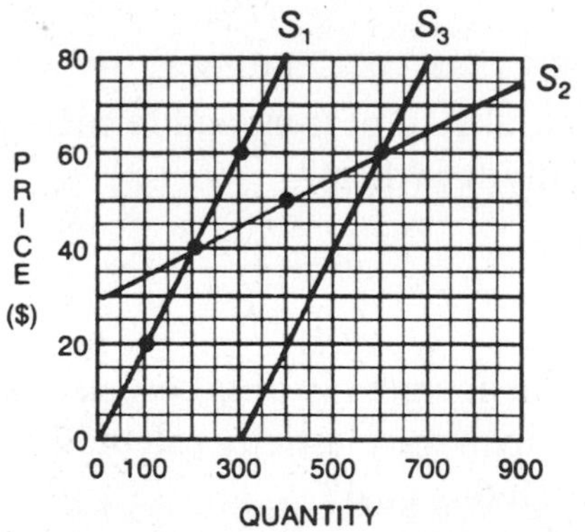

(b) How is the result for S_1 related to the fact that this supply curve passes through the origin?

(c) What does a supply curve such as S_3 imply when price equals zero?

10. The six diagrams represent different combinations of elasticities of demand and supply at the equilibrium price P_E. Indicate which diagram corresponds to each of the following statements. (η_d refers to elasticity of demand, and η_s refers to elasticity of supply.

(a) η_d is greater than one and η_s is unity _____

(b) η_d is unity and η_s is infinity _____

(c) η_d is unity and η_s is unity _____

(d) η_d is greater than one and η_s is zero _____

(e) η_d is zero and η_s is unity _____

(f) η_d is infinity and η_s is unity _____

Figure 5-5

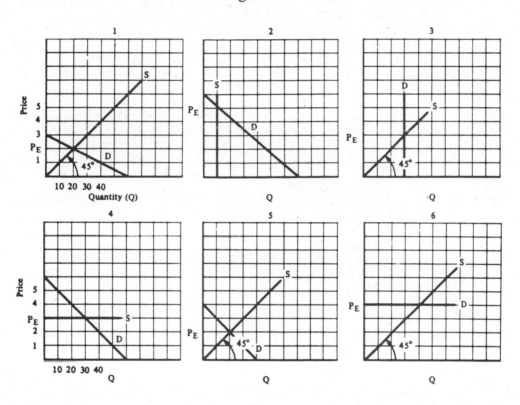

◆ **APPENDIX EXERCISE**

The following exercise is based on the material in the appendix to this chapter. Read the appendix before attempting this exercise.

11. The appendix discusses the distinction between *point* and *arc* elasticity. Point elasticity measures elasticity at a particular point on the demand curve rather than over an interval (arc elasticity). This exercise requires you to calculate point and arc elasticities for the demand curve drawn in the following diagram. (Note: The demand curve is linear with a constant slope of $\Delta P/\Delta Q = -1/2$, or equivalently, $\Delta Q/\Delta P = -2$.)

63

Figure 5-6

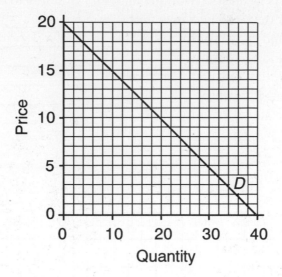

(a) Calculate the *point* elasticity of demand at a price of $10.

(b) Calculate the *arc* elasticity of demand for the following price changes (calculations should be to two decimal places).

Price Change	Arc Elasticity
$18 to $10	_____
$14 to $10	_____
$12 to $10	_____
$11 to $10	_____

(c) What happens to the difference between arc elasticity and point elasticity as the price change gets smaller? When is arc elasticity likely to be a good approximation of point elasticity?

◆ ANSWERS

Multiple-Choice Questions

1. (a) 2. (d) 3. (a) 4. (b)   5. (b) 6. (c) 7. (a) 8. (d) 9. (d) 10. (d) 11. (c) 12. (b) 13. (a) 14. (a) 15. (d) 16. (d) 17. (c) 18. (d) 19. (e) 20. (a) 21. (d) 22. (e) 23. (c) 24. (a) 25. (a) 26. (c) 27. (b)

Exercises

1.   (a) $\eta = 2.0 = (20,000/500 \times 2,500/50,000)$; elastic demand.
        (b)   Elasticity of unity.
        (c)   Perfectly Inelastic demand.
        (d) η cannot be determined because the demand curve has shifted.
        (e) $\eta = 2.5 = ((20,000/80,000) \times 100)$ percent $\div$ 10 percent; elastic demand.
        (f)   Perfectly inelastic demand.
        (g) η cannot be determined because the demand curve shifts.

2.   (a)

Figure 5-7

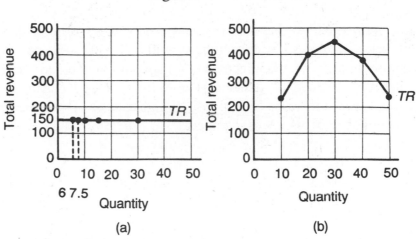

(a)   (b)

       (b)   Panel (a): Since total revenue does not change along the demand curve, the price elasticity of demand is equal to unity at every point along this demand curve.

              Panel (b): Since total revenue increases as price falls from \$25 to \$20 to \$15, demand is elastic over this range. Total revenue is at its maximum value of \$450 when price equals \$15; this corresponds to unit elasticity. For further price decreases from \$15 to \$10 to \$5, total revenue decreases, and hence demand is inelastic along this portion of the demand curve.

3.   (a)   down; (b) none; (c) 1; (d) down; (e) up.

4.   (a)   The following measures express elasticity as: $(\Delta Q/\Delta P)(P_A/Q_A)$, where Q_A and P_A are the average quantity and price, respectively.

              A-B, $\eta = (100/10)(65/50) = 13.0$; B-C, $\eta = (200/20)(50/200) = 2.5$;

              C-D, $\eta = (200/20)(30/400) = 0.75$; D-E, $\eta = (200/20)(10/600) = 0.167$.

       (b) $\eta = (\Delta Q/\Delta P)(P_A/Q_A) = (100/10)(35/350) = 1.0$. Over this interval, total revenue is constant. With further declines in price, total revenue will decline as we move into the inelastic portion of the demand curve.

*5. (a) Calculate arc elasticity from \$1.25 to \$1.35 so that the average price corresponds to the current fare of \$1.30.

$$\eta = \frac{2{,}000}{0.10} \times \frac{130}{20{,}000} = 1.3$$

(b) Since demand is elastic, any increase in price only serves to decrease total revenue. Thus you should recommend that the price be decreased in order to increase total revenue.

(c) Try successively lower fares until total revenue begins to decrease. The maximum total revenue is found to be \$26,450, which obtains at a fare of \$1.15 and a ridership of 23,000 passengers per day.

6. The Honourable Mr. D. Runken assumes a downward sloping demand curve for alcohol—as price increases, its consumption will fall. However, he also assumes that total expenditure on alchohol also decreases. This would only be correct if demand were elastic; in the case of alchohol, demand is more likely to be inelastic so that total expediture on alchohol would increase in response to higher taxes. The impact of this bill would be the exact opposite of what was intended.

7. (a) $\eta_s = 15/10 = 1.5$.

(b) The neceassary price change is 20 percent. It is obtained by dividing the output increase of 30 percent by the elasticity of 1.5. Since $\eta_s = \%\Delta Q/\%\Delta P$, it follows that $\%\Delta P = \%\Delta Q/\eta_s$.

(c) The fall in output is 7.5, which is calculated by multiplying the price decrease of 5 percent by the elasticity of 1.5.

*8. (a) Elasticity measures are calculated under the *ceteris paribus* assumption that other factors affecting demand are unchanged. Between periods 4 and 5, not only has income changed, but so have the prices of x and y.

(b) periods (1) to (2), price elasticity for x =
$$-\frac{9-10}{28-25} \times \frac{(28+25)/2}{(9+10)/2} = 0.93$$
periods (2) to (3), price elasticity for y =
$$-\frac{35-40}{15-10} \times \frac{(15+10)/2}{(35+40)/2} = 0.33$$
periods (3) to (4), income elasticity for x =
$$\frac{9-8}{11{,}000-10{,}000} \times \frac{(11{,}000+10{,}000)/2}{(9+8)/2} = 1.24$$
periods (3) to (4), income elasticity for y =
$$\frac{36-35}{11{,}000-10{,}000} \times \frac{(11{,}000+10{,}000)/2}{(36+35)/2} = 0.30$$
periods (1) to (2), cross-elasticity of demand for y with respect to the price of x
$$= \frac{40-42}{28-25} \times \frac{(28+25)/2}{(40+42)/2} = -0.43$$
periods (2) to (3), cross-elasticity of demand for x with respect to the price of y
$$= \frac{8-9}{15-10} \times \frac{(15+10)/2}{(8+9)/2} = -0.29$$

9.   (a)   Starting from the origin for S_1, the elasticities of supply are: $(100/20)(10/50) =$ $(100/20)(30/50) = (100/20)(50/250) = 1.0$.
For S_2 when price rises from 40 to 50, the price elasticity of supply is: $(200/10)(45/300) = 3.0$, but when price rises from 50 to 60, the elasticity is $(200/10)(55/500) = 2.2$.

      (b)   Because S_1 passes through the origin, P and Q always change in the same proportion, which gives an elasticity value of 1.

      (c) S_3 implies that firms are willing to supply the good (300 units) even when the price they receive is zero.

10.   (a)   1 and 6.   (b)   4.
      (c)   5.   (d)   2.
      (e)   3.   (f)   6.

11.   (a)   Point elasticity = -1.00 = (-2 x 10/20), or 1.00 neglecting the negative sign.

      (b)

Price Change	Arc Elasticity
$18 to $10	2.33
$14 to $10	1.50
$12 to $10	1.22
$11 to $10	1.11

      (c)   As the change in price gets smaller, the values of arc elasticity and point elasticity converge. Thus arc elasticity serves as a good approximation of point elasticity for small changes in price.

Chapter 6

Supply and Demand in Action

◆ LEARNING OBJECTIVES

After studying this chapter, you should be able to:

✔   evaluate how a tax on the sale of a commodity is likely to affect consumers and producers;

✔   understand and explain the effects of government controls on prices;

✔   predict the consequences of rent controls;

✔   appreciate the historical problems that have confronted Canadian agriculture;

✔   show the importance of elasticity of demand in explaining the "farm problem";

✔   describe the objectives and economic implications of government intervention in agricultural markets.

◆ HINTS AND TIPS

Some common examination errors on the material in this chapter are due to students' failure to:

✔   determine if demand is elastic or inelastic which, in turn, determines the resulting relationship between total revenue and a price change;

✔   remember that effective price floors are set above equilibrium price, and effective price ceilings are set below equilibrium price;

✔   use the analytical methods of economic theory to derive the implications of government policy.

◆ MULTIPLE-CHOICE QUESTIONS

1. Since the Goods and Services Tax (GST) is added to the price a consumer must pay for a commodity the
    (a) entire burden of the tax is borne by consumers.
    (b) consumer price increases by the amount of the tax.
    (c) seller price is unaffected.
    (d) burden is borne by producers who must collect the tax.
    (e) distribution of the burden depends upon the elasticities of demand and supply.

2. Consumers bear a greater share of the burden of the tax, the more
    (a) inelastic is supply.   (b) elastic is supply.
    (c) inelastic is demand.   (d) elastic is demand.
    (e) Both (b) and (c) are correct.

3. At a disequilibrium price,
    (a) profits of sellers are eliminated.
    (b) changes in demand must be matched by changes in supply.
    (c) there are always unsold goods.
    (d) there is always excess demand.
    (e) the quantity bought and sold is determined by the lesser of quantity demanded or quantity supplied.

4. Price ceilings below the equilibrium price and price floors above the equilibrium price will both lead to
    (a) production controls.   (b) rationing.
    (c) a drop in quality.   (d) a reduction in quantity exchanged.
    (e) surplus output.

5. A black market may occur whenever
    (a) producers' prices cannot be controlled but retailers' prices can be controlled.
    (b) there is an excess supply of a commodity at the controlled price.
    (c) consumers are prepared to pay more than the ceiling price and exchange between retailer and consumer cannot be enforced at the ceiling price.
    (d) a ceiling price is maintained above the equilibrium price.
    (e) there is an effective price floor.

6. In a free market economy, the rationing of scarce goods is done primarily by
    (a) the price mechanism.   (b) the government.
    (c) business firms.   (d) consumers.
    (e) marketing boards.

7. Allocation by sellers' preferences is feasible when
    (a) there is a disequilibrium price.
    (b) quantity supplied is less than quantity demanded.
    (c) there is a binding price floor.
    (d) there is excess supply.
    (e) the controlled price is sct above the equilibrium price.

8. A price control that leads to the formation of a black market may nonetheless be consistent with government policy if the government's objective is to
    (a) keep the price low.
    (b) encourage output in this industry.
    (c) help producers obtain a more reasonable price for their output.
    (d) restrict output for conservation reasons.
    (e) All of the above.

Questions 9 to 12 refer to the following graph.

Figure 6-1

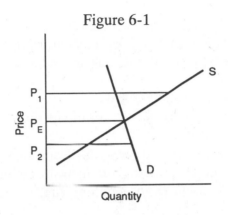

9. A price ceiling equal to P_1
    (a) results in excess supply.
    (b) results in excess demand.
    (c) results in neither excess demand nor excess supply.
    (d) can lead to a black market.
    (e) None of the above.

10. A price control fixed at P_2
    (a) leads to a level of consumption that is greater than quantity supplied.
    (b) results in a greater quantity produced than is actually sold.
    (c) is often justified as a means of helping producers.
    (d) may result in allocation by sellers' preferences.
    (e) results in unsold inventories.

11. A price floor equal to P_E would result in excess supply if
    (a) demand decreases due to a change in tastes.
    (b) supply falls due to an increase in labor costs.
    (c) the demand curve shifts to the right.
    (d) either curve shifts in a direction that causes upward pressure on price.
    (e) None of the above.

12. Suppose that the government decides that P_E is too high and therefore imposes a price ceiling equal to P_2. Further suppose that a black market develops that is able to sell all output at the highest attainable price. The black market price is
    (a) equal to P_E.   (b) greater than P_E.
    (c) greater than P_2 but less than P_E.   (d) equal to P_2.
    (e) None of the above.

71

13. Line-ups (or queues) are one possible allocative mechanism when there is
    (a) excess supply.
    (b) a binding price floor.
    (c) government intervention in the market that controls price above equilibrium level.
    (d) an effective price ceiling.
    (e) Both (b) and (d) are correct.

14. Rent controls are likely to produce all but which one of the following effects?
    (a) Rental housing shortage in the long-run.
    (b) Development of a black market.
    (c) Rental housing short-run supply increases.
    (d) Resource allocation away from the rental housing industry.
    (e) Less expenditure by landlords on upkeep and maintenance.

15. The rental housing market is characterized by
    (a) long- and short-run supply elasticities of equal magnitude.
    (b) inelastic demand.
    (c) short-run inelastic supply and long-run elastic supply.
    (d) short-run elastic supply and long-run inelastic supply.
    (e) elastic supply in both the short- and long-run.

Questions 16 and 17 refer to the following figure, in which the demand for rental housing increases from D_0 to D_1 (*SR* and *LR* refer to the short-run and the long-run, respectively).

Figure 6-2

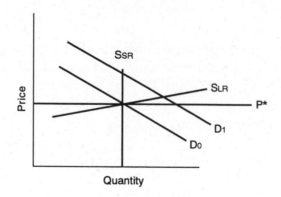

16. If demand increases from D_0 to D_1 and there are no rent controls,
    (a) there will be a greater quantity increase in the short-run than in the long-run.
    (b) the short-run price overshoots its long-run equilibrium level.
    (c) the amount of rental housing will not be affected in the long-run.
    (d) rents will rise more in the long-run than in the short-run.
    (e) the long-run price exceeds the short-run price.

17. Assume that rents are controlled at price P^*. Which of the following best describes the likely events if demand increases from D_0 to D_1?
    (a) There will be no shortage of rental units in either the short-run or the long-run.
    (b) Landlords will have less opportunity to discriminate among prospective tenants.
    (c) Landlords will tend to spend more on maintenance of apartments.
    (d) The apartment shortage will tend to worsen in the long-run.
    (e) All consumers will have access to more affordable housing.

18. One of the long-term trends in Canadian agriculture has been
    (a) an increase in farm incomes relative to urban incomes.
    (b) an increasing proportion of the Canadian labor force working in the agricultural sector.
    (c) a relatively high income elasticity of demand for agricultural output by Canadians.
    (d) a decreasing demand for agricultural output.
    (e) growth in agricultural productivity that has been above the economy's average.

19. The main reason for agricultural price supports is to
    (a) attempt to stabilize farm incomes.
    (b) make certain that there are always extra stocks of goods on hand.
    (c) give the government control over agriculture.
    (d) reduce competition.
    (e) provide assistance to needy consumers.

20. Unplanned changes in output lead to greater fluctuations in price
    (a) the more inelastic is demand.
    (b) the flatter is the demand curve.
    (c) the more elastic is demand.
    (d) the more inelastic is the planned supply curve.
    (e) when demand is perfectly elastic.

21. Most farm receipts vary inversely with output levels
    (a) whenever buyers' preferences change.
    (b) because most farm products have inelastic demands.
    (c) because lower outputs mean higher total costs.
    (d) as long as supply is elastic.
    (e) because world demand is perfectly elastic.

22. A low-yield crop would not alter total farm receipts if demand were
    (a) elastic.   (b) perfectly elastic.
    (c) perfectly inelastic.   (d) of unit elasticity.
    (e) of zero elasticity.

23. A price completely stabilized at the equilibrium level by a government buying surpluses and selling its stocks when there are shortages means that
    (a) poor farmers will benefit the most.
    (b) government has imposed a perfectly inelastic demand curve on farms.
    (c) farmers' revenues will be proportional to output.
    (d) all farms will have satisfactory incomes and farm receipts will be stabilized.
    (e) total farm receipts will increase.

73

24. When domestic farmers sell on world markets at a price that is unaffected by domestic output, they in effect face
    (a)   perfectly elastic demand.   (b)   perfectly inelastic demand.
    (c)   inelastic demand.   (d)   unit-elastic demand.
    (e)   demand of zero elasticity.

25. If domestic output is sold at a *given world price*, the incomes of domestic producers
    (a)   are independent of domestic output.
    (b)   vary in the direction opposite that of domestic output.
    (c)   fluctuate in the same direction as fluctuations in domestic output.
    (d)   increase during domestic crop failures and decrease during domestic bumper crops.
    (e)   are constant.

26. When domestic output is sold at a *given world price*, the most desirable means of stabilizing total farm receipts due to fluctuations in annual output is
    (a)   for the government to introduce a price support at the world price.
    (b)   for farmers to stabilize the annual quantity sold by adding to storage in years with above average crops and depleting stocks in years with below average outputs.
    (c)   to sell each year's output and save the above average revenue from the good years until it is needed in a bad year and in the meantime earn interest.
    (d)   for the government to establish quotas at the average annual output.
    (e)   None of the above.

27. Suppose that annual *domestic output is constant* but is sold at a *world price that fluctuates* from year to year. Suppose further that the current year's price is unusually low and is expected to rise. The most desirable policy for maximizing average annual receipts is to
    (a)   sell all output at an average world price.
    (b)   store output in order to sell at a higher future price.
    (c)   sell output and invest the revenue to earn interest.
    (d)   sell each year's output at the current price..
    (e)   either store or sell the output, depending on storage costs, the future price, and the interest rate.

28. When there are fluctuations in output in a market with inelastic demand, quotas equal to the average annual output have the effect of
    (a)   stabilizing annual output.
    (b)   stabilizing annual receipts.
    (c)   increasing average annual receipts.
    (d)   increasing average annual output.
    (e)   Both (a) and (b) are correct.

29. An unplanned increase in output
    (a)   will allow producers to sell more and thereby increase their income.
    (b)   will always result in lower total receipts for producers.
    (c)   may increase or decrease total income, depending on whether the output is sold on domestic or world markets.
    (d)   may increase or decrease total income, depending on whether demand is inelastic or elastic.
    (e)   may increase or decrease total income, depending on whether price rises or falls.

30. Quotas that lead to higher profits in some industry will in the long-run
    (a)   result in more producers in the industry.
    (b)   make it more costly to enter this industry.
    (c)   result in a larger output for each producer.
    (d)   help individuals who are just entering this industry.
    (e)   All of the above are correct.

31. The Canadian Wheat Board is a good example of a marketing board that
    (a)   acts as a selling agency for Canadian wheat in the international market.
    (b)   actively engages in supply management schemes in order to influence price.
    (c)   supports a market price that is well above the equilibrium price.
    (d)   administers an effective price ceiling.
    (e)   actively enforces production quotas.

32. If markets are highly regulated and controlled,
    (a)   costs can be lowered below those in unregulated markets.
    (b)   the signals required for the allocation of resources will not operate.
    (c)   relative prices will still change to reallocate resources.
    (d)   the distribution of income will be unchanged from that observed in an unregulat-
            ed market.
    (e)   consumers benefit from lower prices and producers benefit from higher profits.

33. One of the central effects of imposing effective price controls in a market is to
    (a)   shift the costs among consumers, producers, and taxpayers.
    (b)   lower the cost of providing a given quantity of a good.
    (c)   allow price to serve as the primary allocative mechanism.
    (d)   increase the actual quantity exchanged.
    (e)   benefit both consumers and producers.

◆ EXERCISES

1. The following diagrams depict the demand and supply curves for the beer and orange
    juice markets in Ontario. Suppose a sale tax of $t per litre is imposed in both of these
    markets.

Figure 6-3

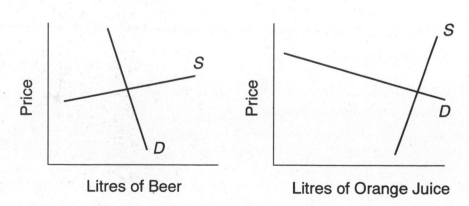

(a) Shift the appropriate curve to show the impact of the tax in each market. Label the new consumer price and seller price in the beer market P_{cb} and P_{sb}, respectively. In the market for orange juice, label them P_{cj} and P_{sj}, respectively.

(b) In which market is most of the burden of the tax borne by consumers? How would you characterize the elasticities of demand and supply in this market?

(c) In which market is most of the tax borne by producers? How would you characterize the elasticities of demand and supply in this market?

(d) In which market is the difference between the consumer price and the seller price greater?

2. Given the two market situations described in the graphs, answer the following questions.

Figure 6-4

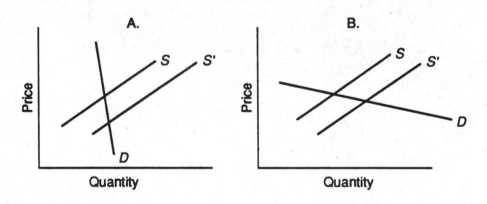

(a) If S and D denote the original supply and demand curves, indicate, by vertical hatching |||, the total receipts (i.e., revenue) in both markets.

(b) If the supply curve shifts to S' in both markets, indicate the new receipts by horizontal hatching ═.

(c) Which market shows the larger loss in total receipts? What is the nature of the demand curve in that market?

(d)   Suppose that there was a price floor equal to the original equilibrium price (before the shift in supply) and the government was committed to purchasing unsold stocks at this price. Given the shift in supply in both markets, would there be any difference in the quantity the government would have to purchase in the two cases? Explain.

3.   The graph on the next page depicts Canadian domestic supply and demand curves, S_c and D_c, respectively, for a commodity in a market for which Canada is assumed to face a fixed world price.

Figure 6-5

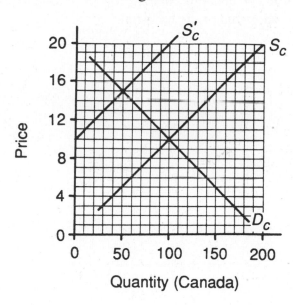

(a)   At a world price of $5, Canadian producers sell _____ units, while Canadian consumers purchase _____ units. Canada therefore (imports, exports) _____ units of this commodity.

(b)   If the world price increases to $12 per unit, Canadians would now consume _____ units but produce _____ units. Thus Canada now (imports, exports) _____ units.

(c)   Should domestic supply shift to S'_c while the world price remains at $12, domestic production would now be _____ units and domestic consumption _____ units. Canada would therefore be an (importer, exporter) of _____ units.

4.   The graph illustrates two situations in the rental housing market: (a) a short-run situation with the supply relatively inelastic, and (b) a long-run situation with a more elastic supply. The subscripts for the demand curves indicate demand for subsequent periods of time within either the short-run or the long-run.

Figure 6-6

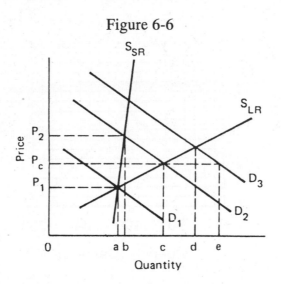

(a)   Suppose that demand for rental housing shifts from D_1 to D_2. In the short-run, price would be expected to increase from _____ to _____, and the equilibrium quantity from _____ to _____.

(b)   (i)   Assume that the predicted sharp increase in price alarms the public, so the government controls the price at P_c. Is this rent control an effective price ceiling? Explain.

(ii)   In the long-run, quantity supplied will increase to _____, and P_c will be the_____ price. The main effects of the price control will be a short-run shift of income from (landlords, tenants) to (landlords, tenants). The long-run allocation of resources will be (efficient, inefficient), given P_c, because of short-run (overshooting, undershooting) of price.

(c)   If P_c is maintained in the face of a further shift of the demand curve to D_3, P_c becomes a price (floor, ceiling), and the excess quantity demanded in the long-run will be _____.

5.   A small town in Saskatchewan has the following monthly demand and supply schedules for kumquats:

Price	Quantity demanded	Quantity supplied
$0.40	3,800	800
0.50	3,600	1,200
0.60	3,400	1,600
0.70	3,200	2,000
0.80	3,000	2,400
0.90	2,800	2,800
1.00	2,600	3,200
1.10	2,400	3,600
1.20	2,200	4,000
1.30	2,000	4,400
1.40	1,800	4,800

(a)   Plot the demand and supply curves for kumquats and label them D_1 and S_1, respectively.

Figure 6-7

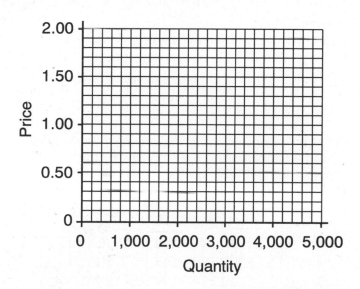

(b)   What are the equilibrium price and quantity in this market?

79

The local government plans to assist kumquat producers by increasing the price of kumquats. It is studying the following two alternative schemes as a means of increasing price.

(c)   In this first scheme, the government offers to purchase, at a price of $1.10 each, any amount of kumquats that are produced but not sold to consumers (it then intends simply to destroy its purchases). Producers therefore face a new demand that is the sum of consumer and government demand.

    (i)   Draw this new demand curve (on the above grid), label it D_2, and determine the new equilibrium price and quantity in this market.

    (ii)   How many kumquats are consumers purchasing, and how many is the government destroying?

    (iii)   How much does this scheme cost the government? Shade in the area on your graph that represents the cost to the government. (*Note:* Ignore all administrative and disposal costs.)

(d)   As an alternative scheme, suppose that the government decides to purchase, at a price of $1.10, all of the kumquats produced. It then puts all of its purchases on the market for resale to consumers at whatever price consumers are willing to pay for that quantity.

    (i)   Draw the demand curve facing producers under this scheme (on the grid below), label it D_3, and determine the equilibrium price and quantity.

    (ii)   What price will the government receive when it resells all of its purchases?

    (iii)   What is the cost to the government of this scheme? Shade in with hatched lines the appropriate area on your graph to illustrate this cost (again, ignore administrative costs).

Figure 6-8

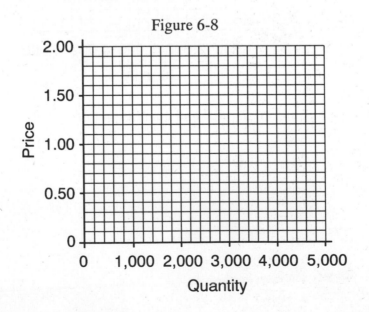

(e)   What do you think are the relative merits of these two alternative policies?

6.   The following diagram illustrates the demand and supply curves for an agricultural product whose output varies due to erratic weather conditions.

Figure 6-9

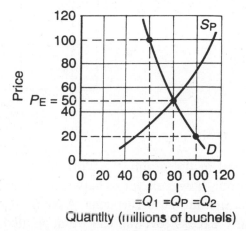

All output is sold in a domestic market where the demand curve is denoted D in the graph. S_P represents planned supply, so the expected equilibrium price is P_E, or \$50, and the planned quantity supplied is Q_P, or 80 million bushels. Suppose that actual output is either Q_1 (a crop failure, 60 million bushels) or Q_2 (a bumper crop, 100 million bushels) and that each is equally likely. (For convenience, you should assume that good and bad crop years always occur consecutively.)

(a)   Are producers in this market better off as a group in the year with a crop failure or the one with a bumper crop? Explain.

(b)   What is average annual farm income in this market?

(c)   Suppose that producers organize and operate a scheme whereby any year's output exceeding average annual output is added to storage and withdrawn in those years with below average outputs. Thus Q_P is offered for sale in each and every year. What are annual farm receipts?

(d)   Now consider government intervention in this market in the form of a quota equal to Q_P. That is to say, any output in excess of Q_P must be destroyed. What would average annual receipts of producers be now?

(e)   Which of these schemes do you think producers would prefer? Which do you think consumers of this product would prefer least? Why?

81

*7. This question addresses the problem of stabilizing domestic annual farm receipts in the presence of a fluctuating output that is sold entirely in export markets at some given world price.

Figure 6-10

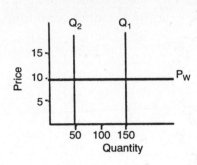

As illustrated in the graph, the world price is $10 and is expected to remain constant. Annual output, however, varies between 150 and 50 units, with each being equally likely, so that average output is 100 units. Assume that the cost of storing a unit of output is $5 and that any excess revenue can be deposited in a savings account that pays a rate of return equal to 10 percent.

Suppose that current output is 150 units and it is certain that next period's output will be 50 units. Should the producers' association stabilize annual receipts by ensuring that exactly 100 units are offered for sale each year, or should it sell all 150 units now?

*8. As in Exercise 6, all output is again sold entirely in export markets at the current world price. However, domestic output is now stable from year to year, and it is the world price that fluctuates. As the following graph illustrates, the constant level of annual output is 100 units. However, the world price is currently at $5 per unit but is expected to be $15 next period.

Figure 6-11

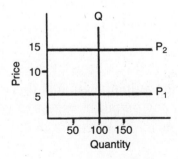

Suppose that the producers' association is committed to paying producers $1,000 each year even if it has to borrow in the first year to meet this obligation. Assume that storage costs are $5 per unit and that the association can borrow money at a 10 percent interest rate. Should the association attempt to stabilize annual receipts at $1,000 by putting all 100 units into storage in order to sell next year when price is high, or should it sell everything now and thereby avoid storage and large borrowing costs?

The following itemized statement of receipts and payments under each scheme will help you do this exercise.

	Receipts	Payments
If first year's output is stored:		
Proceeds from loan	$	$
Payment to producers in year 1		
Borrowing costs: (0.10 x $1000)		
Storage costs: ($5 x 100)		
Crop revenue in year 2: ($15 x 200)		
Loan repayment		
Payment to producers in year 2		
Total	$_____	$_____

	Receipts	Payments
If first year's out put is sold:		
Crop revenue in year 1: ($5 x 100)	$	$
Proceeds from loan		
Payment to producers in year 1		
Borrowing costs: (0.10 x $500)		
Crop revenue in year 2: ($15 x 100)		
Loan repayment		
Payment to producers in year 2		
Total	$_____	$_____

◆ ANSWERS

Multiple-Choice Questions

1. (e) 2. (e) 3. (e) 4. (d) 5. (c) 6. (a) 7. (b) 8. (d) 9. (c) 10. (d) 11. (a) 12. (b) 13. (d) 14. (c) 15. (c) 16. (b) 17. (d) 18. (e) 19. (a) 20. (a) 21. (b) 22. (d) 23. (c) 24. (a) 25. (c) 26. (c) 27.(e) 28. (c) 29. (d) 30. (b) 31. (a) 32. (b) 33. (a)

Exercises

1.   (a)

Figure 6-12

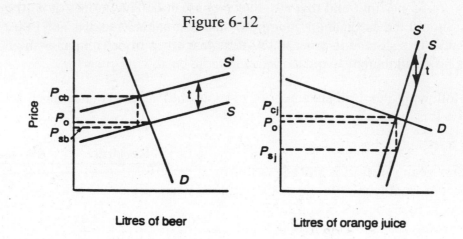

Litres of beer   Litres of orange juice

    (b)   The tax on beer is borne primarily by consumers. The relative slopes of the demand and supply curves in these markets suggest that the demand for beer is relatively inelastic, while its supply is relatively elastic.

    (c)   The tax on orange juice is borne primarily by producers. Demand in this market is relatively elastic, while supply is inelastic.

    (d)   The differences between consumer and seller prices are the same in each market. Specifically, the vertical distance by which each supply curve shifts is $t in each market.

2.   (a) and (b)

Figure 6-13

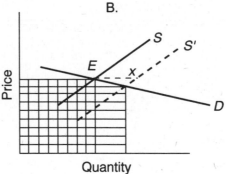

    (c)   Market **A**. The demand is inelastic compared to market **B**.

    (d)   No. The shift in supply is identical, and at a price equal to original equilibrium price, the quantity of unsold goods (*EX* in both markets) is the same.

3.   (a)   50; 150; imports; 100.

    (b)   80; 120; exports; 40.

    (c)   20; 80; importer; 60.

4. (a) P_1 to P_2; a to b.

  (b) (i) Yes, in the short-run, since it is below the equilibrium price. (It would not be effective in the long-run since it equals the equilibrium price as the quantity supplied expands (along S_{LR}) to meet the demand—c on D_2.)

  (II) c; equilibrium, landlords to tenants; efficient; overshooting.

  (c) Ceiling; quantity e - c.

5. (a)

Figure 6-14

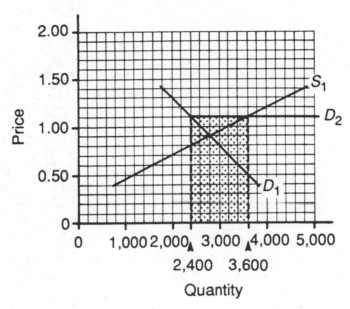

  (b) At the intersection of D_1 and S_1 in the graph, the equilibrium price is 90 cents and the equilibrium quantity is 2,800 units per month.

  (c) (i) As shown in the graph, the new demand curve is perfectly elastic at a price of $1.10. For prices greater than $1.10, the demand curve is D_1. The equilibrium now obtains at the intersection of D_2 and S_1, where $P = \$1.10$ and $Q = 3,600$ per month.

  (ii) At a price of $1.10, quantity demanded by consumers is 2,400, so the remaining 1,200 units are purchased and destroyed by the government.

  (iii) The government is purchasing 1,200 units at $1.10 each, so total cost (to taxpayers) is $1,320 per month.

  (d) (i) In effect, producers face a perfectly elastic demand at a price of $1.10. As shown in the following graph, the new equilibrium occurs at the intersection of D_3 and S_1 with the same equilibrium price of $1.10 and equilibrium quantity of 3,600 per month.

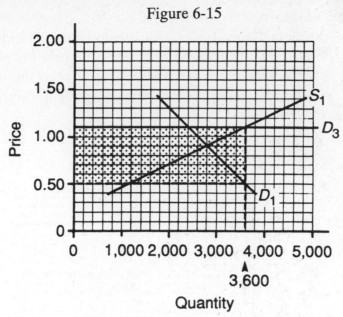

Figure 6-15

(ii)   Consumers are willing to purchase 3,600 units when price is 50 cents.
(iii)   The government pays $1.10 for each of its 3,600 units purchased and receives only 50 cents for each resale. Therefore, the cost to the government is 3,600 x ($1.10 -$0.50) = $2,160 per month.

(e)   Although the second scheme costs the government more, it may be less costly for society as a whole in that everything that is produced is actually consumed, thereby yielding some benefits for consumers as well. The destroyed output in the first scheme is a net cost to society, since resources (which have an alternative use) are used up without any resulting benefits.

6.   (a)   In a crop failure year, output is 60 million bushels and price per bushel is $100; therefore, total receipts are $100 x 60 million = $6 billion. In a bumper crop year, total harvest is 100 million bushels, and price is $20, so total revenue is $2 billion. Therefore, in terms of total income, these producers as a group are better off in years with crop failures. The reason for the negative relationship between total output and total receipts is that demand for this product is inelastic.

(b)   Since large and small harvests are equally likely, average annual farm receipts for this crop are $4 billion: ($6 billion + $2 billion)/2.

(c)   When 100 million bushels are actually produced, 20 million are stored and only 80 million are offered for sale. In a year with a production level of only 60 million bushels, 80 million bushels are again put on the market for sale by withdrawing 20 million from stocks. Therefore, 80 million bushels are sold each year, and the equilibrium price each year is $50. Thus total receipts each year are $4 billion: $50 x 80 million.

(d)   When output is 60 million bushels, it is sold for $6 billion. When output is 100 million, only the quota of 80 million bushels is sold, and the remaining 20 million bushels are destroyed. The 80 million bushels sell at a price of $50 so that total revenue is $4 billion. Average annual receipts are therefore $5 billion: ($6 billion + $4 billion)/2.

(e)   Average annual revenue of producers is greatest with the quota. Therefore, in terms of income, producers as a group are better off with the quota. Since total revenue of producers is equal to total expenditure by consumers, consumers spend the most for this product under the quota scheme. Further, average annual consumption is lowest under the quota than under any other scheme: 70 million bushels as opposed to 80 million. Therefore, consumers would prefer the quota scheme the least.

*7.   With a constant world price, it is always best to stabilize producers' annual income by selling the entire crop. Revenue from the 150 units is $1,500. Of this, $1,000 must be paid to producers, leaving $500 to invest at a 10 percent rate of return, which yields another $50 revenue. Next period, when output is below average, the $500 savings is added to the second year's crop revenue of $500 ($10 x 50) to keep total farm receipts at $1,000. Thus the association has stabilized incomes at the annual average of $1,000 and has a surplus revenue of $50 for further distribution. Had the association stored the 50 units exceeding average annual output in the first year, it would have incurred a storagecost of $250 ($5 x 50) and would not have the additional interest revenue from the investment. It would therefore be $250 short in its attempt to stabilize income at $1,000.

*8.   Regardless of whether the association stores or sells the first year's output, it must under these circumstances borrow in order to meet its obligation of paying producers $1,000 in the first year. If it stores the crop, it has no crop revenue and must therefore borrow all $1,000. If it sells at the current price, it receives revenue of $500, implying that an additional $500 must be borrowed. The following is an itemized account of the receipts and payments associated with each scheme:

	Receipts	Payments
If first year's output is stored:		
Proceeds from loan	$1,000	
Payment to producers in year 1		$1,000
Borrowing costs: (0.10 x $1000)		100
Storage costs: ($5 x 100)		500
Crop revenue in year 2: ($15 x 200)	3,000	
Loan repayment		1,000
Payment to producers in year 2		1,000
Total	$4,000	$3,600
If first year's out put is sold:		
Crop revenue in year 1: ($5 x 100)	$500	
Proceeds from loan	500	
Payment to producers in year 1		$1,000
Borrowing costs: (0.10 x $500)		50
Crop revenue in year 2: ($15 x 100)	1,500	
Loan repayment		500
Payment to producers in year 2		1,000
Total	$2,500	$2,550

Therefore, storing year 1's output in order to sell next period when the price is high yields a net revenue (i.e., receipts less payments) of $400. Conversely, selling immediately so as to avoid storage costs yields a net revenue of -$50. Thus, in this particular numerical example, the association maximizes net revenues for producers by storing output. Unlike Exercise 6, there is no single best strategy when world price fluctuates. Rather, the decision whether to store or sell depends on prices in each period, storage costs, and the interest rate.

PART THREE

CONSUMPTION, PRODUCTION AND COST

Chapter 7

Household Consumption Behavior

◆ LEARNING OBJECTIVES

After studying this chapter, you should be able to:

✔ use price and income data to construct a budget line;

✔ show how changes in relative prices and income affect the budget line;

✔ illustrate how a demand curve for a commodity can be derived;

✔ distinguish among normal goods, inferior goods, and Giffen goods;

✔ explain what gives rise to consumers' surplus and the importance of the concept.

◆ HINTS AND TIPS

The most frequent sources of errors on examinations are attributable to:

✔ an incomplete understanding of income and substitution effects;

✔ a lack of appreciation of the difference between money and real incomes.

◆ MULTIPLE-CHOICE QUESTIONS

1. A budget line
   (a) describes the demand for two goods.
   (b) describes the quantity demanded at each and every price.
   (c) ranks bundles of goods according to a household's preferences.
   (d) separates bundles of goods that a household can afford to purchase at current income and prices from those that it cannot afford.
   (e) slopes upwards as income increases.

2. An increase in income
   (a) makes the budget line steeper.
   (b) shifts the budget line uniformly outward.
   (c) does not affect relative prices and therefore does not affect the budget line.
   (d) rotates the budget line outward on the axis with the more expensive good.
   (e) makes the budget line upward sloping.

3. An increase in income by 10 percent and an increase in all prices by 10 percent will
   (a) not affect the budget line.
   (b) shift the budget line uniformly outward by 20 percent.
   (c) shift the budget line uniformly inward by 20 percent.
   (d) shift the budget line uniformly outward by 1 percent.
   (e) rotate the budget line by 20 percent.

4. An increase in the absolute price of one good increases
   (a) money income.
   (b) real income.
   (c) purchasing power.
   (d) the opportunity cost of buying that good.
   (e) the relative price of other goods.

5. A change in relative prices always implies
   (a) a change in real income.
   (b) a change in purchasing power.
   (c) a change in the opportunity cost of buying goods.
   (d) that only one absolute price has changed.
   (e) All of the above.

6. If the budget line shifts outward in parallel fashion,
   (a) prices increase by the same amount.
   (b) relative prices have increased.
   (c) prices and income increase in the same proportion.
   (d) price increases exactly offset decreases in income.
   (e) relative prices remain constant.

Questions 7 to 11 refer to the following graphs, which depict an initial budget line labelled *ab* and a new budget line *a'b'*, which is caused by some change in income, prices, or both.

Figure 7-1

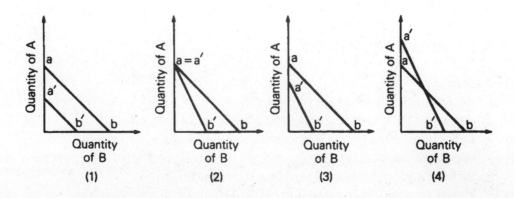

92

7.   Which graph (or graphs) depicts the shift in a budget line that results from a decrease in income?
      (a)   1.   (b)   2.
      (c)   3.   (d)   4.
      (e)   1 and 3.

8.   Which shift (or shifts) in the budget line could be explained by an increase in the price of good *B*?
      (a)   1.   (b)   2.
      (c)   3.   (d)   4.
      (e)   2 and 3.

9.   Which shift (or shifts) could be explained by increases in the prices of both goods?
      (a)   1.   (b)   3.
      (c)   1 and 3.   (d)   3 and 4.
      (e)   1 and 4.

10.   Which shift (or shifts) are consistent with a decrease in the price of good *A* and an increase in the price of good *B*?
      (a)   2.   (b)   3.
      (c)   4.   (d)   3 and 4.
      (e)   2 and 3.

11.   Which graphs describe the shift in a budget line that results from decreases in both the price of good *A* and income?
      (a)   2.   (b)   2 and 4.
      (c)   2 and 3.   (d)   3 and 4.
      (e)   2, 3 and 4.

12.   In response to a price change, the substitution effect is isolated from the income effect when
      (a)   relative prices are held constant.
      (b)   real income is held constant.
      (c)   money income is held constant.
      (d)   the quantities demanded are held constant.
      (e)   None of the above.

Questions 13 to 16 refer to the following graph, which depicts several budget lines for food and clothing. The individual is initially on budget line *ab* and consuming at point *e*. The price of food then increases.

Figure 7-2

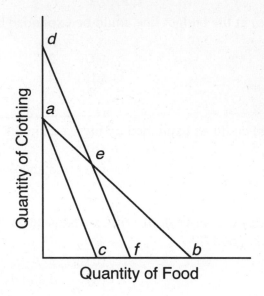

13. After the price increase, the individual selects a new consumption bundle somewhere on the line segment
    (a)   *eb*.   (b)   *ac*.
    (c)   *de*.   (d)   *ef*.
    (e)   *ae*.

14. The substitution effect of this price increase induces the individual to choose a consumption bundle somewhere on line segment
    (a)   *de*.   (b)   *ac*.
    (c)   *ae*.   (d)   *ef*.
    (e)   *eb*.

15. The income effect of this price increase is represented by a change in the consumption bundle somewhere on *de* to a point on
    (a)   *ac*.   (b)   *eb*.
    (c)   *ae*.   (d)   *ef*.
    (e)   *ab*.

16. If an individual chooses bundle *e* when confronted with budget line *ab* and selects a bundle between *e* and *f* when confronted with budget line *df*, then
    (a)   food is a normal good.
    (b)   clothing is an inferior good.
    (c)   real income has decreased.
    (d)   money income has increased.
    (e)   this individual would not be behaving in a consistent manner.

94

17. The price change and its associated substitution effect on quantity purchased are
    (a)   in the same direction for inferior goods.
    (b)   in the same direction for Giffen goods.
    (c)   always in opposite directions.
    (d)   in opposite directions for only downward-sloping demand curves.
    (e)   always opposite in direction to the income effect.

18. A positively sloped demand curve (i.e., a Giffen good)
    (a)   is typical of all inferior goods.
    (b)   describes all goods for which the income and substitution effects are in opposite directions.
    (c)   implies an inferior good for which the income effect outweighs the substitution effect.
    (d)   implies a good for which the price change and the substitution effect are in the same direction.
    (e)   implies that income has increased.

19. Demand curves for normal goods slope downward because
    (a)   the substitution effect of a price change is greater than the income effect.
    (b)   substitution and income effects work in the same direction.
    (c)   the income effect is greater than the substitution effect.
    (d)   the income effect dominates the substitution effect.
    (e)   None of the above; demand curves for normal goods slope upward.

20. The slope of the budget line with product Y on the vertical axis and product X on the horizontal axis is
    (a) $-(P_y/P_x)$.   (b) -1.
    (c) $-(X/Y)$.   (d) $-(P_x/P_y)$.
    (e)   dependent upon both prices and income.

21. Consumers' surplus derived from the consumption of a commodity
    (a)   is the difference between the total value placed on a certain amount of consumption and the total payment made for it.
    (b)   will always be less than the total amount paid for the commodity.
    (c)   will always be more than the total amount paid for the commodity.
    (d)   equals the total value of that commodity to consumers.
    (e)   any of the above could be correct.

22. If an individual is prepared to pay $3 for the first unit of a commodity, $2 for the second, and $1 for the third unit, and the market price is $1,
    (a)   consumers' surplus is $3.
    (b)   the individual will purchase three units of the commodity.
    (c)   the individual's demand curve for this commodity is downward-sloping.
    (d)   consumers' surplus on the last unit purchased is zero.
    (e)   All of the above.

23.   If I am willing to pay $50 for a particular pair of blue jeans, but when I arrive at the store they are on sale for $30,
        (a)   I should buy all the blue jeans in the store.
        (b)   the value I place on the consumption of these blue jeans is lowered by $20.
        (c)   I receive consumer surplus of $20 if I purchase the pair of blue jeans.
        (d)   my valuation of consuming these blue jeans is now $70.
        (e)   my consumer surplus decreases by $20.

24.   The total value Mr. Wimpy places on his consumption of hamburgers equals
        (a)   the amount he pays for them.
        (b)   price times marginal value.
        (c)   marginal value multiplied by quantity demanded.
        (d)   price multiplied by quantity demanded.
        (e)   his total expenditure on hamburgers plus his consumers' surplus.

25.   Consumers' surplus can be measured by the area between the demand curve and the
        (a)   quantity axis.
        (b)   supply curve.
        (c)   horizontal line at the market price.
        (d)   vertical line at the quantity demanded.
        (e)   price axis.

◆ APPENDIX QUESTIONS

The following questions are based on material in the two appendixes to this chapter. Read them before answering these questions.

Appendix A

26.   An indifference curve indicates
        (a)   constant quantities of one good with varying quantities of another.
        (b)   the prices and quantities of two goods that can be purchased for a given sum of money.
        (c)   all combinations of two goods that will give the same level of satisfaction to the household.
        (d)   combinations of goods whose marginal utilities are always equal.
        (e)   all combinations of goods that can be purchased with a given income and constant prices.

27.   The relative prices of two goods can be shown by the
        (a)   slope of the budget line.   (b)   slope of an indifference curve.
        (c)   marginal rate of substitution.   (d)   price-consumption line.
        (e)   indifference map.

28.   At the point where the budget line is tangent to an indifference curve,
        (a)   equal amounts of goods give equal satisfaction.
        (b)   the ratio of prices of the goods must equal the marginal rate of substitution.
        (c)   the prices of the goods are equal.
        (d)   a household cannot be maximizing its satisfaction.
        (e)   the marginal rate of substitution is zero.

29. A household's demand curve can be derived from
    (a) a single indifference curve.   (b) a single budget line.
    (c) a price-consumption line.   (d) an income-consumption line.
    (e) the indifference map.

Appendix B

30. The hypothesis of diminishing marginal utility states that
    (a) the less of a commodity one is consuming, the less the additional utility obtained by an increase in its consumption.
    (b) the more of a commodity one is consuming, the more the additional utility obtained by an increase in its consumption.
    (c) the more of a commodity one is consuming, the less the additional utility obtained by an increase in its consumption.
    (d) the more of a commodity one is consuming, the less will be total utility.
    (e) marginal utility cannot be measured, but total utility can.

31. According to utility theory, a consumer will maximize total satisfaction when A and B are consumed in quantities such that MU_A/MU_B
    (a) equals the ratio of the price of A to the price of B.
    (b) equals the ratio of total utility of A to that of B.
    (c) equals the ratio of the price of B to the price of A.
    (d) equals the ratio of the quantities demanded.
    (e) always equals unity.

32. If a household's marginal utility is positive, but decreases as more of a commodity is consumed, its total utility
    (a) is increasing.
    (b) is also decreasing.
    (c) is constant.
    (d) may be increasing, decreasing, or constant.
    (e) increases at the same rate.

◆ **EXERCISES**

1. A household has an annual budget of $600 to spend on two recreation activities: skiing (at $20 per day) and golf (at $12 per 18-hole round).
    (a) Draw the budget line for recreation expenditures on the graph below. Label the budget line BL_A.
    (b) Is a combination of 20 units of skiing and 20 rounds of golf attainable? Explain.

(c)   Suppose an increase in income allowed a 50 percent increase in the recreation budget. Graph the new budget line and label it BL_C — assume prices are unchanged.

Figure 7-3

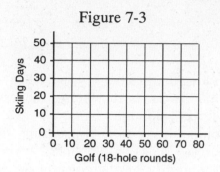

(d)   Suppose now that the price of skiing increases to $30 per day, ceteris paribus. Draw the new budget line and label it BL_D.

(e)   Finally, suppose that the price of a round of golf increases to $18. Graph the new budget line (BL_E). Compare BL_E and BL_A. Explain your findings.

2.   The text discusses two types of changes in income: a change in money income and a change in real income. This exercise illustrates the difference between these two concepts.

A household has a weekly money income of $300 to spend on two goods, A and B. The price of good A is $10 a unit, and the price of good B is $20 a unit.

(a)   Plot the budget line on the following grid.

Figure 7-4

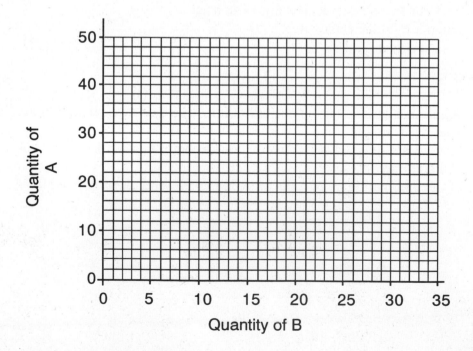

(b)   Assume that money income remains at $300 per week but that relative prices change. Specifically, assume that the price of good B falls to $10 a unit and that the price of good A remains at $10. Plot the new budget line.

(c)   Calculate the change in real income induced by the relative price change when the household's original consumption bundle, at the money income and prices in (a), is
(i)   10 units of good A and 10 units of good B.

(ii)   20 units of good A and 5 units of good B.

(iii)   30 units of good A and none of good B.
(*Hint:* Draw the budget line that would just permit the household to afford to purchase its original consumption bundle at the new prices.)

3.   The following table provides budget data for an individual under three different combinations of income and prices. The table also gives quantities demanded of goods A and B by this individual with each budget constraint.

Budget	Money income	Price of good A	Price of good B	Quantity demanded of good A	Quantity demanded of good B
1	$100	$ 5	$10	10	5
2	150	10	10	8	7
3	100	10	10	4	6

(a)   Plot each budget line, and identify the corresponding consumption bundle as E_1, E_2, and E_3 for budgets 1, 2, and 3, respectively.

Figure 7-5

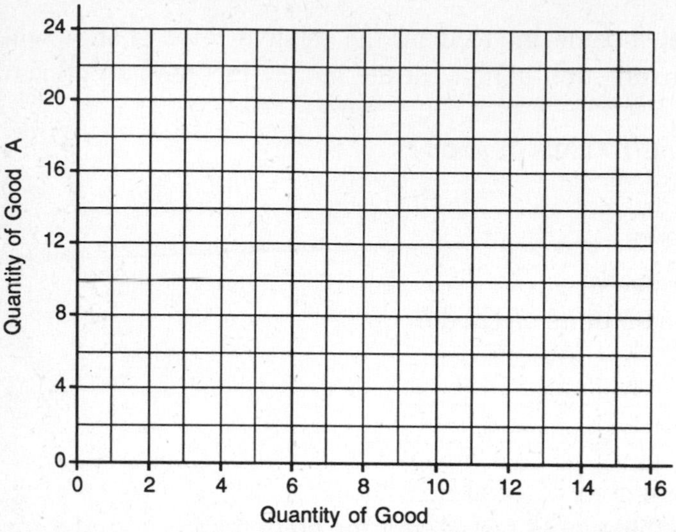

Figure 7-6

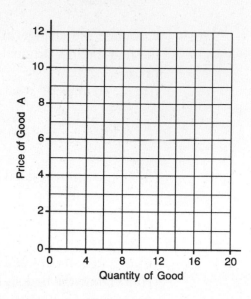

(b)   Suppose that the individual initially faces budget 1, and then the price of good A increases. Assuming that the demand curve is linear, use the data in the table to plot the demand curve.

(c)   What is the new ratio of relative prices?

(d)   What is the substitution effect from the increase in the price of good A?

(e)   What is the income effect induced by the price change?

(f)   Are goods A and B normal or inferior?

4.   During the 1970's the Government of Ontario adopted the objective of promoting the conservation of electricity. At the same time, it did not want to adversely affect the real incomes of households. The following example illustrates how a tax-and-rebate scheme which takes advantage of income and substitution effects can achieve these twin objectives. The student should note how relevant this policy remains in the 1990's.

Assume a typical household in Ontario has $300 per month to spend on consumption of electricity or entertainment. Suppose the price of a kilowatt hour (kwh) of electricity is

100

$0.10 while a unit of entertainment is $1.00. In its initial equilibrium, the household is consuming 2000 kwh's of electricity and 100 units of entertainment.

(a)   Draw the household's initial budget line on the following graph, and label its initial equilibrium E_A.

Figure 7-7

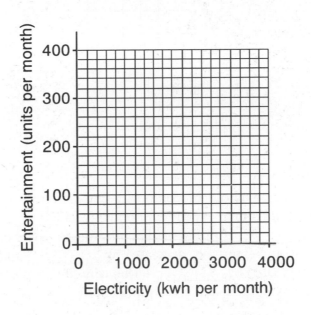

(b)   Now suppose a tax of 50 percent is imposed on electricity so that the consumer price of a kwh is now $0.15. This typical Ontario household responds by changing its consumption bundle to 90 units of entertainment and 1400 kwh's of electricity. Draw the new budget line and label the new equilibrium point E_B.

(c)   The government now decides to compensate households for the electricity tax by using the resulting revenue to send each household a monthly rebate that restores its real income. What will be the amount of this rebate for the typical household represented in this example? Explain.

(d)   Draw the budget line the typical household would face in the presence of the tax on electricity and the rebate scheme. Where on this new budget line would the household be consuming? Could the Government of Ontario have achieved its twin objectives with this tax-and-rebate scheme? Explain.

5. The following graph depicts a household's demand for widgets, which have a current price of $2 per unit.

Figure 7-8

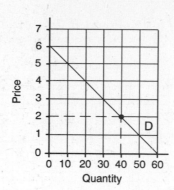

The total value this household places on its consumption of widgets is _____. However, the household's total expenditure on widgets is _____, so it receives consumers' surplus of _____. If the market price drops to $1, this household's total valuation of widgets would (increase, decrease) by _____ and its consumers' surplus would (increase, decrease) by _____. The value this household places on consumption of the twentieth widget is, and it is willing to pay _____ for 20 widgets.

6. An individual's weekly demand for playing squash is given by:

$$Q^D = 10 - 2P$$

where Q^D is hours of squash time demanded per week and P is the price per hour (for each player) of court time (assume that this person can always find a partner).
(a)   Plot this individual's demand curve for squash.

Figure 7-9

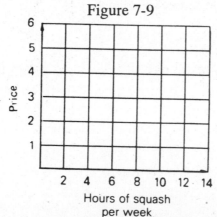

(b)   The only squash courts available are at The Racquet Club, Inc., where each player is charged $2 per hour. How much squash does this person play per week?

(c)   What is this individual's total valuation of the games consumed per week?

102

(d)   How much does this person actually spend on squash each week?

(e)   What is this individual's consumer surplus?

(f)   The Racquet Club, Inc., is considering a pricing scheme whereby individuals still pay $2 per hour of court time, but in addition they must also pay a mandatory membership fee. What is the largest fee The Racquet Club, Inc., could charge for a weekly membership without losing this individual as a customer?

(g)   As an alternative pricing scheme, suppose that The Racquet Club, Inc., introduces a membership fee but does not charge members for court time (i.e., members are entitled to unlimited use of the facility). What is the maximum amount this individual is willing to pay for a weekly membership under these circumstances?

*7.   A certain chief executive officer (CEO) with a large corporation instructs her personal secretary (a recent graduate of a prestigious M.B.A. program) to purchase tickets to the Stanley Cup playoffs. Specifically, she tells him, "If the tickets are $150 each, buy one ticket for me; at $100 each, buy two; and, if the price is $50 each, buy me three." The young secretary (eager to make an impression) responds, "Madame, your instructions appear to be inconsistent. You are saying that you are *willing to pay* more in total for two tickets than for three!" Is the secretary correct? Explain. (*Hint:* Sketch the CEO's demand curve for tickets.)

◆ **APPENDIX EXERCISES**

The following exercises are based on material in the two appendixes to this chapter. These should be read before attempting these exercises.

Appendix A

8.   (a)   The following table provides information on the quantities of food and clothing that are contained on indifference curves I, II, and III.

	Units of food			Units of clothing		
	I	II	III	I	II	III
	45	50	55	0	10	20
	30	35	40	5	15	25
	20	25	30	10	20	30
	15	20	25	15	25	35
	10	15	20	25	35	45

(i)   Graph indifference curves I, II, and III on the grid provided.

Figure 7-10

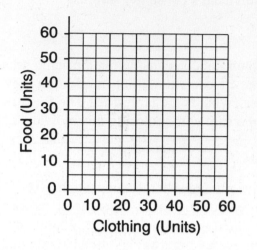

(ii)   Draw a budget line on the graph that represents a budget constraint of $350 and food and clothing prices of $10 and $15, respectively.

(iii) Given (i) and (ii), what combination of food and clothing will maximize consumer satisfaction? Explain.

(b)   Extend the analysis and use the same graph to show the derivation of a demand curve for clothing by proceeding as follows (assume that "food" stands for "everything consumed except clothing").

(i)   Change the price of clothing so that a budget line with the same food intercept (35) is tangent to each of the indifference curves I, II, and III. Extend the X axis as necessary.

The X intercepts for budget lines tangent to indifference curves I, II, and III are approximately _____, _____, and _____, respectively.

The prices of clothing represented by the budget lines are approximately _____, _____, and _____, respectively.

(ii)   Draw the price-consumption line on the graph.

(iii) Describe how the information on the price-consumption line can be used to derive a demand curve for clothing.

104

9. On the following graph, a household moves from one equilibrium E_0 to a new equilibrium E_1 after a decline in the price of commodity X.

Figure 7-11

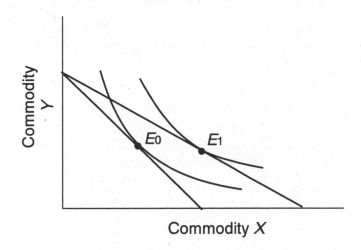

(a)   Illustrate on the graph the size of the substitution effect.
(b)   Illustrate on the graph the size of the income effect.
(c)   Is commodity X an inferior good? Explain.

Appendix B

10. The following table relates total utility and the number of milkshakes consumed per weekend.

Number of milkshakes per weekend	Total utility
0	0
1	50
2	90
3	120
4	130
5	130
6	120

Figure 7-12

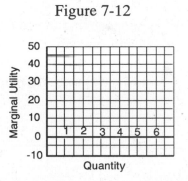

(a)   Plot the marginal utility schedule on the grid provided above.

(b)   At what point does the consumer experience disutility (i.e., after how many milk-shakes per weekend)?

11.   Suppose that a consumer spends recreation time and income on two leisure activities: tennis and fishing. The consumer has the basic equipment to pursue both activities. The costs associated with these activities are court fees for tennis and the expense of boat rental for fishing. The marginal utility schedules for hours spent on these activities are shown in the table below.

| Hours per week | Marginal utility schedule | |
	Fishing	Tennis
1	20	20
2	18	19
3	16	18
4	14	17
5	12	16
6	10	15
7	8	14
8	6	13

(a)   If the cost per hour of each activity is $1 and the consumer spends five hours per week on recreation activity, how many hours would be spent on each activity in order to maximize total utility?

(b)   Suppose that the cost of tennis increased 19 percent. What change in the "mix" of tennis and fishing would be required to maximize utility? Explain, using marginal utility to price ratios, why this is the case. (Consider the initial cost of both activities in (a) to be $1 per hour.)

◆ ANSWERS

Multiple-Choice Questions

1. (d) 2. (b) 3. (a) 4. (d) 5. (c) 6. (e) 7. (a) 8. (b) 9. (c) 10. (c) 11. (e) 12. (b) 13. (b) 14. (a) 15. (a) 16. (e) 17. (c) 18. (c) 19. (b) 20. (d) 21. (a) 22.(e) 23. (c) 24. (e) 25. (c) 26. (c) 27. (a) 28. (b) 29. (c) 30. (c) 31. (a) 32. (a)

Exercises

1.   (a)   Intercepts on the graph are 30 days of skiing and 50 rounds of golf.

(b) The combination of 20 units of each activity lies outside the budget line. It is therefore unattainable (unaffordable) at these prices with a total expenditure of $600.

(c) Intercepts are now 45 days of skiing and 75 rounds of golf.

(d) The intercept for golf would remain at 75 rounds; the skiing intercept changes to 30 days.

(e) The skiing intercept is 30 units and the golf intercept is now 50 rounds. BL_E and BL_A are identical because absolute prices and money income have changed in exactly the same proportions (i.e., by 50 percent).

2. (a) budget line *ab*

Figure 7-13

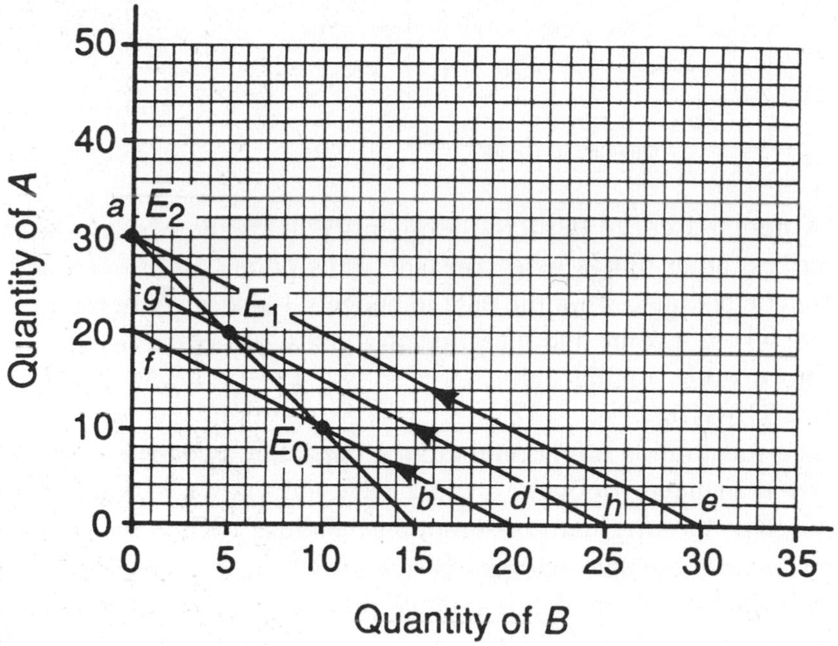

Quantity of B

(b) budget line *ae*

(c) (i) $100. Budget line *fd* just enables the household to afford to purchase its original bundle E_0 at the new prices. The shift from budget *fd* to *ae* is equivalent to giving the household an additional $100 money income.

(ii) $50. Budget line *gh* allows the household to repurchase E_1 at the new prices.

(iii) There is no change in real income in this case. The budget line that can repurchase the original bundle E_2 at the new prices is simply *ae*, the actual budget line that results from the new prices.

3.   (a)

Figure 7-14   Figure 7-15

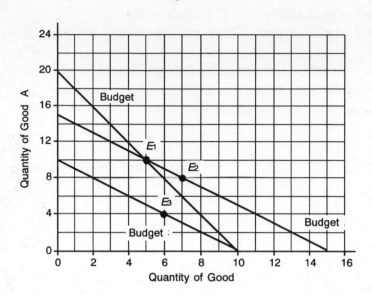

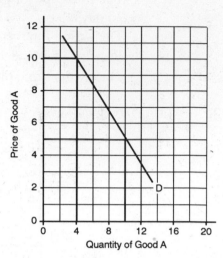

(b)   A demand curve depicts the quantity demanded of a commodity at different prices, other things held constant. Thus points on the demand curve for good *A* can be obtained from the data in budgets 1 and 3 where the price of good *A* varies but where income and the price of good *B* are held constant. The demand curve is shown above on the right.

(c) $1 = \$10/\$10$.

(d)   The substitution effect refers to the impact of a change in relative prices on quantity demanded. Budgets 1 and 2 have the same *real* income so that each passes through the original consumption bundle E_1. Thus the change in consumption between these two budgets is due strictly to the change in relative prices. The substitution effect of this relative price change on the demand for good *A* is -2 since consumption falls from 10 to 8.

(e)   The income effect refers to the change in demand resulting from a change in income, holding new relative prices constant. This corresponds to a shift from budget 2 to budget 3. The income effect on the demand for good *A* is -4 since consumption falls from 8 to 4. The total reduction in quantity demanded of good *A* is 6.

(f)   In the shift from budget 2 to budget 3, income decreases and the quantity demanded of each good also decreases. Therefore, each is normal.

4.   (a)   The initial budget line is *ab* in the following graph.

Figure 7-16

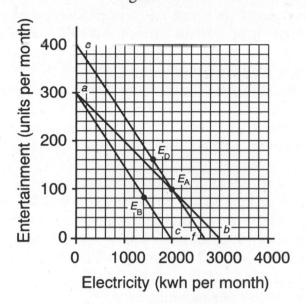

(b)   The resulting budget line is *ac* in the above graph.
(c)   If the household's real income (i.e., purchasing power) were restored, it would be able to purchase its original consumption bundle E_A at the new prices. Thus, it would be able to purchase 100 units of entertainment and 2000 kwh's of electricity at prices of $1 and $0.15, respectively. This requires a total expenditure of $400. Since the household only has $300 to spend, it will require a rebate of $100.
(d)   The final budget line is *ef*. The household will consume a bundle on budget line *ef* between *e* and E_A. Except for the rare case in which a household remains at E_A, most households will decrease their consumption of electricity relative to the initial consumption level of 2000 kwh's (for example, the household may consume bundle E_D). Yes, the Government could have realized its twin objectives because any bundle between *e* and E_A constitutes a reduction in electrical consumption, but the same real income as before intervention.

5. $160; $80; $80; increase; $15; increase; $45; $4; $100.

6.   (a)

Figure 7-17

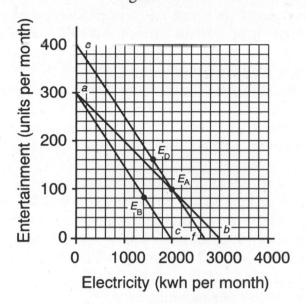

(b)   Six hours per week.
(c) $21 (obtained by calculating the area under the demand curve up to a quantity of 6).

109

(d) $12 (i.e., $2 x 6).

(e) $9 (obtained by calculating the area below the demand curve and above the price line).

(f)   For consumption of six hours, this person is willing to pay the total valuation of $21. At a price of $2, current payment is $12 for six hours. Therefore, this individual is willing to pay an additional $9 to play six hours of squash, which may be collected as a membership fee.

(g)   By joining the club, the price per hour is zero, so as a member this person would now play 10 hours of squash each week. The value this individual places on 10 hours of squash is $25. Thus $25 could now be charged for a membership in The Racquet Club, Inc., without losing this person as a member.

*7.   No, the secretary is not correct. The CEO's demand curve is sketched in the following diagram. The CEO is willing to pay $150 for the first ticket, $100 for the second, and $50 for the third. Thus for two tickets she is willing to pay $250: ($150 + $100), and for three she is willing to pay $300: ($150 + $100 + $50). If the price is $100 per ticket, she has only to pay $200 for two, and if the price is $50, she has only to pay $150 for three. What she is willing to pay is determined by the value she places on the consumption of these goods, not on the cost of purchasing them.

Figure 7-18

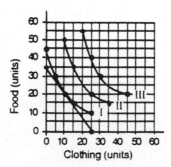

Appendix A

8.   (a)   (i) and (ii) The indifference curves and budget line are shown on the following graph.

Figure 7-19

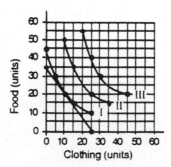

        (iii)   F = 20; C = 10. Given the budget constraint, curve I is the highest indifference curve attainable.

110

(b)   (i)   Quantities: 23.3; 58; 105. Prices: $15; $6; $3.33.

       (ii)   Connect points of tangency.

       (iii)   Plot the corresponding price-quantity combinations on a graph with price on the Y axis and quantity demanded on the X axis.

9.   (a)   The substitution effect is AB in the graph.

       (b)   The income effect is BC in the graph.

       (c)   No. If X were an inferior good, there would have to be a negative income effect.

Figure 7-20

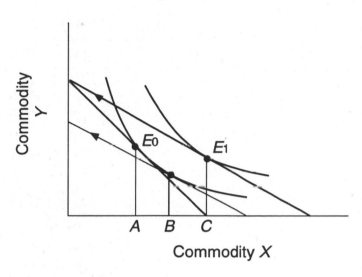

Appendix B

10.   (a)   The graph should show the following points (marginal utility is given in parentheses next to number of milkshakes consumed): 1(50), 2(40), 3(30), 4(10), 5(0), 6(-10).

       (b)   After the fifth milkshake.

11.   (a)   Utility maximization requires that $MU_T/P_T = MU_F/P_F$. When tennis and fishing are priced the same (e.g., $1.00 each) and a total of 5 hours must be allocated across these activities, the utility maximization condition is satisfied when 18/1 = 18/1. This implies: three hours on tennis and two hours on fishing.

       (b)   With the price of tennis increased to $1.19 (19 percent), the condition is met when 19/1.19 = 16/1 (approximately). Thus three hours are now allocated to fishing and two to tennis.

Chapter 8

Using Demand Theory

◆ LEARNING OBJECTIVES

After studying this chapter, you should be able to:

✔   resolve the paradox of value;

✔   distinguish between free goods and scarce goods;

✔   discuss consumer behaviour under conditions of uncertainty;

✔   explain why there is a market for insurance and discuss the effects of moral hazard and adverse selection;

✔   understand the roles of risk pooling and risk sharing in the development of insurance markets.

◆ HINTS AND TIPS

You might be guided by the fact that frequent errors on examinations are attributable to:

✔   confusion between the concepts of marginal and total values of consumption, and their relationship to price; and

✔   an inability to correctly calculate expected values.

◆ MULTIPLE-CHOICE QUESTIONS

1.   The existence of a relatively stable, negatively sloped market demand curve requires that
      (a)   all households behave as assumed in the theory at all times.
      (b)   all households behave "rationally".

(c)   all households have stable, negatively sloped demand curves.
(d)   erratic or irrational consumers be excluded from the data.
(e)   at any moment in time, most households are behaving as predicted by the theory.

2. The "paradox of value" arises from the fact that
    (a)   people are irrational in consumption choices.
    (b)   free goods are essential for life.
    (c)   there is no necessary positive relationship between the marginal and total values households place upon consumption.
    (d)   the higher the price of a good, the greater is the total value of consumption.
    (e)   the price of a good and its market value are unrelated.

3. Diamonds have a higher price than water because
    (a)   household total consumption value of diamonds is greater than that of water.
    (b)   household total consumption value of water is greater than that of diamonds.
    (c)   the marginal consumption value of diamonds is greater than that of water.
    (d)   households are willing to pay more in total for diamonds than for water.
    (e)   marginal value and total values are negatively related.

4. Good A is more of a luxury commodity than good B if
    (a)   the price of A is greater than B.
    (b)   the price elasticity of demand for A is greater than that for B.
    (c)   the area under A's demand curve is less than that under B's.
    (d)   the quantity demanded of A is more responsive to price changes than the quantity demanded of B.
    (e)   the marginal consumption value of A is greater than that of B.

5. The price elasticity of demand for a good depends on
    (a)   only whether the good is a necessity or a luxury.
    (b)   the value households place on the consumption of one unit more or less.
    (c)   the total value placed on consumption.
    (d)   the market value of a good.
    (e)   None of the above.

6. A good with a market price of zero is indicative of
    (a)   a good that nobody wants at any price.
    (b)   a good for which quantity supplied exceeds quantity demanded at a price of zero.
    (c)   a scarce good.
    (d)   an inferior good.
    (e)   a necessity.

7. As the value individuals place on the consumption of an additional unit of a good increases the
    (a)   more inelastic is demand.
    (b)   greater is its total consumption value.
    (c)   more the good can be classified as a necessity.
    (d)   more the good can be classified as a luxury.
    (e)   greater is the area under the good's demand curve.

8. That voters in a town could believe that an excellent school system is an important public asset but then vote down a school tax levy
   (a) is clearly irrational behavior because of the high value placed on education.
   (b) suggests bias in the poll that led to an overassessment of the importance given to public education.
   (c) indicates a low voter turnout except for antitaxers.
   (d) could be quite consistent since high total values do not rule out low marginal values, especially in ranges of high total expenditure.
   (e) is indicative of a low total value of consumption.

9. A law requiring that water be provided free to everyone
   (a) ensures that only households with the highest marginal values will consume water.
   (b) ensures that all households will consume equal quantities of water.
   (c) is likely to result in some households with a low marginal value of water getting water while others with a higher marginal value do without.
   (d) ensures that households can consume water until the marginal value of water is zero.
   (e) would reduce the total consumption value of water.

10. The total market value of a commodity
    (a) exceeds the value consumers place on the consumption of a given quantity of the commodity.
    (b) is measured by the area under the demand curve at the quantity purchased.
    (c) is the amount everyone spends to purchase it.
    (d) varies negatively with its market price.
    (e) is what consumers are willing to pay for a given quantity of the good.

11. The degree of risk attached to a given choice
    (a) refers to the dispersion in the possible results from that choice.
    (b) is always negatively related to the expected value.
    (c) is always positively related to the expected value.
    (d) varies among risk-averse, risk-neutral, and risk-loving individuals.
    (e) is zero for all "fair" games.

Questions 12 and 13 assume the following information: Consider a game involving repeated tosses of a fair coin. If the result is a head, $1 is won; if the result is a tail, $1 is lost.

12. The expected value of this game is
    (a) $1 (0.5) + $1 (0.5) = $1.　　　　(b) $1 (1.0) + $1 (1.0) = $2.
    (c) $1 (1.0) - $1 (1.0) = $0.　　　　(d) $1 (0.5) - $1 (0.5) = $0.
    (e) $1 - $1 = $0.

13. Risk-averse individuals
    (a) would play the game without a risk premium.
    (b) should be indifferent about playing the game.
    (c) would choose to play the game only if the number of tosses were sufficiently large.
    (d) would not play the game.
    (e) None of the above.

14. The main explanation of why insurance companies can afford to absorb their customers' risks is their ability to engage in
    (a) insuring against events such as war where a common cause acts on all insured units.
    (b) risk pooling and risk sharing.
    (c) adverse selection.
    (d) moral hazard.
    (e) "fair" games.

15. A "fair" game is one in which
    (a) the expected value of the outcome is zero.
    (b) the expected winnings equal the expected losses.
    (c) the average gain or loss per play will tend to approach zero as the number of repetitive plays increases.
    (d) a player expects to break even.
    (e) All of the above are correct.

16. A risk-neutral individual would
    (a) never participate in a fair game.
    (b) be indifferent about participating in a fair game.
    (c) not buy a $1,000 insurance policy to protect against a 1/100 chance of losing $100,000.
    (d) avoid all risky situations.
    (e) take on any and all risks.

17. One reason insurance firms offer policies with only partial coverage is
    (a) moral hazard.
    (b) risk-loving customers.
    (c) that it permits the insurer to pool its risks.
    (d) risk spreading.
    (e) All of the above.

◆ EXERCISES

1. The table that follows provides data on the total value a household places upon the consumption of different quantities of pizza per week.

Pizzas per week	Total value	Marginal value
1	$14	_____
2	24	_____
3	31	_____
4	36	_____
5	40	_____

(a) Calculate the marginal value the household places on each successive pizza consumed.

(b)   If the price of a pizza is $5, how many will this household purchase per week?

(c)   Calculate the associated consumers' surplus at a market price of $5 by subtracting total expenditure from total consumption value.

(d)   Calculate consumers' surplus by summing the incremental consumers' surplus derived from each successive unit purchased.

2.   The following table presents the amount a consumer is willing to pay for successive units of yogurt and movies during a weekly time period.

Unit consumed per week	Willingness to pay for each container of yogurt	Willingness to pay for each movie
1st	$8.00	$4.00
2nd	4.00	3.75
3rd	3.10	3.50
4th	2.40	3.25
5th	1.80	3.00
6th	1.40	2.75
7th	1.10	2.50
8th	0.90	2.25
9th	0.80	2.00
10th	0.75	1.75

Suppose that the price of yogurt is 90 cents and the price of a movie is $3.00.

(a)   How many of each of these goods does this individual consume on a weekly basis?

(b)   What are the market values of each of these consumption levels?

(c)   What total value does this consumer place on the consumption of these goods at the current market prices?

(d)   What consumers' surplus is derived from each good?

3.   Suppose that there is one chance in a 100 that your $100,000 house will be damaged by flooding. You are considering the purchase of an insurance policy to cover the possible loss. You can either purchase the policy at a price of $1,000 and eliminate the risk or not buy it and risk the damage.

(a)   Calculate the expected value of both courses of action.

(b)   If you were risk-averse, would you buy the policy? Explain.

(c)   If you were risk-neutral, would you buy the policy? Explain.

(d)   Assume that the cost of the policy rises to $1,200. Would a risk-neutral person purchase it? A risk-averse person? Explain.

*4.   Consider a farmer who can plant wheat or corn (but not both) on a given piece of land. If the weather is good, the wheat harvest will yield a profit of $4,000, whereas corn would yield a profit of $1,800. However, if the weather is bad, the wheat harvest would have a profit of only $1,000, but the corn profit would be $3,000. Assume that good and bad weather are equally likely and that the farmer's objective is to get as large a profit as possible.

(a)   If the farmer is risk-neutral, what will she plant on this piece of land?

(b)   Would your answer change if she were risk-averse?

◆ ANSWERS

Multiple-Choice Questions

1. (e) 2. (c) 3. (c) 4. (c) 5. (b) 6. (b) 7. (a) 8. (d) 9. (c) 10. (c) 11. (a) 12.(d) 13. (d) 14. (b) 15. (e) 16. (b) 17. (a)

Exercises

1. (a)

Pizzas per week	Total value	Marginal value
1	$14	14
2	24	10
3	31	7
4	36	5
5	40	4

(b) 4.

(c) consumers' surplus = total valuation - total expenditure = $36 - ($5 x 4) = $16.

(d) Consumers' surplus from each unit consumed equals the marginal value minus market price. Thus consumers' surplus on the first unit is $9, on the second $5, on the third $2, and zero on the last unit consumed. Summing these yields $16.

2. (a) Quantity demanded for yogurt is 8 and for movies it is 5.

(b) The market value of consumed yogurt is $7.20 (i.e., 8 x $0.90), and for movies the market value is $15 (i.e., $3 x 5).

(c) Consumer total valuation of yogurt consumption is $22.70: ($8 + $4 + ... + $0.90), while for movie consumption it is $17.50: ($4 + $3.75 + ... + $3).

(d) Consumers' surplus for yogurt is $15.50 and for movies it is $2.50.

3. (a) Expected value of buying: -$1,000; expected value of not buying: -$100,000 (0.01) + $0 (0.99) = - $1,000.

(b) Yes, because the expected value of the two choices (buy/not buy) are the same (-$1,000), but not buying the insurance is much riskier than buying it.

(c) A risk-neutral person would be indifferent between buying the insurance policy and not buying it since both courses of action have the same expected value (assuming that there are no other considerations).

(d) At $1,200 the expected net gain of buying the policy is negative. A risk-neutral person would not buy it. A risk-averse person would still buy the policy if the value of reducing the risk was worth more than the additional $200 cost.

4. (a) The risk-neutral farmer plants wheat, which has the higher expected profit: expected profit from wheat = 1/2 ($4,000) + 1/2 ($1,000) = $2,500; expected profit from corn = 1/2 ($1,800) + 1/2 ($3,000) = $2,400.

(b) Uncertain. Although corn yields a lower expected profit, the dispersion of profit for corn due to weather is less than that for wheat. For a risk-averse individual, the lower expected profit of $100 may be more than offset by the lower risk associated with planting corn.

Chapter 9

The Role of the Firm

◆ LEARNING OBJECTIVES

After studying this chapter, you should be able to:

✔   identify the major differences among single proprietorships, partnerships, and corporations;

✔   distinguish between debt and equity financing;

✔   understand the meaning of opportunity cost, and its implications for decision-making by the firm;

✔   distinguish economic profits from accounting profits, and;

✔   explain how profits provide important signals for the allocation of resources.

◆ HINTS AND TIPS

Frequent examination errors on the material in this chapter are attributable to:

✔   an incomplete understanding of imputed costs and their treatment in the calculation of profits.

◆ MULTIPLE-CHOICE QUESTIONS

1.   One of the major differences between a partnership and a corporation is that
      (a)   the owners of a corporation always outnumber the owners of a partnership.
      (b)   a corporation always has more assets.
      (c)   the owners of a corporation have limited liability, whereas partners have unlimited liability.
      (d)   corporations are always more profitable.
      (e)   corporations are listed on a stock market such as the Toronto Stock Exchange.

2. One of the significant disadvantages of a corporation is
   (a) the double taxation of income.
   (b) limited liability.
   (c) that the only way it can raise capital is by borrowing.
   (d) that it must issue annual dividends.
   (e) All of the above.

3. Which of the following groups of claimants would be the last to have their claims honored in a corporate bankruptcy?
   (a) Bondholders.
   (b) Stockholders.
   (c) Commercial creditors.
   (d) Employees owed back wages.
   (e) Governments owed back taxes.

4. Corporations can finance their operations by
   (a) reinvesting profits.
   (b) issuing bonds.
   (c) issuing new equity.
   (d) borrowing.
   (e) All of the above.

5. The assumption that firms maximize profit
   (a) has yielded predictions of firms' behavior that have been substantially correct.
   (b) is irrefutable.
   (c) has been observed to be always true.
   (d) implies that profits are the only factor that influence business decisions.
   (e) Both (b) and (c) are correct.

6. Debt financing by firms involves
   (a) issuance of common stock only.
   (b) selling bonds to the public or borrowing from financial institutions.
   (c) issuance of common and preferred stock.
   (d) retention of undistributed profits.
   (e) Both (b) and (c) are correct.

7. A major assumption in the economic theory of the firm is that
   (a) decisions within the firm are made by consensus between labor and management.
   (b) regardless of their size, firms are assumed to act as a single consistent decision-making unit.
   (c) every firm behaves in a fundamentally different and unpredictable way.
   (d) objectives of firms depend primarily on firm size.
   (e) objectives of corporations differ from those of proprietorships.

8. Which of the following firms are examples of public enterprises in Canada?
   (a) CBC or VIA Rail.
   (b) Bell Canada or Canadian Pacific.
   (c) Any firm that serves the public, such as Harvey's Hamburgers or Famous Players' Theatres.
   (d) Any firm listed on the stock exchange, such as the Ford Motor Company of Canada.
   (e) Any firm that makes its financial statements public.

9. Suppose that you own a dairy store that makes and sells homemade ice cream, using an ice cream maker that has no alternative use and no resale value. It cost $1,500 when it was purchased 15 years ago. The opportunity cost of its use is
    (a) $100, representing the annual depreciation.
    (b) zero.
    (c) some number greater than zero but under $100, representing the annual depreciation.
    (d) the amount of imputed interest on the cost of a replacement machine.
    (e) its replacement cost.

10. Economic profits are defined as the difference between
    (a) accounting profits and normal profits.
    (b) total revenues and opportunity costs.
    (c) total revenues and the monetary costs of hiring resources for current use.
    (d) net income before and after taxes.
    (e) total revenues and imputed costs.

11. Opportunity cost refers to
    (a) what must be given up to secure the next best alternative.
    (b) unexpected profits for the firm.
    (c) the best rate of return possible on an investment.
    (d) the return to using something in the most profitable way.
    (e) the cost of hiring labour or renting equipment.

12. Applying the concept of opportunity cost to the firm is difficult because
    (a) it requires imputing certain costs when a resource is not directly hired or purchased.
    (b) most of a firm's costs are monetary costs.
    (c) many labour contracts include fringe benefits.
    (d) the firm uses many different tyes of inputs.
    (e) revenues are sometimes unknown.

13. Which of the following is most likely to represent an imputed cost to the firm?
    (a) Wages paid to current employees.
    (b) Rent for use of a leased plant.
    (c) Interest paid on borrowed funds.
    (d) Interest that could have been received on money currently invested in inventory.
    (e) Dividends paid to shareholders.

14. When a firm uses its own funds to finance a project,
    (a) the cost of these funds is zero.
    (b) profits are greater because the firm does not have to borrow.
    (c) the forgone interest that could have been earned by these funds is an imputed cost of the project.
    (d) future profits diminish when revenues are used to replace internal investment funds.
    (e) profits are greater because interest does not have to be paid.

15. Depreciation, defined as the loss of value of an asset associated with its use in production,
    (a)   is clearly a monetary cost.
    (b)   is a function only of wear and tear in use.
    (c)   is not an economic cost if the asset has no market value or alternative use.
    (d)   does not apply to used equipment.
    (e)   does not affect economic profit so long as the asset has been fully paid for.

16. Accounting profits are
    (a)   always positive.
    (b)   usually greater than economic profits.
    (c)   the same as normal profits.
    (d)   the result of technologically inefficient production.
    (e)   less than normal profits.

17. Normal profits refer to
    (a)   what all firms, on average, obtain as a return on investment.
    (b)   the base used by Revenue Canada to levy business taxes.
    (c)   the imputed return to capital and risk-taking required to keep firms in the industry.
    (d)   the level of profits necessary to ensure that the firm covers its day-to-day operating expenses.
    (e)   a return to capital that is comparable to rates of return earned on bank deposits.

18. Sunk costs are
    (a)   the costs to a firm of using its own capital.
    (b)   costs incurred in the past that involve no current opportunity cost.
    (c)   costs that must be accounted for only if the firm is producing current output.
    (d)   depreciation costs on any fully owned plant and equipment.
    (e)   imputed costs.

19. If economic profits are zero for all firms in an industry, then
    (a)   firms are earning less than normal profits and will shift resources toward alternative investments.
    (b)   revenues equal the monetary costs of operation.
    (c)   resources are earning a return in this industry at least equal to that available elsewhere.
    (d)   firms will cease production immediately.
    (e)   firms will exit the industry.

20. The major role of economic profits, as seen in this chapter, is to
    (a)   provide income for shareholders.
    (b)   provide income for entrepreneurs.
    (c)   serve as a signal to firms concerning the desirability of devoting additional resources to a particular activity.
    (d)   encourage labor to reform the system.
    (e)   provide a revenue base for business taxation.

21. Equity financing includes
    (a) selling newly issued shares.   (b) reinvesting profits.
    (c) investing dividends.   (d) selling bonds.
    (e) Both (a) and (b) are correct.

22. Which of the following is *not* an imputed cost?
    (a) Use of a firm's own funds.
    (b) Depreciation.
    (c) A return that compensates for risk taking.
    (d) An owner-manger's time.
    (e) The cost of an asset with no resale value.

23. A firm's real (or physical) capital is
    (a) money borrowed from banks.
    (b) the value of the firm's stocks.
    (c) start-up financing provided by the original owners.
    (d) comprised of plant and equipment.
    (e) its undistributed profits.

24. For a firm that is operated by an owner-manager
    (a) economic profits invariably exceed accounting profits.
    (b) economic and accounting profits are equal.
    (c) economic profits are large because a manager does not have to be hired.
    (d) there are no imputed costs because all costs are known.
    (e) the salary forgone from alternative employment of the owner-manager must be included in calculating economic profits.

25. A firm has total revenues of $100,000, total monetary outlays of $75,000, and imputed costs of $25,000. It is correct to say that
    (a) economic profits are $25,000   (b) normal profits are $25,000.
    (c) accounting profits are zero.   (d) accounting profits are negative.
    (e) economic profits arc zero.

◆ EXERCISES

1. After five years of working, Mary Kaufman left a $25,000 job to start her own business with the use of $20,000 she had saved. She charged the business $15,000 a year for her services but made no allowance for the 10 percent she might have earned on her savings in an investment of equal risk. In 1993 her accounting profits were $10,000. Had the business been economically profitable to that point? What needs to be known to decide whether it is economically profitable to continue the business?

2. The following table presents last year's annual income statement for Harry's Hardware Store. Harry worked full-time at the store. He also used $25,000 of his savings to furnish and stock the store (included in costs). At the beginning of last year, he had been offered a $20,000 annual salary to work in another hardware store.

Annual Income Statement

Revenues		Costs	
Sales of merchandise	$90,000	Wholesale purchases	$60,000
Service revenues	5,000	Store supplies	2,000
		Labor costs (hired)	10,000
		Utilities	1,000
		Rent	5,000
		Depreciation on fixtures	2,000
Total revenues	$95,000	Total costs	$80,000

(a) Calculate the last year's accounting profits for Harry's Hardware Store.

(b) What are some imputed costs that Harry should include in estimating the total costs of owning his business?

(c) Assume an interest rate of 10 percent. What are the total costs of Harry's owning this business?

(d) Calculate his economic profits.

3. (a) For $10,000 a firm purchases a machine with an estimated 10 years of economic life and zero salvage value. What is the straight-line depreciation per year?

(b) At the end of five years, this firm finds that the machine has a market value of only $1,000, which is expected to decline to zero after the five remaining years. What is the economically relevant depreciation per year now?

4. Arrange the following items and use the information presented to obtain:

(a) net profit before taxes, (b) economic profit before taxes, (c) economic profit after taxes. (*Hint:* See Table 9-1 in the text.)

- Revenue from sale of goods: $5 million
- Tax rate: 50 percent of net profit before tax
- Depreciation: $500,000
- Salaries: $1 million
- Imputed charges for use of own capital and risk taking: $500,000
- Cost of raw materials: $2 million

(a) Net profit before taxes = _____
(b) Economic profit before taxes = _____
(c) Economic profit after taxes = _____

5. Jean-Marc, a third-year honours economics student at Laurentian University, is considering the possibility of setting up his own business for the summer. Specifically, Jean-Marc plans to provide door-to-door delivery of the *Financial Post*, the *Wall Street Journal*, and the *New York Times* to cottagers in the Muskoka and Haliburton resort regions of Ontario. Because he will be graduating and seeking permanent employment next year, this enterprise is for one summer only and is an alternative to earning $3,000 after-tax income as a lifeguard. The following list itemizes the particulars:

- Jean-Marc expects total revenues of $24,000 for the season.
- To deliver the papers, he must purchase a van for $6,000, which he is certain to sell at season's end for $4,000.
- The license for distributing newspapers in these regions costs $3,000 and lasts for three years. However, it is nontransferable (i.e., it cannot be sold or used by anyone else).
- To finance the purchase of the van and the license, Jean-Marc will withdraw $9,000 from his savings account for a period of six months. This account pays an annual interest rate of 10 percent.
- It will cost $8,000 to purchase the newspapers in bulk. To get this special price, Jean-Marc agrees to pay the $8,000 up front (i.e., at the beginning of the season). He borrows this amount from a bank for six months at an annual interest rate of 15 percent.
- Costs of promotion, gas, and other incidentals come to $2,500.
- Although Jean-Marc expects $24,000 in revenues, it may actually be less. Thus there is some risk involved. He feels that $1,000 would compensate him for taking the risk.
- The tax rate on his business is 50 percent of net income.

(a) What are Jean-Marc's direct and indirect costs for hired and purchased factors? (*Note:* Include any depreciation of assets.)

(b)   What are Jean-Marc's imputed costs?

(c)   What is Jean-Marc's net profit before taxes and after taxes?

(d)   What are his economic profits after taxes?

(e)   If the business tax rate were applied to economic profits rather than to net income, would Jean-Marc be more or less likely to undertake this enterprise?

◆ ANSWERS

Multiple-Choice Questions

1. (c) 2. (a) 3. (b) 4. (e) 5. (a) 6. (b) 7. (b) 8. (a) 9. (b) 10. (b) 11. (a) 12.(a) 13. (d) 14. (c)
15. (c) 16. (b) 17. (c) 18. (b) 19. (c) 20. (c) 21. (e) 22. (e) 23. (d) 24. (e) 25. (e)

Exercises

1.   No, she would have been $2,000 better-off by working and investing separately. In deciding whether or not to continue it is current alternatives that count: Can she still get $25,000 in the old job (or another)? Can she sell her business assets for $20,000 and reasonably expect a $2,000 return? What are her expectations regarding sales increases next year?

2.   (a) $15,000.
       (b)   Harry's imputed costs include foregone annual interest on the $25,000 investment (assuming that he could recover it), and $20,000 opportunity cost for his own salary.
       (c)   Total costs would be accounting costs of $80,000 plus foregone interest earnings of $2,500 and $20,000 salary.
       (d)   A *loss* of $7,500 is indicated for the past year.

3.   (a) $1,000.
       (b) $200, the amount of market value given up by using the machine one more year.

4. Revenue $5.0 million
        Less direct cost (salaries and materials)   -3.0 million
        Less indirect cost (depreciation)   -0.5 million
    (a) Net profit before taxes: $1.5 million
         Less imputed cost of capital and risk taking   -0.5 million
    (b) Economic profit before taxes: $1.0 million
         Less taxes (0.5 x $1.5 million)   -0.75 million
    (c) Economic profit after taxes: $0.25 million

5. (a) Direct costs:
              License $ 3,000
              Interest payments on loan   600
              Bulk purchase   8,000
              Promotion, gas, etc.   2,500
         Indirect costs:
              Depreciation of van   2,000
         Total direct and indirect costs   **$16,100**
    (b) Imputed costs:
              Interest forgone on savings $ 450
              Risk compensation   1,000
              Forgone lifeguard earnings   3,000
         Total imputed costs   **$4,450**

    (c) Net profit before taxes = revenue - (direct costs + indirect costs) =
         $24,000 - $16,100 = $7,900.
         Net profit after taxes = $7,900 X 0.50 = $3,950.

    (d) Economic profit after taxes = net income after taxes - imputed costs
         = $3,950 - $4,450 = -$500.
    (e) Economic profit before taxes = revenue - imputed costs - (direct + indirect costs)
         = $24,000 - $4,450 - $16,100 = $3,450.
         Economic profit after taxes = $3,450 x 0.50 = $1,725.

    Jean-Marc is more likely to undertake this enterprise if the business tax is applied
    to economic profits instead of net profit. By taxing net income, Revenue Canada
    does not allow Jean-Marc to deduct real (albeit imputed) costs and thereby con-
    verts his economic profit into a loss of $500.

Chapter 10

Production and Cost in the Short Run

◆ LEARNING OBJECTIVES

After studying this chapter, you should be able to:

✔   explain how the different time horizons (the short, long, and very long runs) affect decision making by firms;

✔   explain the law of diminishing returns;

✔   show how total, average, and marginal product curves summarize production information in alternative ways;

✔   relate the family of product curves to the family of cost curves;

✔   explain the economic definition of capacity.

◆ HINTS AND TIPS

Your performance on examinations will significantly improve if when reading this chapter you

✔   fully understand the relationships among all product curves, and all cost curves;

✔   learn how to derive short run cost curves from product curves;

✔   understand the common sense of the relationship between marginal and average product (or cost) curves, and;

✔   understand the economic reasoning behind the shapes of the various curves.

1. The short run is defined as a period
    (a)   of less than a month.
    (b)   during which there is insufficient time to change the employment level of any factor.
    (c)   during which some factors are fixed and others are variable.
    (d)   during which new firms can enter an industry and old firms can exit.
    (e)   during which there is insufficient time to change output.

2. The long run time horizon
    (a)   is the same for all firms.
    (b)   allows the impact of new inventions to be felt.
    (c)   is defined as the minimum length of time it takes to vary output.
    (d)   is a length of time that is sufficient for all factors to be variable.
    (e)   allows for changes in only labor employment levels.

3. Which of the following is an example of a short run production decision?
    (a)   A firm decides to relocate.
    (b)   A contractor decides to work his crew overtime to finish a job.
    (c)   A railway decides to eliminate all passenger service.
    (d)   A paper company installs antipollution equipment.
    (e)   An airline expands its fleet of aircraft.

4. The production function relates
    (a)   outputs to inputs.
    (b)   outputs to labor inputs only.
    (c)   outputs to costs.
    (d)   costs to inputs.
    (e)   an economy's attainable combinations of output to alternative resource allocations.

5. Assuming that capital is a fixed input and that labor is variable, the total product curve relates
    (a)   output to various levels of capital and labor employment.
    (b)   output to various levels of labor employment with capital held constant.
    (c)   labor cost to the level of output.
    (d)   total cost to various levels of labor employment.
    (e)   output to the cost of labor.

6. An increase in the fixed input
    (a)   shifts the total product curve upward.
    (b)   does not affect the total product curve.
    (c)   lengthens the firm's long run time horizon.
    (d)   lengthens the firm's short run time horizon.
    (e)   Both (c) and (d) are correct.

7. When a firm increases employment of a variable input, it
   (a) shifts the production possibility curve.
   (b) shifts its total product curve upward.
   (c) alters its production function.
   (d) is making a long run decision.
   (e) moves along its total product curve.

8. If labor is the variable factor, average product is defined as
   (a) total product divided by total output.
   (b) the quantity of labor divided by total product.
   (c) the additional output produced by the last unit of labor.
   (d) output per unit of labor.
   (e) total product divided by capital.

9. The change in output that results when another unit of the variable factor is employed is referred to as
   (a) marginal product.   (b) average product.
   (c) average fixed product.   (d) total product.
   (e) average total product.

10. If average product is falling, marginal product
    (a) is less than average product.
    (b) is equal to average product.
    (c) is greater than average product.
    (d) can be greater than, equal to, or less than average product.
    (e) is negative.

11. If marginal product is falling, marginal product
    (a) is always less than average product.
    (b) is always equal to average product.
    (c) is always greater than average product.
    (d) can be greater than, equal to, or less than average product.
    (e) is negative.

12. The law of diminishing returns states that
    (a) as output increases, the rate of increase in costs will eventually decrease.
    (b) as output increases, profits will eventually decline.
    (c) the incremental output achieved by increases in a variable factor will eventually decrease.
    (d) as more labor is employed, the wage rate will increase and thereby increase costs.
    (e) as more labor is employed, the total product curve eventually has a negative slope.

13. A firm's wage bill in the short run equals its
    (a) short run total costs.
    (b) total variable costs.
    (c) total fixed costs.
    (d) marginal costs.
    (e) average total cost multiplied by output.

14. "Spreading one's overhead" is equivalent to
    (a)   increasing capital to spread total costs.
    (b)   decreasing average fixed costs.
    (c)   increasing output to decrease average total costs.
    (d)   any decrease in total costs.
    (e)   increasing employment of the variable factor.

15. Using the notation in the text, *AFC* equals
    (a)   *ATC - AVC*.   (b)   *AVC + MC*.
    (c)   *ATC* at its minimum point.   (d)   *TC - TVC*.
    (e)   *ATC + AVC*.

16. *AVC* equals
    (a)   *MC + AFC*.   (b)   *TVC* per unit of labor.
    (c)   *ATC + AFC*.   (d)   *MC* at the minimum point of *AVC*.
    (e)   *ATC + MC*.

Questions 17 to 21 refer to the following graph, which illustrates a firm's average total cost (*ATC*) and average variable cost (*AVC*) curves.

Figure 10-1

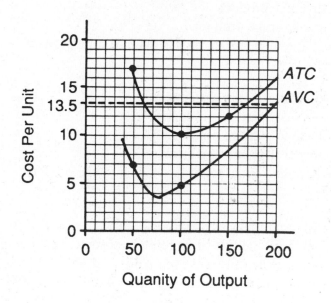

17. When the firm is producing 200 units of output, total costs in the short run are
    (a) $3,200.   (b) $2,700.
    (c) $16.   (d) $13.50.
    (e)   Indeterminable with data provided.

18. When output equals 100 units, marginal cost is
    (a) $5.   (b) $15.
    (c) $10.   (d) $500.
    (e)   Indeterminable with data provided.

134

19. At a total product of 200 units, *AFC* is
    (a) $2.50.   (b) $13.50.
    (c) $16.   (d) $2,700.
    (e) Indeterminable with data provided.

20. If the level of production is 50 units, *TFC* is
    (a) $350.   (b) $7.
    (c) $500.   (d) $10.
    (e) Indeterminable with data provided.

21. At an output of 200, *TFC* is
    (a) $500   (b) $3,200
    (c) $2.50   (d) $2,700
    (e) Indeterminable with data provided.

22. Total cost is $30 at 10 units of output and $32 at 11 units of output. In this range of output, marginal cost is
    (a) equal to average total cost.   (b) greater than average total cost.
    (c) less than average total cost.   (d) less than average fixed cost.
    (e) Indeterminable with the information provided.

23. If the difference between average total cost (*ATC*) and average variable cost (*AVC*) at 100 units of output is $1, at 200 units of output the difference between *ATC* and *AVC* must be
    (a) $2.   (b) $1.
    (c) 50 cents.   (d) $1.50
    (e) zero.

24. A firm's capacity
    (a) continuously declines as output increases.
    (b) is the output level corresponding to minimum average total cost.
    (c) is the size of its plant.
    (d) varies with its labor employment.
    (e) is the maximum output that can physically be produced with a given amount of capital.

25. The law of diminishing marginal returns implies
    (a) decreasing average variable costs.   (b) increasing marginal costs.
    (c) decreasing marginal revenue.   (d) increasing average fixed costs.
    (e) decreasing average fixed cost.

26. A change in the wage rate paid to the variable factor labor will shift
    (a) the *ATC* curve.   (b) the *AVC* curve.
    (c) the *MC* curve.   (d) the *AFC* curve.
    (e) the *ATC*, *AVC* and *MC* curves.

27. The fact that the marginal cost curve is U-shaped reflects
    (a) the law of diminishing returns.
    (b) eventually diminishing marginal product.
    (c) a negatively sloped total product curve.
    (d) a total cost curve that initially increases, but eventually decreases.
    (e) Both (a) and (b) are correct.

◆ **EXERCISES**

1. The data in the following table relate employment levels of a variable factor to the resulting output.

Variable factor	Total product	Average product	Marginal product
1	10	_____	
2	160	_____	_____
3	330	_____	_____
4	480	_____	_____
5	600	_____	_____
6	670	_____	_____
7	680	_____	_____

(a) Fill in the blanks. (Recall that marginal product refers to a change in output from one level of labor input to another. It is therefore shown *between* the lines referring to input levels.)

(b) Graph the total product curve in panel (i) and the average product and marginal product curves in panel (ii). (Remember that marginal product is plotted at the midpoint on the horizontal axis—See Table 10-1 in the text.)

Figure 10-2

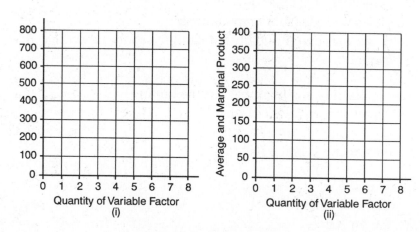

(c) At what output do diminishing returns begin?

136

2.   This exercise is designed to illustrate the relationship between productivity and cost with very few figures. Take $30 as the cost associated with the fixed factors and $10 as the cost of each variable unit. Consider, for example, an agricultural situation in which the variable factors are seed, labor, fertilizer, and equipment and the fixed factor is land.
     (a)   Complete the following table.

Units of variable factor	Total product	Marginal product	Average product	Total cost	Marginal cost	Average total cost
0	0		0.0	$30		∞
		2			$5.00	
1	2		2.0	40		$20.00
		3				
2	5		___	___	___	___
3	7	___	___	___	___	___
4	8	___	___	___	___	___
5	8	___	___	___	___	___

(b)   Graph the total, average, and marginal product curves in panel (a) and the three cost curves in panel (b). Remember that these "marginal" points are plotted at the midpoints of the intervals on the horizontal axis.

Figure 10-3

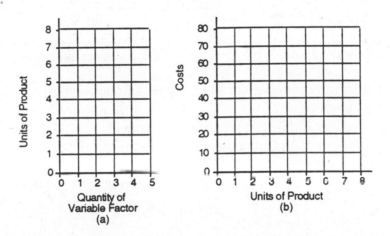

3.   The graph on the following page presents the marginal cost curve for a particular firm. Because marginal cost is plotted at the midpoint, the marginal cost of producing (for example) the first unit of output is $50. In addition, suppose that the firm's fixed costs are $100.

137

Figure 10-4

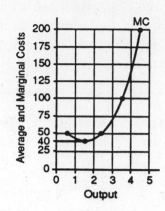

(a)   Use the firm's *MC* curve together with the level of fixed costs to determine total variable costs (*TVC*), total costs (*TC*), average variable costs (*AVC*), and average total costs (*ATC*).

Output	MC	TVC	TC	AVC	ATC
0		——	——	——	——
1	$50	——	——	——	——
2	——	——	——	——	——
3	——	——	——	——	——
4	——	——	——	——	——
5	——	——	——	——	——

(b)   Plot (approximately) the *AVC* and *ATC* curves on the graph.

4.   Given the family of cost curves for a hypothetical firm shown in the diagram below, answer the following questions.
(a)   The capacity of this firm occurs at an output of _____.
(b)   The effect of diminishing marginal returns occurs after an output level of _____.

(c)   The effect of diminishing average returns occurs after an output level of _____.

Figure 10-5

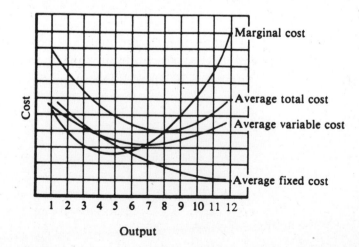

*5. Assume that you are in the business of producing a commodity for which short run total cost is represented by the following equation:

$$TC = 30 + 3Q + Q^2$$

where Q is output of the commodity and TC is total costs.

(a)   What are total fixed costs equal to?

(b)   What is the equation that represents total variable costs?

(c)   Derive the equation for average total costs (ATC).

(d)   Fill in the blanks in the following table.

Q	TVC	TFC	TC	ATC	MC
0	___	___	___	___	
1	___	___	___	___	___
2	___	___	___	___	___
3	___	___	___	___	___
4	___	___	___	___	___
5	___	___	___	___	___
6	___	___	___	___	___
7	___	___	___	___	___
8	___	___	___	___	___
9	___	___	___	___	___
10	___	___	___	___	___

(e)   What is the capacity of this firm?

(f)   What is marginal cost at this capacity output?

(g)   The equation for this firm's MC curve is:

$$MC = 3 + 2Q$$

(Those students that are familiar with calculus should note that this is the first derivative of the TC curve). To understand why marginal cost is plotted at the midpoints, use the equation for MC to calculate MC at outputs of 5, 5.5, and 6. Compare these answers with the marginal cost you derived in (d), which was calculated by taking the difference in TC between outputs of 5 and 6.

139

◆ ANSWERS

Multiple-Choice Questions

1. (c) 2. (d) 3. (b) 4. (a) 5. (b) 6. (a) 7. (e) 8. (d) 9. (a) 10. (a) 11. (d) 12. (c) 13. (b)
14. (b) 15. (a) 16. (d) 17. (a) 18. (c) 19. (a) 20. (c) 21. (a) 22. (c) 23. (c) 24. (b) 25. (b) 26.
(e) 27. (e)

Exercises

1. (a)

Variable factor	Total product	Average product	Marginal product
1	10	10	
			150
2	160	80	
			170
3	330	110	
			150
4	480	120	
			120
5	600	120	
			70
6	670	112	
			10
7	680	97	

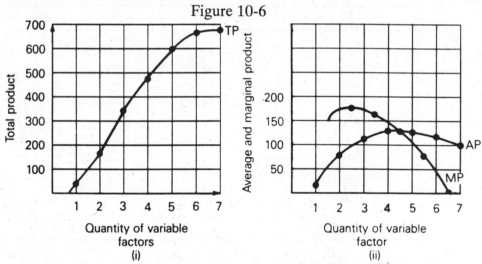

Figure 10-6

(c) Maximum *MP* is 170, which obtains for the third unit of the variable factor (plotted at 2.5 units). Thus diminishing returns begin after employment of the third variable factor.

2. (a)

Units of variable factor	Total product	Marginal product	Average product	Total cost	Marginal cost	Average total cost
0	0		0.0	$30		∞
		2			$5.00	
1	2		2.0	40		$20.00
		3			3.33	
2	5		2.5	50		10.00
		2			5.00	
3	7		2.3	60		8.57
		1			10.00	
4	8		2.0	70		8.75
		0			∞	
5	8		1.6	80		10.00

140

(b)

Figure 10-7

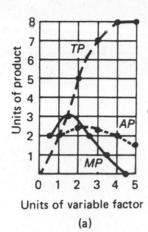

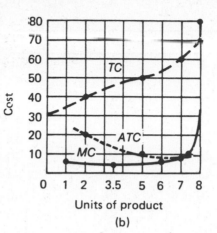

(a)

(b)

3. (a)

Output	MC	TVC	TC	AVC	ATC
0		$0	$100	—	—
1	$50	50	150	$50.00	$150
2	40	90	190	45.00	95
3	50	140	240	46.67	80
4	100	240	340	60.00	85
5	200	440	540	88.00	108

(b)

Figure 10-8

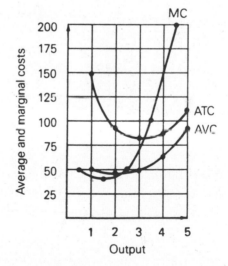

4. (a) 8.   (b) 5.
   (c) 7.

*5. (a) 30.

(b) $TVC = 3Q + Q^2$.

(c) $ATC = TC/Q = (30 + 3Q + Q^2)/Q = 30/Q + 3 + Q$.

(d)

Q	TVC	TFC	TC	ATC	MC
0	$ 0	$30	$30	-	$ 4
1	4	30	34	34	6
2	10	30	40	20	8
3	18	30	48	16	10
4	28	30	58	14.5	12
5	40	30	70	14	14
6	54	30	84	14	16
7	70	30	100	14.3	18
8	88	30	118	14.8	20
9	108	30	138	15.3	22
10	130	30	160	16	

(e) Somewhere between output levels 5 and 6.

(f) 14.

(g) The marginal costs of outputs 5, 5.5, and 6 are 13, 14, and 15, respectively. The difference in TC between outputs 5 and 6 is 14, which is precisely the MC at the midpoint of 5.5 units of output.

142

Chapter 11

Production and Cost in the Long Run and the Very Long Run

◆ LEARNING OBJECTIVES

After studying this chapter, you should be able to:

✔   apply the principle of substitution in explaining a firm's input use;

✔   distinguish the long run and the very long run from the short run;

✔   explain why increasing returns (economies of scale) occur;

✔   discuss the relationship between long run average cost and economies of scale;

✔   understand how long run and short run cost curves are related, and what causes them to shift;

✔   understand how productivity is measured, and;

✔   recognize the role of technological change in determining future productivity.

◆ HINTS AND TIPS

You might be guided by the fact that frequent errors on examinations are attributable to:

✔   confusion between what causes a movement along a cost curve, and what causes a shift in cost curves;

✔   failure to remember that decreasing costs, increasing returns or economies of scale all refer to the same concept.

◆ MULTIPLE-CHOICE QUESTIONS

1.   In addition to choosing the level of output, a firm in the long run must also select
     (a)   the appropriate technology.
     (b)   the amount of overtime for its labor force.
     (c)   the cost-minimizing combination of inputs.
     (d)   the profit-maximizing quantity of labor to employ with its fixed plant.
     (e)   All of the above.

2.   The cost-minimizing factor mix obtains when
     (a)   the marginal products of all factors are equalized.
     (b)   the marginal product per dollar expended on each factor is equalized.
     (c)   the marginal product of each factor divided by total expenditure on that factor is equalized across all factors.
     (d)   the cost of employing an additional unit of each factor is equalized across all factors.
     (e)   each factor's marginal cost is equalized.

3.   The profit-maximizing combination of capital (K) and labor (L) occurs when these factors are employed such that
     (a) $MP_K/P_K = MP_L/P_L$.   (b) $MP_K/K = MP_L/L$.
     (c) $MP_K/P_L = MP_L/P_K$.   (d) $P_K K = P_L L$.
     (e) $MP_K/P_K K = MP_L/P_L L$.

4.   Suppose that the marginal product of capital in a particular firm is 5 and that of labor is 10, and the price of capital is $2 and that of labor is $1. To minimize costs, this firm will
     (a)   substitute more capital for less labor.
     (b)   substitute more labor for less capital.
     (c)   not alter its factor mix.
     (d)   hire more capital and keep labor constant.
     (e)   reduce labor employment.

Questions 5 and 6 refer to the following table, which presents four possible combinations of capital (K) and labor (L) and their associated marginal products. Each combination produces exactly 100 units of output. Assume that the firm wishes to minimize production costs.

Combination	K	MP_K	L	MP_L
A	14	12	1	10
B	12	14	3	7
C	8	16	4	4
D	6	20	7	2

5.   If the ratio of the price of capital to the price of labor is 2, a firm will employ combination
     (a)   A.   (b)   B.
     (c)   C.   (d)   D.
     (e)   Either C or D.

144

6. If the relative price of capital to labor falls, the firm may (depending on the magnitude of the fall) wish to use combination
   (a)   A.   (b)   B.
   (c)   C.   (d)   D.
   (e)   Indeterminable with data provided.

7. A firm's long run average cost curve depicts
   (a)   what costs will be attainable with technological improvement.
   (b)   the lowest attainable unit costs when all factors are variable.
   (c)   a firm's profit-maximizing output choices.
   (d)   the lowest attainable average cost when all factor prices vary.
   (e)   the lowest attainable average cost when technology is variable.

8. The long run average cost curve is determined by
   (a)   technology and tastes.   (b)   long run supply.
   (c)   population growth.   (d)   technology and input prices.
   (e)   All of the above.

9. If the long run average cost curve is upward sloping, the firm is experiencing
   (a)   long run decreasing returns.   (b)   diseconomies of scale.
   (c)   increasing costs.   (d)   All of the above.
   (e)   None of the above.

10. Constant long run average costs for a firm means that
   (a)   there are greater advantages to small than to large plants.
   (b)   an unlimited amount of output will be produced.
   (c)   any scale of production costs the same per unit as any other.
   (d)   total cost is independent of the level of output.
   (e)   marginal cost equals zero.

11. Suppose that a firm doubles employment of all of its factors and, as a result, output increases from 100 units to 300 units. This firm is operating under
   (a)   diseconomies of scale.   (b)   long run decreasing returns.
   (c)   decreasing costs.   (d)   decreasing total cost.
   (e)   increasing costs.

12. A firm experiencing long run increasing returns that decides to increase output should do so by
   (a)   substituting more labor and less capital.
   (b)   employing a new technology.
   (c)   employing less of each factor.
   (d)   building smaller plants.
   (e)   building larger plants.

13. One possible explanation for economies of scale is
   (a)   invention and innovation.
   (b)   the introduction of new, improved inputs.
   (c)   a decrease in a factor price.
   (d)   increased specialization of production tasks.
   (e)   technological improvement.

14. An upward shift in the family of short run cost curves as well as the long run average cost curve could be explained by
    (a) economies of scale.
    (b) an increase in the fixed factor such as plant size.
    (c) a increase in a factor price.
    (d) a larger capital-labor ratio.
    (e) technological improvement.

15. Which of the following is the best measure of productivity?
    (a) Total output.
    (b) Total output per hour.
    (c) Total output per unit of resource input.
    (d) Total output per dollar of cost.
    (e) Total output per dollar of revenue.

16. Which of the following is *not* a type of technological change?
    (a) Process innovation.   (b) Lean production.
    (c) Product innovation.   (d) Improved inputs.
    (e) Economies of scale.

17. The very long run
    (a) introduces changes in factor prices.
    (b) always involves a greater range of output than the short run or the long run.
    (c) applies to a period in which new production methods can be introduced.
    (d) extends long run analysis to higher production levels.
    (e) introduces allowance for variable plant size.

18. An *economically efficient* method of production is one that
    (a) uses the smallest number of resource inputs.
    (b) necessarily involves the use of roundabout methods of production.
    (c) costs the least.
    (d) cannot also be technologically efficient.
    (e) minimizes the use of scarce capital.

19. A major source of the current international competitive advantage of Japanese automobile manufacturers is their
    (a) use of mass production.
    (b) ability to exploit economies of scale.
    (c) use of assembly-line production techniques.
    (d) ability to take full advantage of economies from the division of labor.
    (e) use of lean production techniques.

20. In a country where labor is relatively abundant and capital is scarce, it is likely that
    (a) firms will use capital intensive production methods, *ceteris paribus*.
    (b) virtually any combination of inputs would be economically efficient.
    (c) firms will employ labor intensive production techniques.
    (d) there is a strong incentive to introduce labor-saving innovations.
    (e) Both (c) and (d) are correct.

The following questions are based on material in the appendix to this chapter. Read the appendix before answering these questions.

21. If the marginal rate of substitution is -2 at a point on an isoquant involving two factors,
    (a) the ratio of factor prices is +1:2.
    (b) the ratio of factor prices is -2:1.
    (c) the ratio of marginal products is 2:1.
    (d) the ratio of factor prices is +2.
    (e) one factor of production has negative marginal product.

22. An isocost line for two factors C and L (their respective prices are P_C and P_L) could have which of the following equations?
    (a) $LC = \$100$.
    (b) $\$100 = P_C + P_L$.
    (c) $\$100 = P_L L + P_C C$.
    (d) $\$100 = P_L P_C$.
    (e) $LC = P_L L + P_C C$.

23. If two factors C and L are graphed in the same unit scale with C on the vertical axis, and an isocost line has a slope = -2, then
    (a) $P_L = 2P_C$.
    (b) $P_C/P_L = 2$.
    (c) $C = 2L$.
    (d) $L = 2C$.
    (e) $P_L L = 2P_C C$.

24. At the point of tangency of the isocost line in question 23 with an isoquant,
    (a) the desired factor combination has $2C$ for each L.
    (b) the marginal product of labor is twice that of capital.
    (c) the desired factor combination has $2L$ for each C.
    (d) the marginal product of capital is twice that of labor.
    (e) the marginal rate of substitution is -0.5.

♦ EXERCISES

1. Well into the post-World War II period, Inco (then International Nickel) possessed monopoly power based on the rich nickel ore body around Sudbury, Ontario. However, discoveries elsewhere gradually eroded its power to control prices. During the metal slump of the early 1980's, Inco posted losses of $1 billion (1981-1984). In 1981, Inco introduced a technique of "bulk mining" columns of ore 300 feet high. Only two tunnel shafts were required. The upper shaft was used for crews to drill the ore column and deposit explosives; the lower shaft, 300 feet below, was used to load the fallen ore. This innovation replaced a technique of drilling 20-foot sections. As a result, Inco made a profit of $45 million in 1985 (even though nickel prices remained depressed and volume static) with 21,000 employees as compared to 35,000 in 1981.

(a) Economists would term this a _____ run development, which is characterized by (upward/downward) shifts of the _____ run and _____ run cost curves.

(b) Assuming the same volume of output, labor productivity increased by roughly _____ percent between 1981 and 1985.

(c) Does this problem lend credence to the adage that "necessity is the mother of invention"? Explain.

2. In the table that follows, three different firms are able to combine capital (K) and labor (L) in various ways, resulting in pairs of marginal products as shown. (Note that higher number combinations substitute more capital for less labor, which decreases MP_K and increases MP_L.) For all firms, the price of a unit of capital is $10, and the price of labor is $5.

Combination number	Firm A		Firm B		Firm C	
	MP_K	MP_L	MP_K	MP_L	MP_K	MP_L
1	10	1	6	3	25	2
2	8	2	5	4	20	4
3	6	3	4	6	14	7
4	4	4	3	8	10	8
5	2	5	2	10	5	10

(a) Firm A is currently using combination 3, Firm B is using combination 2, and Firm C is using combination 4. Which firm is minimizing its costs? Explain.

(b) How would the firms that are not minimizing their costs have to alter their use of capital and labor to do so?

148

3. At the beginning of some time period, it is observed that a firm producing 1,000 bottles of wine per month uses the following inputs of capital (K) and labor (L) per month: $K = 5$ units and $L = 100$ units. The price of capital is $20, and the price of labor is $4 per unit.

As the firm increases its output over a period of time, the following changes in the use of capital and labor are observed:

Output per month	K	L
2,000	10	180
4,000	18	300
6,000	25	400
8,000	34	650
10,000	60	1,000

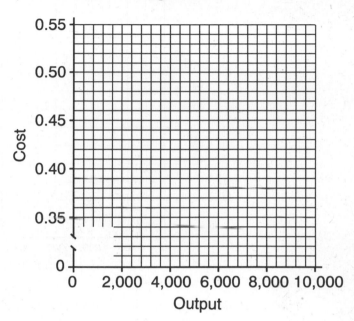

Figure 11-1

(a) Calculate and graph the long run average cost curve.

(b) At what output level do long run increasing returns cease?

*4. A firm is operating in an industry in which it is technologically possible to construct only two classes of plant. The first, Class A, is highly automated and requires an initial investment of $1,000,000; production in this plant takes place at a marginal cost of $3 per unit of output. The Class B plant employs a more labor-intensive production process and therefore requires a relatively smaller fixed cost of $500,000. However, this class of plant has a relatively higher marginal cost of $4 a unit. Thus the total cost curve for each class of plant can be represented by the following equations:

Class A plant: $TC_A = \$1,000,000 + 3Q$
Class B plant: $TC_B = \$500,000 + 4Q$

149

(a)   Plot the firm's long run average cost curve (i.e., the lowest attainable average cost for each output with plant size variable).

Figure 11-2

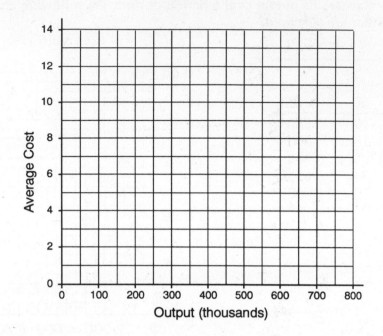

(b)   If this firm plans to produce 400,000 units of output, which plant should it employ? Explain.

(c)   Over what range of output do economies of scale occur for each class of plant? Why?

5.   A firm has four alternative methods of producing 100 gizmos. Each method represents different combinations of three factors: labor, lathe time, and raw materials. The inputs required by each method are given in the following table.

| | Production Method | | | |
	A	B	C	D
Labor hours	100	90	60	80
Lathe hours	25	75	80	70
Raw materials (pounds)	160	150	120	100

(a)   Suppose that the price per unit of each factor is $1. Determine the cost of each production method and indicate which is economically efficient.

(b)   Suppose that the price of an hour of lathe time increases to $2 (other prices remaining constant). What method(s) would a profit-maximizing firm now use?

(c)   Which of these methods is technically inefficient? Explain.

Appendix Exercises

The following exercises are based on material in the appendix to this chapter. Read the appendix before attempting them.

*6.   The table that follows shows six methods of producing 10 widgets per month using capital and labor.

(a)   Complete the last three columns in the table.

Method	Units of capital	Units of labor	Δ Capital	Δ Labor	Estimated MRS of capital for labor
A	10	80			
B	15	58			
C	25	40			
D	40	24			
E	58	15			
F	80	9			

(b)   On the graph, plot the isoquant indicated by the data in the table. (Assume these are the only feasible methods, and connect points by straight line segments.)

Figure 11-3

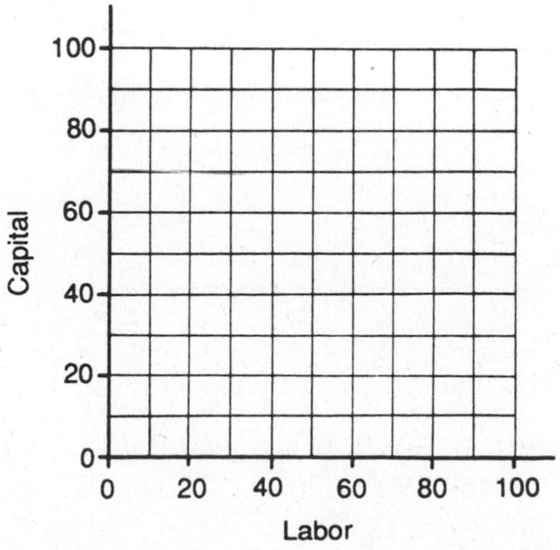

151

(c)   For each of the following price combinations, calculate the slope of the isocost line P_L/P_K and determine the economically efficient method of production by drawing in the minimum isocost line.

	Price of labor	Price of capital	P_L/P_K	Method
(1)	$1,000	$ 500		
(2)	1,000	1,000		
(3)	1,000	2,000		

7.   The graph illustrates how several levels of output could be produced with different combinations of capital and labor.

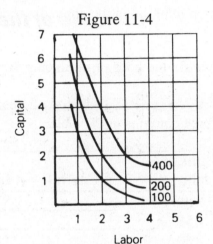

Figure 11-4

(a)   If the relative price of labor to capital were 1, how many units of capital and labor would this firm employ to produce 100 units of output (at minimum cost)?

(b)   If the price of capital were to change to one-half its original level, and the firm wanted to produce 200 units of output at minimum cost, how much capital and labor would it now employ? Explain.

(c)   By examining these three isoquants what, if anything, can be said about returns to scale?

◆ ANSWERS

Multiple-Choice Questions

1. (c) 2. (b) 3. (a) 4. (b) 5. (b) 6. (a) 7. (b) 8. (d) 9. (d) 10. (c) 11. (c) 12. (e) 13. (d)
14. (c) 15. (c) 16. (e) 17. (c) 18. (c) 19. (e) 20. (c) 21. (c) 22. (c) 23. (a) 24.(b)

Exercises

1.   (a)   Very long; downward; short; long.

       (b)   67%. Since 3/5 of the number of workers are producing the same output, productivity increased to 5/3 its original level or, equivalently, by 2/3.

       (c)   The losses with the erosion of monopoly power and the slump in the metal market created the necessity.

2.   (a)   Firm A is minimizing costs since, with combination 3, the ratio of the marginal products of capital and labor are equal to the ratio of their cost per unit of the factor employed (6/3 = 10/5).

       (b)   Firm B would have to move to combination 1 by using less capital, and thereby raise the MP_K, and more labor, thereby reducing the MP_L. Firm C would have to move to combination 3, increasing MP_K (reducing capital use) and decreasing MP_L (increasing labor use).

3.   (a)

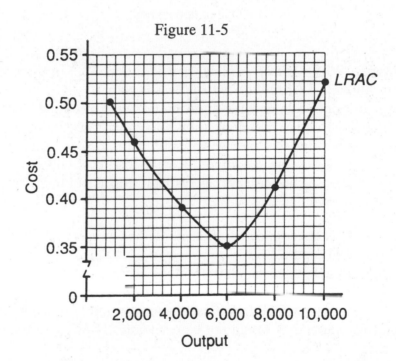

Figure 11-5

       (b)   6,000.

*4. (a)

Figure 11-6

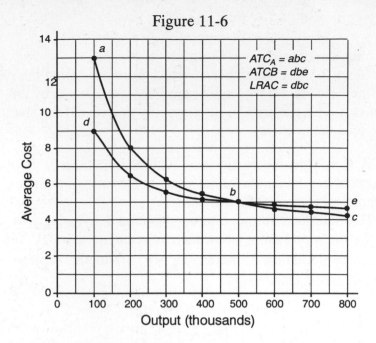

(b) Class B. With a Class A plant, it would cost $2.2 million to produce 400,000 units but only $2.1 million with a Class B plant.

(c) Economies of scale occur over the entire range of output from 1 to infinity. Each total cost curve is characterized by a fixed cost and constant marginal cost. It is easy to determine that average variable cost is also constant (and equal to marginal cost). Under these conditions, average total cost will continuously decrease as output increases because average variable cost is not rising to offset the impact of a declining average fixed cost.

5. (a) Method D is economically efficient. Method A costs $285, B costs $315, C costs $260, and D costs $250.

(b) Method A, which costs $310. (Method B now costs $390, C costs $340, and D costs $320.)

(c) Method B is technically inefficient since method D uses fewer units of *each* factor. Thus method B would not be economically efficient under any set of factor prices.

*6. (a)

Method	Δ Capital	Δ Labor	Estimated *MRS* of capital for labor
A	—	—	—
B	+ 5	- 22	- 0.23
C	+10	- 18	- 0.56
D	+15	- 16	- 0.94
E	+18	- 9	- 2.00
F	+22	- 6	- 3.67

154

(b)

Figure 11-7

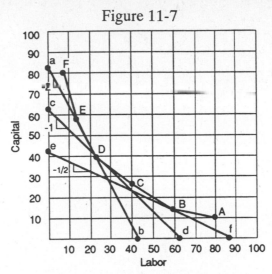

(c) For price combination 1, the relative price of labor to capital is 2, and the minimum isocost line for producing 100 widgets is *ab* in the graph. The tangency of the isocost line and the straight line segment joining *E* and *D* implies that either method E or D could be employed. Combination 2 has a price ratio of 1, and a minimum isocost line *cd*, which implies method D. Combination 3 has a price ratio of 0.5, a minimum isocost line *ef*, which implies that method B should be employed.

7. (a) One unit of capital and two units of labor.
   (b) The slope of an isocost line is now -2, which yields a tangency with the isoquant representing 200 units of output at approximately two units of capital and two units of labor.
   (c) Yes, these isoquants indicate economies of scale. Take any factor mix such as two units each of capital and labor. Double these to four units of each. Since factor prices are constant, doubling all factors serves to double total cost exactly. However, the combination of four units of each factor lies above the isoquant representing 100 units of output. Therefore, doubling all factors results in more than double the output. A doubling of costs and a more than doubling of output implies that long run average cost is decreasing.

PART FOUR

MARKETS AND PRICING

Chapter 12

Competitive Markets

◆ LEARNING OBJECTIVES

After studying this chapter, you should be able to:

✔ understand the distinction between competitive behavior and competitive structure;

✔ explain the behavioral rules for a profit-maximizing firm;

✔ understand why individual competitive firms are price takers and face a horizontal demand curve;

✔ define average revenue, marginal revenue, and price under perfect competition;

✔ explain how the short run industry supply curve can be derived;

✔ describe the role of entry and exit of firms in achieving long run market equilibrium;

✔ distinguish short run and long run equilibrium of competitive firms and industries;

✔ understand why an industry's response to changing technology depends on whether it is growing or declining.

◆ HINTS AND TIPS

You might be guided by the fact that frequent errors on examinations are attributable to:

✔ an inadequate understanding of the two rules for profit maximization;

✔ failure to remember that for a price taker average renevue, marginal revenue and price are equal;

✔ confusion between the supply curves of the firm and the industry, and;

✔ a lack of appreciation for the process by which the pursuit of profits eliminates profits.

159

◆ MULTIPLE-CHOICE QUESTIONS

1.   A perfectly competitive market structure is best described by firms that
     (a)   allocate a substantial share of their budget to advertising.
     (b)   engage in cutthroat competition by denigrating each others' products.
     (c)   are subjected to government controls ensuring fair competition.
     (d)   do not engage in active competitive behavior.
     (e)   actively undercut their competitors' prices.

2.   Which of the following characteristics is *not* an important determinant of the type of market structure?
     (a)   The number of sellers and the number of buyers.
     (b)   Whether the firms are foreign-owned transnational corporations.
     (c)   The firm's ability to influence demand by advertising.
     (d)   The ease of entry and exit in the industry.
     (e)   The similarity of competitors' products.

3.   If output occurs where marginal cost equals marginal revenue, then
     (a)   the last unit produced adds the same amount to costs as it does to revenue.
     (b)   the firm is maximizing profits.
     (c)   there is no reason to reduce or expand output, as long as TR is greater than or equal to TVC.
     (d)   the difference between TR and TC is maximized.
     (e)   All of the above.

4.   A profit-maximizing firm, regardless of market structure, should shut down and suffer a loss equal to its fixed cost if
     (a)   average revenue is less than average variable cost.
     (b)   average revenue is less than average total cost but greater than average variable cost.
     (c)   total revenue is less than total cost but greater than total variable cost.
     (d)   its economic profits are negative and smaller in absolute value than total fixed cost.
     (e)   profits are negative.

5.   Should it decide to produce a positive output, any profit-maximizing firm should produce the output level for which
     (a)   the incremental change in revenue equals the incremental change in costs.
     (b)   total revenue exceeds total costs.
     (c)   average revenue equals average total costs.
     (d)   average costs are minimized.
     (e)   total revenue equals total costs.

6.   The assumption that each firm in a perfectly competitive market is a price taker basically means that
     (a)   market price is independent of the level of industry output.
     (b)   each firm's supply curve is perfectly elastic.
     (c)   the industry supply curve is perfectly elastic.
     (d)   regardless of how much an individual firm produces, it will never have any impact on market price.
     (e)   for reasonable variations in a single firm's output, the impact on market price is negligible.

7. Which one of the following characteristics of a market would you expect to be *inconsistent* with price-taking behavior?
   (a) There are a large number of firms in the industry.
   (b) Each firm produces a product that is somehow distinguishable from that of its competitors (e.g., in terms of quality or brand name).
   (c) Each firm's share of total industry output is insignificant.
   (d) Each firm behaves as though it faces a perfectly elastic demand curve.
   (e) Firms do not actively engage in competitive behaviour.

8. A firm that faces a perfectly elastic demand curve has a
   (a) linear total revenue curve with a slope equal to the market price.
   (b) horizontal total revenue curve.
   (c) constant total revenue regardless of the level of output.
   (d) total revenue curve shaped like an inverted *U*.
   (e) negatively sloped total revenue curve.

9. In a perfectly competitive market, each firm's demand curve is coincident with the
   (a) average revenue curve.
   (b) marginal revenue curve.
   (c) horizontal line drawn at the market price.
   (d) All of the above.
   (e) None of the above.

10. A perfectly competitive firm does not try to sell more of its product by lowering its price below the market price because
    (a) this would be considered unethical price chiseling.
    (b) its competitors would not permit it.
    (c) its demand is inelastic, so total revenue would decline.
    (d) it can sell whatever it produces at the market price.
    (e) consumers might believe this firm's product to be inferior, and therefore cease buying it.

11. Assuming that Rule 1 for profit maximization is satisfied, a perfectly competitive firm is in short run equilibrium when it produces the output where
    (a) price equals average total cost.
    (b) price equals short run marginal cost.
    (c) short run marginal cost equals average total cost.
    (d) marginal revenue equals average variable cost.
    (e) All of the above.

12. A firm producing a positive output level, covering variable costs but making a loss in the short run,
    (a) is not maximizing profits.
    (b) should definitely shut down.
    (c) should exit the industry.
    (d) should either expand or contract its plant size.
    (e) may nonetheless be doing the best that it can with respect to profits.

Questions 13 to 20 refer to the following graph, which depicts the short run cost curves of a perfectly competitive firm.

Figure 12-1

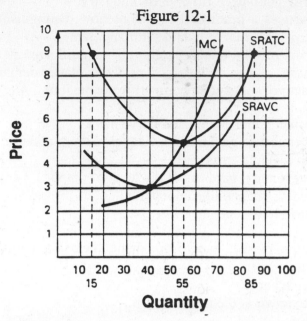

13. If the current market price is $9, the profit-maximizing output of this firm is
    (a)   15.   (b)   70.
    (c)   55.   (d)   85.
    (e)   40.

14. At this output, total costs are equal to
    (a) $135.   (b) $765.
    (c) $630.   (d) $420.
    (e) $350.

15. The firm's total profit is equal to
    (a) $210.   (b) $220.
    (c) $280.   (d) $70.
    (e)   Indeterminable with data provided.

16. Should the market price fall to $4, this firm will
    (a)   shut down and make zero profit.
    (b)   shut down and suffer a loss equal to fixed cost.
    (c)   continue operating in the short run and suffer a loss that is less than its fixed cost.
    (d)   produce 55 units and make a loss equal to total variable cost.
    (e)   produce 40 units and suffer a loss equal to its total fixed cost.

17. This firm's maximum attainable profit level would equal zero if
    (a)   it were in short run equilibrium.
    (b)   it produces any output where marginal cost equals marginal revenue.
    (c)   the market price were $5.
    (d)   the market price were $3.
    (e)   it shut down.

18. This firm would shut down production if the market price were below
    (a) $5.   (b) $3.
    (c) marginal cost.   (d) average total cost.
    (e) Indeterminable with data provided.

19. The short run supply curve for this firm is its
    (a) marginal cost curve.
    (b) marginal cost curve at or above $3.

    (c) marginal cost curve at or above $5.
    (d) SRATC curve at or above $5.
    (e) SRAVC curve at or above $3.

20. With a market price of $5, an output of 55 units would be the firm's long run equilibrium output if
    (a) the firm expected price to rise in the future.
    (b) its long run average cost curve is minimized at 55 units of output.
    (c) other firms were barred from entering this industry.
    (d) this firm could not exit the industry.
    (e) the firm was experiencing decreasing returns to scale.

21. The existence of positive profits in a perfectly competitive industry
    (a) is a signal for existing firms to lower their price.
    (b) is a signal for existing firms to maintain their plant size.
    (c) provides an incentive for new firms to enter the industry.
    (d) encourages all firms to expand their production levels.
    (e) signals firms to increase price.

22. Long run equilibrium in a perfectly competitive industry is characterized by
    (a) each firm in the industry earning maximum attainable profits.
    (h) each firm in the industry making zero economic profits.
    (c) no firm desiring to enter or exit this industry.
    (d) no firm desiring to alter its plant size.
    (e) All of the above.

23. The conditions for long run competitive equilibrium include *all but which* of the following?
    (a) $P = AVC$.   (b) $P = MC$.
    (c) $P = SRATC$.   (d) $P = LRAC$.
    (e) $MR = MC$.

24. When all firms in a perfectly competitive industry are producing at minimum efficient scale and just covering costs,
    (a) it is physically impossible for existing firms to increase output.
    (b) new firms could enter, produce at minimum efficient scale, and also cover their costs.
    (c) profits could be made only with larger plants.
    (d) the industry is in long run equilibrium.
    (e) some firms will exit the industry.

25. Which of the following characteristics is true of a perfectly competitive industry that is subject to continuous technological change?
    (a) Only plants of recent vintage and thus greater efficiency will operate.
    (b) The market price equals the minimum average total cost of the most efficient plants.
    (c) The market price equals the minimum average total cost of the least efficient plant still in use.
    (d) Plants with a greater than average level of efficiency will make positive profits.
    (e) Any plant without the most recent and efficient technology will be closed.

26. In which of the following situations should a profit-maximizing firm leave its output unaltered?
    (a) $MR > MC$ and $TR > TC$.   (b) $MR = MC$ and $TR > TVC$.
    (c) $MR > MC$ and $TR = TC$.   (d) $MR < MC$ and $TR < TC$.
    (e) $MR = MC$ and $TR < TVC$.

27. Long run economic profits will not exist in a perfectly competitive industry because
    (a) new firms will enter the industry and eliminate them.
    (b) corporate income taxes eliminate profits.
    (c) competitive firms are too small to be profitable.
    (d) increasing costs will eliminate profits in the long run.
    (e) firms in this industry engage in cutthroat price cutting.

28. If a competitive industry faced a steady decrease in demand, economic theory predicts that in the long run
    (a) firms will gradually leave the industry, thereby shrinking its productive capacity.
    (b) firms will modernize plant and equipment in order to increase efficiency.
    (c) existing firms will expand output levels as a means of recovering losses.
    (d) the industry will expand with newer, more efficient firms entering.
    (e) Both (b) and (d) are correct.

◆ EXERCISES

1. The graph below depicts the short run cost structure of a hypothetical perfectly competitive, profit-maximizing firm.
    (a) Use the graph to fill in the blanks in the table.

If market price is	$10.00	$ 7.50	$5.50
(i) equilibrium output is	_____	_____	_____
At this output,			
(ii) total revenue is	_____	_____	_____
(iii) total cost is	_____	_____	_____
(iv) profit is (+ or -)	_____	_____	_____
(v) marginal revenue is	_____	_____	_____
(vi) marginal cost is	_____	_____	_____
(vii) average total cost is	_____	_____	_____
(viii) profit per unit is	_____	_____	_____

164

Figure 12-2

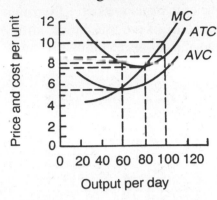

Output per day

(b)   Why is neither $10.00 nor $5.50 the long run market price?

2.   Consider the following information regarding output levels, costs, and market price for two perfectly competitive firms operating in different industries. Each firm has an upward-sloping marginal cost curve.

Firm A: output = 5,000   total variable cost   = $2,500
           price = $1.00   total fixed cost   = $2,000
                                marginal cost   = $1.20

Firm B: output = 5,000   average total costs = $1.00
           price = $1.20   (at their minimum level)

		Firm A	Firm B
(a)	Are these firms making profits?	___	___
(b)	If so, how much?	___	___
(c)	Are these firms making maximum profits?	___	___
(d)	Should these firms produce more, less, or the same output? Explain.	___	___

3.   Output of peanuts in the United States, it is assumed, is 2 million tons in a given year. One of the many producers, Mr. Shell, has experienced a doubling of his output over his previous year's output of 40 tons. All other producers report no change in their output. The market elasticity of demand is estimated to be 0.20.

(a)   Calculate the effect on the world price of peanuts from Mr. Shell's increase in output (in percentage terms).

(b)   Calculate the elasticity of demand Mr. Shell's firm faces.

(c)   Does your answer for (b) indicate that the firm is likely to act as a price taker? Explain.

4.   The following graphs page present the marginal cost curves of three firms, which, for simplicity, are assumed to be the only firms in a perfectly competitive industry. Minimum average variable costs for the three firms are as follows: Firm A, $3; Firm B, $5; Firm C, $7. Further, minimum average total costs are as follows: Firm A, $5; Firm B, $7; Firm C, $8.

Figure 12-3

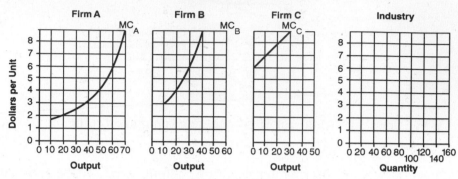

(a)   Derive the industry short run supply curve, and plot it in the industry grid.

(b)   If market price were $6.50, what quantity would be supplied by this industry, and what would be the output of each of the three firms? (approximate answers)

(c)   For each of the three firms, indicate if it would be making a profit or a loss.

5.   This exercise traces some of the long run adjustments that take place in a perfectly competitive market in response to a change in demand (we ignore adjustments that current firms may make to plant size). Assume that each firm—currently in the industry as well as potential entrants—has the cost structure depicted in panel (i) of the following graph (where the notation is identical to that in the text). Panel (ii) shows the industry's short run supply curve S and the current market demand curve D.

(a)   What are equilibrium price and quantity in this market?

(b)   What is the output of each firm in this industry, and what is the resulting level of profit?

Figure 12-4

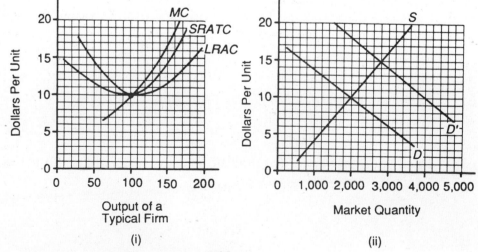

166

(c)   How many firms are operating in this industry?

(d)   Is the industry in long run equilibrium? Explain.

(e)   Now suppose that the demand for this good shifts to D' What are the new equilibrium market price and quantity in the short run?

(f)   What is the short run quantity response of each firm in the industry?

(g)   What is each firm's profit in this short run equilibrium?

(h)   Explain what will happen to the industry short run supply curve once sufficient time has elapsed for entry and exit to occur.

(i)   Once the new long run equilibrium is established, what are the market price and quantity?

(j)   What are the level of output and associated profit of each firm in the new long run equilibrium?

(k)   How many firms will be active in this industry?

6. An industry's short run supply (SRS) and long run supply (LRS) curves are depicted in panel A. The initial equilibrium output of X is disturbed by a shift in demand to D'D'. The new short run equilibrium output is Y, and long run equilibrium output is Z. In panel B show these equilibria and the adjustments for a firm. Use demand, short run marginal and average cost, and long run average cost curves. Denote the corresponding output per firm x, y and z.

Figure 12-5

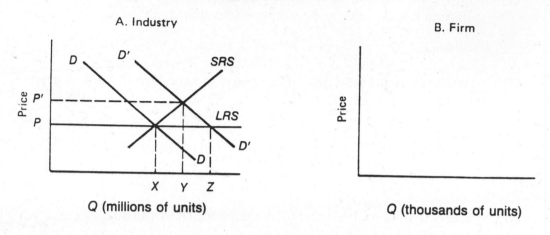

*7. This exercise addresses the impact of a change in technology in a perfectly competitive market. For simplicity we shall consider only two vintages of technology, the old and the new. For the moment, assume that the new technology has not yet been invented, so that all firms employ the current (soon to be old) production technology that results in the cost structure depicted in panel (i) of the following graph. To keep the graph tidy, the *LRAC* curve has not been drawn; however, you should assume that minimum efficient scale for these firms occurs at 10 units of output. Panel (ii) provides the market demand curve (*D*) and the industry short run supply curve (*S*).

Figure 12-6

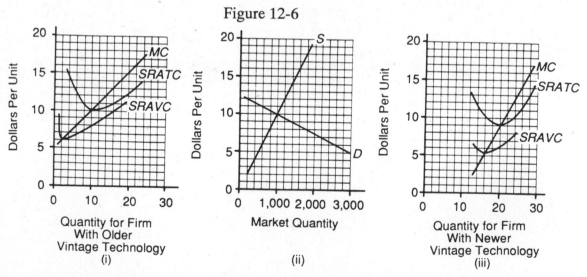

(a) What are the long run equilibrium market price and quantity?

(b)   What is each firm's output and profit level in the long run equilibrium? How many firms are in the industry?

(c)   Now suppose that a new technology is invented so that any firm now entering this industry can do so with the cost structure depicted in panel (iii). Assume that the minimum efficient scale for these firms occurs at 20 units of output. Will new firms enter the industry? Explain.

(d)   When will entry into this industry cease?

(e)   In the new long run equilibrium,
        (i)   what are market price and quantity?

        (ii)   what are the output level and profit of firms using the newer-vintage technology?

        (iii)   what are the output level and profit of firms employing the older-vintage technology?

        (iv)   how many firms in the industry use the newer technology and how many use the older, less efficient technology?

(f)   Should all of the plants using the less efficient technology be replaced by those with the newer production technology?

◆ ANSWERS

Multiple-Choice Questions

1. (d) 2. (b) 3. (e) 4. (a) 5. (a) 6. (e) 7. (b) 8. (a) 9. (d) 10. (d) 11. (b) 12. (e) 13. (b) 14. (d) 15. (a) 16. (c) 17. (c) 18. (b) 19. (b) 20. (b) 21. (c) 22. (e) 23. (a) 24. (d) 25. (b) 26. (b) 27. (a) 28. (a)

Exercises

1. (a) (i) 100; 80; 60.

(ii) $1,000; $600; $330.

(iii) $850; $600; $480.

(iv) $150; 0; -$150.

z(v) $10.00; $7.50; $5.50.

(vi) $10.00; $7.50; $5.50.

(vii) $8.50; $7.50; $8.00.

(viii) $1.50; 0; -$2.50.

(b) At $10.00, profits will induce entry; at $5.50, losses will induce exit of firms, so the industry supply curve shifts.

2. (a) Yes, for both firms

(b) Firm A: $500; Firm B: $1,000

(c) No, for both firms. Neither firm is producing where $P = MC$ (note that for Firm B, $MC = \$1$ because at minimum ATC, $ATC = MC$).

(d) Firm A should produce less output. At current output $P < MC$; since P is constant for a perfectly competitive firm and MC is positively sloped, a decrease in output changes MC toward P. For Firm B, $P > MC$; this firm will therefore maximize profits by producing more output.

3. (a) The market elasticity of demand (η) is given by the formula

$$\eta = \frac{\text{percentage change in output}}{\text{percentage change price}}$$

Here,

$$0.20 = \frac{40/2,000,000}{\text{percentage change price}}$$

Thus, the percentage change in price = 0.0001.

(b) The firm's elasticity of demand is the percentage change in the output of the firm divided by the percentage change in the price [calculated in (a)]. This is equal to

$$\frac{40/60}{.0001} = 6,667$$

(c) Yes. For practical purposes the elasticity is (negative) infinity (perfectly elastic), and the firm has no effect on price.

4. (a)

Figure 12-7

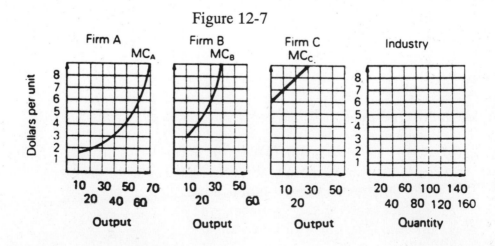

170

Each firm's short run supply curve corresponds to the portion of its *MC* curve that is greater than or equal to *AVC*. Thus no firm produces at a price less than $3. Between $3 and just slightly below $5, only Firm A produces output. When the price hits $5, Firm B abruptly raises output from zero to approximately 25 units—this explains the horizontal segment of the industry supply curve at $5. Similarly, the discrete jump in output by Firm C when price reaches $7 explains the other horizontal segment of the industry supply curve. As the number of firms in the industry increases, these discrete jumps in output by additional firms coming on line would become small relative to total industry output, so the industry supply curve would be much smoother.

(b)   At a market price of $6.50, Firm A would produce approximately 62.5 units and Firm B, approximately 32.5 units. Since the market price would be less than Firm C's *AVC* (at every level of output), it would shut down and produce no output in the short run. Thus the quantity supplied by the industry at this price would be approximately 95 units.

(c)   Firm C would make a loss equal to its fixed cost. Firm A would make a profit, but we do not have enough information to determine how much. At 62.5 units of output, we do not know the level of Firm A's *ATC*. However, we do know that the *ATC* curve is rising at this output because it is to the right of minimum *ATC*. Since *ATC* is rising, *MC*(=*P*) is greater than *ATC*, and profit is therefore positive. For Firm B, price is greater than *AVC* (same reason as before) but less than *ATC*. Firm B is therefore making a loss that is less than its fixed cost. Again, we cannot determine the magnitude of the loss because the information provided does not indicate the level of *AVC* at 32.5 units of output.

5.

Figure 12-8

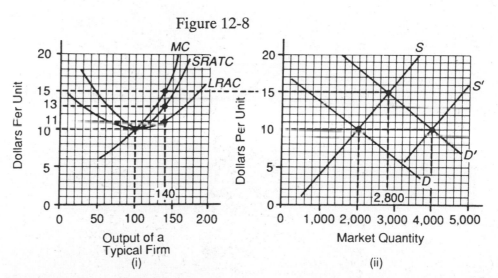

Output of a
Typical Firm
(i)

Market Quantity

(ii)

(a) $10 and 2,000 units, respectively.

(b)   Each firm produces 100 units of output (i.e., where *MC* = *MR* = *P* = $10). Since at an output of 100 units average revenue (*P*) equals *SRATC*, profits are therefore equal to zero.

(c)   20 (= 2,000/100).

(d)   Yes. The typical firm is producing where *MC* = *MR* and is on its *LRAC* curve; thus it is producing the profit-maximizing output at the lowest attainable cost. Further, since the level of economic profit is zero, there is no incentive for new firms to enter or old firms to exit.

(e) $15 and 2,800 units, respectively.

(f)   At a market price of $15, each existing firm increases output to 140 units where $P = MC$.

(g)   Each firm's total revenue is $2,100 (i.e., $15 x 140). The average total cost of producing 140 units (given that the firm cannot adjust plant size) is $13. Thus total cost is $1,820 ($13 x 140). Therefore, short run profit for each firm is $2,100 - $1,820 = $280.

(h)   Since industry profits are positive, new firms will enter. This entry is captured in the graph by the industry short run supply curve shifting to the right and thereby lowering price.

(i)   Long run equilibrium obtains when each firm is doing the best that it can and there is no incentive for further entry. Both conditions are satisfied when price is again equal to $10 at the intersection of the new demand curve D' and a new industry short run supply curve (e.g., S' in the graph). The associated equilibrium market quantity is 4,000 units.

(j)   Each firm produces 100 units and earns an economic profit equal to zero, which is the same as the initial long run equilibrium position of each firm in (b).

(k)   The difference with the initial long run equilibrium is that there will be more firms in the industry; specifically, there will be 40 firms (4,000/100).

6.

Figure 12-9

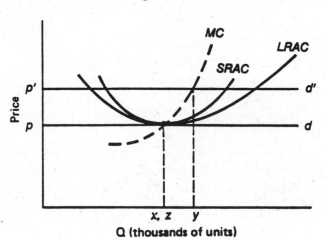

7.

172

Figure 12-10

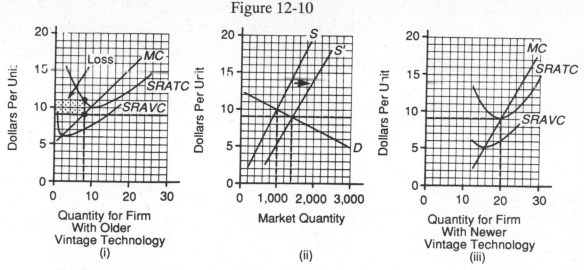

(i) Quantity for Firm With Older Vintage Technology

(ii) Market Quantity

(iii) Quantity for Firm With Newer Vintage Technology

(a) $10 and 1,000 units, respectively.

(b)   Each firm produces 10 units of output and makes zero profits. There are 100 firms in the industry (i.e., 1,000/10).

(c)   Yes. A firm entering with the new technology faces the same price as the existing firms, and by producing 20.5 units (where $MR = MC$ for the newer plants), it can make a positive profit; at this output, average revenue is greater than average total cost.

(d)   Entry will cease when profits of a potential entrant are driven to zero. This occurs when the market price is $9, implying that plants of recent vintage would operate at minimum efficient scale.

(e)   (i) $9 and 1,400 units, respectively.

(ii)   20 units of output and zero profit.

(iii) 8 units of output and a loss of $16.

(iv) Since total revenue exceeds total variable cost for plants employing the older technology, all 100 of these firms remain in the industry. Total output by these firms is therefore 800 units (100 x 8), which leaves 600 units that are produced by the newer vintage plants (1,400 - 800). Each of these produces 20 units, so there are 30 plants with the new technology.

(f)   No. The market value of the output of each of these firms is $72 ($9 x 8), greater than the value of resources that are currently used to produce this output (i.e., total variable cost), which is $63.

Chapter 13

Monopoly

◆ LEARNING OBJECTIVES

After studying this chapter, you should be able to:

✔ explain the relationship between price and marginal revenue for a monopolist;

✔ relate marginal revenue, total revenue, and elasticity;

✔ illustrate potential monopoly profits in any competitive equilibrium;

✔ distinguish between natural and created barriers to entry;

✔ explain why cartels tend to develop and the reasons for their instability;

✔ define price discrimination and identify conditions that make price discrimination both possible and profitable.

◆ HINTS AND TIPS

The following are the sources of some common errors students make on examinations:

✔ failure to remember the relationship between a monopolist's marginal revenue and demand curve;

✔ a lack of appreciation of the dilemma presented by individual incentives and group interests in a cartel, and;

✔ the erroneous belief that the existence of different prices for the same good is sufficient evidence of price discrimination.

◆ MULTIPLE-CHOICE QUESTIONS

1. A fundamental feature of a monopolistic market is that the firm
    (a) can sell any quantity it desires at current market price.
    (b) can obtain any price for any quantity of output.
    (c) faces a perfectly inelastic demand curve.
    (d) faces the price and quantity trade-off depicted by market demand.
    (e) Both (a) and (b) are correct.

2. For the single-price monopolist, the average revenue curve
    (a) is a horizontal line drawn at the market price.
    (b) is the same as the market demand curve.
    (c) is the same as the marginal revenue curve.
    (d) has the same price intercept as the demand curve, but is twice as steep.
    (e) does not exist.

3. If average revenue declines as output increases, marginal revenue must
    (a) increase.
    (b) also decline and be less than average revenue.
    (c) also decline because it is equal to average revenue.
    (d) also decline and be greater than average revenue.
    (e) decline, but may be less than, equal to or greater than average revenue.

4. Since the profit-maximizing monopolist produces that output where marginal cost equals marginal revenue, we can conclude that
    (a) $P = MC$.   (b) $P = MR$.
    (c) $P > MC$.   (d) $P < MR$.
    (e) $P > ATC$.

5. As long as marginal cost is positive, a monopolist will be operating
    (a) on the elastic portion of the demand curve.
    (b) where demand is unit-elastic and total revenue is therefore at a maximum.
    (c) on the inelastic portion of the demand curve.
    (d) on any portion of the demand curve, depending on the supply curve.
    (e) where demand is perfectly inelastic.

6. A linear downward-sloping demand curve has a marginal revenue curve that is
    (a) also linear, with the same price intercept as the demand curve and half the quantity intercept.
    (b) coincident with the average revenue curve.
    (c) horizontal at market price.
    (d) also linear, with half the slope of the demand curve.
    (e) negatively sloped and intersects demand at the equilibrium price.

7. A single-price monopoly is able to make positive profits only if the average total cost curve
    (a) intersects the demand curve.
    (b) is tangent to the demand curve.

176

(c)   declines over a substantial portion of market demand.
(d)   lies above the marginal revenue curve.
(e)   lies above the demand curve.

8.   In perfect competition, the industry short-run supply curve is the horizontal summation of the marginal cost curves (above *AVC*) of all of the firms in the industry. In monopoly, the short-run supply curve
(a)   is the single firm's marginal cost curve.
(b)   is the portion of the single firm's marginal cost curve that lies above average variable cost.
(c)   is the downward-sloping segment of the average total cost curve.
(d)   is the upward-sloping segment of the MC curve.
(e)   does not exist.

Questions 9 to 12 refer to the following graph, which depicts the marginal cost curve of a monopoly and the market demand it faces.

Figure 13-1

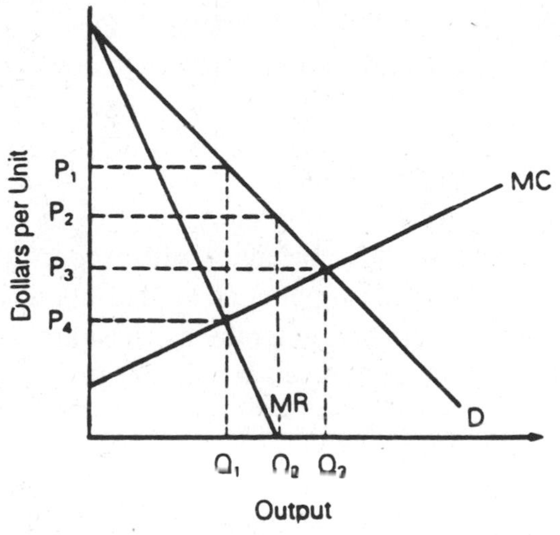

9.   The monopolist's profit-maximizing output is
(a) Q_1.   (b) Q_2.
(c) Q_3.   (d)   greater than Q_1 but less than Q_3.
(e)   Indeterminable with data provided.

10.   The price set by the monopolist for the profit-maximizing output is
(a) P_1.   (b) P_2.
(c) P_3.   (d) P_4.
(e)   Indeterminable with data provided.

11.   The level of output that corresponds to maximum revenue is
(a) Q_1.   (b) Q_2.

(c) Q_3.   (d)   greater than Q_3.
(e)   Indeterminable with data provided.

12.   A monopolist that is able to practice perfect price discrimination will produce output
(a) Q_1.   (b) Q_2.
(c) Q_3.   (d)   greater than Q_3.
(e)   Indeterminable with data provided.

13.   Suppose a firm's minimum efficient scale occurs at an average cost of $4 and an output of 4 million units, while quantity demanded at a price of $4 is 3 million units. Given that the demand curve is downward-sloping, then
(a)   the firm is a natural monopoly.
(b)   the firm's profits can be sustained only if it creates barriers to entry.
(c)   it is always impossible to make positive profits regardless of the output level.
(d)   the firm always breaks even.
(e)   the firm will exit the industry.

14.   Barriers to entry, which sustain a monopoly, may be due to *all but which* of the following?
(a)   Economies of scale.   (b)   Patent laws.
(c)   Long-run increasing average costs. (d)   Large set-up costs.
(e)   Licensing.

15.   A cartel increases the industry's profits by
(a)   fully capturing all economies of scale.
(b)   ceasing all active competitive behavior with respect to price.
(c)   agreeing to sell all current output at an agreed-upon fixed price.
(d)   decreasing industry output and thereby increasing market price.
(e)   agreeing to produce more, but sell at a higher price.

16.   Which of the following is *not* a problem associated with the enforcement of a successful cartel?
(a)   Entry of new firms.
(b)   Government restrictions on output.
(c)   Preventing cartel members from violating the agreed-upon production level.
(d)   Convincing other firms to join the cartel.
(e)   Monitoring the output of cartel members.

17.   Which of the following is the *best* example of price discrimination?
(a)   Some air travelers pay lower air fares as standby passengers.
(b)   A telephone company charges lower rates for long-distance calls after midnight than during the day.
(c)   A local transit company allows senior citizens, the unemployed, and children to ride at reduced fares.
(d)   The London underground charges each individual according to the distance travelled.
(e)   A cinema charges lower prices on Tuesdays than on Fridays or Saturdays.

178

18. Price discrimination is possible because
    (a) different individuals are willing to pay different amounts for the same commodity.
    (b) each individual is willing to pay a different amount for each successive unit of the same commodity.
    (c) different individuals have different incomes.
    (d) demand curves slope downwards.
    (e) Both (a) and (b) are correct.

19. Price discrimination increases a monopoly's profits because it
    (a) increases the willingness of households to pay for a good.
    (b) allows the firm to capture some consumers' surplus.
    (c) allows the firm to exploit economies of scale more fully.
    (d) shifts the demand curve the firm faces.
    (e) restricts output.

20. Which of the following is *not* true of price discrimination?
    (a) Output is generally larger than under a single-price monopoly.
    (b) Any given level of output yields a larger revenue.
    (c) To be successful, resale must be impossible or prevented.
    (d) Lower-income individuals must be charged lower prices.
    (e) Consumers' surplus decreases.

21. Perfect price discrimination implies that
    (a) demand is perfectly elastic.
    (b) demand is perfectly inelastic.
    (c) supply is perfectly elastic.
    (d) the firm produces a lower output than it would as a single price monopolist.
    (e) the firm sells each unit at a different price and captures all consumers' surplus.

22. Natural barriers to entry
    (a) include patent laws and exclusive franchises.
    (b) most commonly arise through economies of scale.
    (c) result from an increasing long run average cost curve.
    (d) imply that small firms have lower ATC curves than larger firms.
    (e) must be sustained by government regulation.

23. If a firm can sell 10 units of output for $15 each or eleven units at $14 each, the additional revenue from selling the eleventh unit is
    (a) $14.   (b) $4.
    (c) $15.   (d) $154.
    (e) $1.

24. Economic theory predicts cartels to be unstable because
    (a) there is an incentive for individual firms to produce beyond their quota.
    (b) governments will invariably dismantle them.
    (c) although industry profits increase, the profits of individual firms decrease.
    (d) individual firms have an incentive to produce less than the restrictions imposed on them by the cartel.
    (e) the industry output that maximizes joint profits for the cartel tends to exceed that of a competitive market.

25.   The process of "creative destruction" refers to
    (a)   the threat of price-cutting behavior.
    (b)   the inherent instability of cartels.
    (c)   an early declaration of bankruptcy as a means of avoiding debts.
    (d)   the takeover of a competitive industry by a monopoly.
    (e)   the replacement of one monopoly by another through invention and innovation.

◆ EXERCISES

1.   The following graph depicts the demand curve and selected cost structure of a monopolist.

Figure 13-2

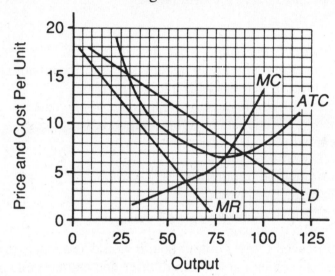

    (a)   At what output are the firm's profits at a maximum? _____
    (b)   What is the price at this output? _____
    (c)   What is total revenue at this output? _____
    (d)   What are the corresponding total costs? _____
    (e)   What is the level of economic profits? _____
    (f)   Within what range of output is there at least some economic profit? _____

2.   The following data relate to a monopolistic firm and its product.
    (a)   Calculate marginal cost (*MC*), marginal revenue (*MR*), total revenue (*TR*), and profit to complete the table.

Output	Total cost	Price	Quantity demanded	TR	MR	MC	Profit
0	$20	$20	0	____			____
1	24	18	1	____	____	____	____
2	27	16	2	____	____	____	____
3	32	14	3	____	____	____	____
4	39	12	4	____	____	____	____
5	48	10	5	____	____	____	____
6	59	8	6	____	____	____	____

180

(b)   Plot average revenue (AR), MR, and MC in panel (i), TC and TR in panel (ii).

Figure 13-3

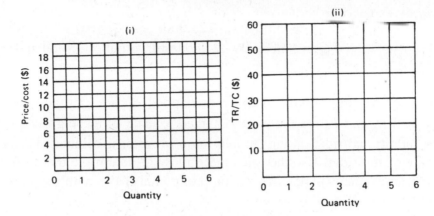

(c)   What is the profit-maximizing output (whole units)?_____

(d)   At what price will the monopolist sell the product (whole units)?_____

(e)   What are the monopolist's economic profits?_____

3.   The following graph shows the cost and revenue curves for a monopolist.

Figure 13-4

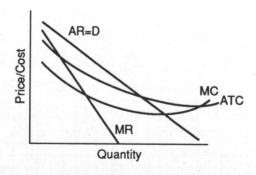

(a)   Illustrate on the graph the price the profit-maximizing monopolist will set and the
       quantity that will be sold. (Label the P_M and Q_M.)
(b)   Indicate monopoly profits by vertical hatching,||||.
(c)   Suppose that the monopolist, to be allocatively efficient, sets price (AR) equal to
       marginal cost. Label the price P_E and the output Q_E. Would this output be sustain-
       able in the long run? Explain with reference to the costs the monopolist faces in
       the graph.

181

*4.   This exercise provides an example of profit maximization through price discrimination. A local amusement park has estimated the following demand curves for its new roller coaster ride, the Double-Loop Monster:

$$Q_a = 1,000,000 - 125,000P_a$$
$$Q_c = 8,000,000 - 2,000,000P_c$$

ATC

where Q_a and Q_c are the annual quantity demanded of rides by adults and children, respectively, and P_a and P_c are the prices charged to each of these groups. The marginal cost of every additional rider on the Double-Loop Monster is calculated to be $1, regardless of the age of the rider. Use the grids that follow to determine the profit-maximizing prices for the amusement park. Indicate (approximately) the number of rides taken by each group.

Figure 13-5

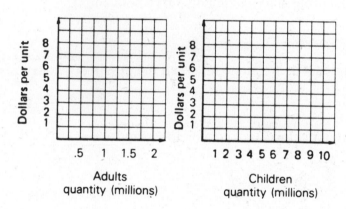

*5.   This exercise focuses on the cartelization of a perfectly competitive industry. The graph on the left presents the cost structure for one of many identical firms in a perfectly competitive industry. On the right you are given the market demand curve and the industry supply curve, which (you should recall) is the horizontal summation of the marginal cost curves of all firms in the industry.

Figure 13-6

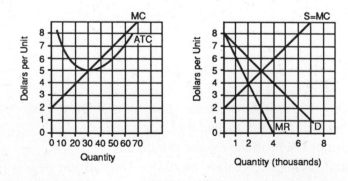

(a)   Suppose that the industry is in long-run competitive equilibrium.
       (i)   What are market price and quantity?

182

(ii)   What is the output of each firm?

(iii)   What is the profit of each firm?

(b)   Now suppose that all firms in the industry collude by forming a cartel to maximize joint profits. What market price and quantity maximize profits for the cartel?

(c)   What output would the cartel instruct each firm to produce?

(d)   What is the level of profits for each firm in the cartel?

(e)   Given the market price established by the cartel, what output would an individual firm like to produce? What are the associated profits? Explain.

6.   The following graph applies to a monopoly. *AL* is the market demand curve and *AK* the marginal revenue curve. *EH* is the long-run supply curve for the industry as well as the *LRAC* curve for the monopolist. (There are no economies of scale so that *LRAC* = *LRMC*.)

Figure 13-7

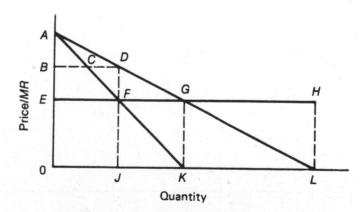

(a)   Assume that the monopolist sets a single price and maximizes profits. Predict the following:
(i)   the monopolistic price _____ and output _____.
(ii)   the amount of consumer surplus at that price _____.
(iii)   the amount of economic profits at that price _____.

183

(b)   Assume that a discriminating monopolist is able to obtain the maximum price for each unit. Predict the following:
      (i)   the price range, from _____ to _____.
      (ii)   the output _____.
      (iii)   the amount of consumers' surplus _____.
      (iv)   the amount of economic profits _____.

◆ ANSWERS

Multiple-Choice Questions

1. (d) 2. (b) 3. (b) 4. (c) 5. (a) 6. (a) 7. (a) 8. (e) 9. (a) 10. (a) 11. (b) 12.(c) 13. (a) 14. (c) 15. (d) 16. (b) 17. (c) 18. (e) 19. (b) 20. (d) 21. (e) 22. (b) 23. (b) 24. (a) 25. (e)

Exercises

1.   (a)   60.
       (b) $11.
       (c) $660.
       (d) $480.
       (e) $180.
       (f)   output: 30 to 90 units; price ranges from $15 to $7.

2.   (a)

Output	TR	MR	MC	Profit
0	$ 0			$-20
		$18	$ 4	
1	18			- 6
		14	3	
2	32			5
		10	5	
3	42			10
		6	7	
4	48			9
		2	9	
5	50			2
		-2	11	
6	48			-11

(b)

Figure 13-8

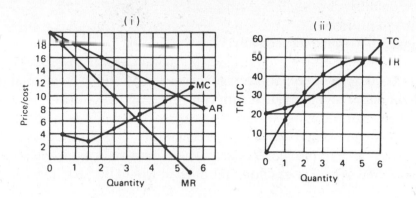

(c)   3 units.

(d) $14 (price to sell output where $MR = MC$).

(e)   At 3 units of output, TR is $42, TC is $32, and profits are $10.

3.   (a) and (b)

Figure 13-9

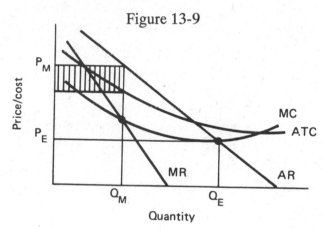

(c)   No, it would not, because the ATC exceeds the price, so business could not be sustained for long.

*4.

Figure 13-10

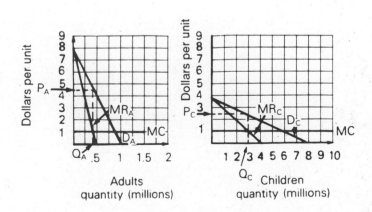

*5.   (a)   (i) $5 and 3,000 units, respectively.
            (ii) 30 units.
            (iii) zero profits.
      (b) $6 and 2,000 units, respectively.
      (c)   20 units; where *MC* of each firm equals market *MR* of $4.
      (d) $10. At 20 units of output, average revenue is $6 and average total cost is $5.50.
      (e)   The output of any individual firm constitutes an insignificant share of total output (in this example, one-hundredth), so market price is negligibly affected by changes in any single firm's output. Therefore, each firm behaves as a price taker and would like to produce 40 units where marginal cost is equal to marginal revenue for the firm. The resulting profit level would be $20 =($6 - $5.50) x 40.

6.   (a)   (i) *OB, OJ*   (ii) *ABD*   (iii) *BDEF*

      (b)   (i) OA to OE   (ii) OK (iii) zero   (iv) AEG

Chapter 14

Patterns of Imperfect Competition

◆ LEARNING OBJECTIVES

After studying this chapter, you should be able to:

✔ explain how imperfectly competitive market structures differ from the perfectly competitive and monopoly models;

✔ explain the importance of product differentiation in monopolistically competitive markets;

✔ distinguish the different types of collusion and their behavioral implications;

✔ understand why oligopolistic prices tend to be "sticky", and;

✔ understand that profits in oligopolistic industries can persist in the long run only if there are significant barriers to entry.

◆ HINTS AND TIPS

You might be guided by the fact that frequent errors on examinations are attributable to:

✔ an incomplete understanding of long run equilibrium in a monopolistically competitive market;

✔ a neglect to remember that each firm's strategic choices in a Nash equilibrium take the choices of competitors as given, and;

✔ many students' inability to properly read the payoff matrix.

◆ MULTIPLE-CHOICE QUESTIONS

1. A concentration ratio is intended to measure
   (a) how much of an industry is concentrated in central Canada.
   (b) the number of firms in an industry.
   (c) how much production in a given market is controlled by a few firms.
   (d) how much of a given industry is concentrated in the hands of foreign-owned transnational corporations.
   (e) the proportion of an industry that concentrates on export markets.

2. Neither the model of perfect competition nor that of monopoly provides a completely satisfactory description of the Canadian economy because there are significant sectors of the economy with
   (a) many small firms that still have some price-setting ability.
   (b) only a few small firms.
   (c) many firms, but with a disproportionate amount of production concentrated in the hands of a few.
   (d) many small firms each selling a differentiated product.
   (e) All of the above.

3. Firms that sell a differentiated product (such as Burger King and Harvey's Hamburgers) each
   (a) face a downward-sloping demand curve.
   (b) have some ability to administer price.
   (c) receive information on market conditions through changes in quantity sold at the set price.
   (d) tend to absorb transitory fluctuations in demand by changing output and holding prices constant.
   (e) All of the above.

4. Which of the following is not a characteristic of a market that features monopolistic competition?
   (a) There is a large number of firms.
   (b) Each firm faces a downward-sloping demand curve.
   (c) The firms sell an identical product.
   (d) There is freedom of entry and exit.
   (e) Each firm's marginal revenue curve lies below its demand curve.

5. The excess capacity theorem in monopolistic competition
   (a) means that these firms will not be producing at minimum average total cost in the long-run equilibrium.
   (b) implies that the trade-off for product variety is a higher unit production cost.
   (c) arises because of the assumptions of freedom of entry and downward-sloping demand curves.
   (d) is a characteristic of long run equilibrium in this market structure.
   (e) All of the above.

6. In the sense used in this chapter, administered prices are
   (a) prices determined by international forces.
   (b) prices controlled by the government.
   (c) prices determined by market forces.
   (d) set by individual firms rather than in response to market forces.
   (e) set by regulatory agencies such as marketing boards.

7. An important feature that distinguishes monopolistic competition from perfect competition is that
   (a) monopolistic competitors sell a differentiated product rather than a homogeneous one.
   (b) the monopolistic competitor's demand curve is the same as the market demand curve.
   (c) in long-run equilibrium, monopolistic competitors earn economic profits, whereas perfectly competitive firms do not.
   (d) there are important barriers to entry in monopolistic competition.
   (e) there is only one firm in a monopolistically competitive market structure.

8. An important prediction of monopolistic competition is that the long-run equilibrium output of the firm is
   (a) where price exceeds average total cost.
   (b) less than the point at which average total cost is at a minimum.
   (c) less than the point at which average total cost equals average revenue.
   (d) less than the point at which marginal cost equals marginal revenue.
   (e) where price equals marginal revenue.

Questions 9 and 10 refer to the following graph.

Figure 14-1

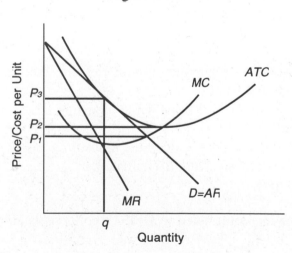

9. The profit-maximizing firm in monopolistic competition will set its price equal to
   (a) P_1.   (b) P_2.
   (c) P_3.   (d) minimum MC.
   (e) marginal cost.

189

10. The situation described by price P_3 and output q is
   (a) a long-run equilibrium in perfect competition since there are no economic profits.
   (b) a long-run equilibrium in monopolistic competition.
   (c) unstable; new firms will enter the industry to eliminate economic profits.
   (d) unstable; firms will exit because profits are zero.
   (e) not the profit-maximizing equilibrium for a monopolistic competitor.

11. The feature that distinguishes perfect competition from all other market structures is that competitive firms
   (a) face negatively sloped demand curves.
   (b) sell an identical product and are price takers.
   (c) actively compete through various forms of nonprice competition such as advertising.
   (d) administer their prices.
   (e) make zero profits in long run equilibrium.

12. In some markets, there may be room for only a few firms because
   (a) of economies of scale and scope.
   (b) the industry produces a homogeneous good.
   (c) individual firms face perfectly elastic demand curves.
   (d) a rising *LRAC* curve
   (e) All of the above.

13. A noncooperative (Nash) equilibrium among oligopolistic firms
   (a) tends to be unstable because each firm has an incentive to cut price and increase output.
   (b) is the same outcome that a single monopoly firm would reach if it owned all the firms in the industry.
   (c) results in each firm producing more, but earning less than it would in a cooperative equilibrium.
   (d) maximizes joint profits for the firms in the industry.
   (e) is characterized by each firm having an incentive to change its output.

14. Other things being equal, oligopolistic industries are likely to come closer to the joint profit-maximizing output level
   (a) the greater the number of firms in the industry.
   (b) when the industry's market is growing rather than contracting.
   (c) when other firms can easily enter the industry.
   (d) if the product can be easily differentiated.
   (e) All of the above.

15. Which of the following contributed to OPEC's collapse as an output-restricting cartel in the late 1980s?
   (a) New productive capacity by non-OPEC countries.
   (b) Individual OPEC members producing in excess of their quotas.
   (c) Development of substitute products and new technologies that were more efficient in their use of oil.
   (d) All of the above.
   (e) Both (b) and (c) but not (a).

16. "Stickiness" in oligopoly theory refers to the fact that
    (a) oligopolists tend to stick together.
    (b) profit levels of competing oligopolists tend to rise and fall together.
    (c) oligopolistic firms tend to keep price constant and vary quantity in response to cyclical demand shifts.
    (d) for oligopolistic firms, demand and supply tend to shift together.
    (e) oligopolists tend to "stick" to collusive agreements.

17. Oligopolistic prices ordinarily change
    (a) whenever there are changes in production costs.
    (b) with seasonal fluctuations in demand.
    (c) in response to large, unexpected shifts in demand.
    (d) rapidly in response to any fluctuations in either demand or cost.
    (e) All of the above.

18. The cooperative, joint profit-maximizing outcome in oligopoly
    (a) is a long run equilibrium so long as there are barriers to entry.
    (b) will be unstable because each firm has an incentive to produce more output to increase profits.
    (c) results in allocative efficiency.
    (d) maximizes the profits of each firm.
    (e) is an equilibrium so long as collusion is explicit as opposed to tacit.

19. Brand proliferation creates a barrier to entry by
    (a) reducing production costs for existing firms.
    (b) reducing the market share for a potential entrant.
    (c) allowing existing firms to fully exploit economies of scale.
    (d) enabling existing firms to operate at minimum efficient scale.
    (e) All of the above.

20. Tacit cooperation among oligopolistic firms that affects prices
    (a) is an effective agreement because it is a legal contract.
    (b) results in long run joint profit-maximizing equilibrium and stability in the industry.
    (c) tends to break down through strategic behavior and technological innovation.
    (d) is more likely the greater the number of firms in the industry.
    (e) is more likely the weaker are the industry's barriers to entry.

21. Advertising expenditures can create a barrier to entry by
    (a) increasing set-up costs for new entrants.
    (b) raising the minimum efficient scale of production.
    (c) allowing existing firms to announce to potential entrants the intention to engage in predatory pricing.
    (d) making a market contestable.
    (e) Both (a) and (b).

22.	Which of the following qualify as possible barriers to entry that oligopolistic firms may erect?
	(a)	Production of many competing brands of a good by a single firm.
	(b)	Large advertising budgets.
	(c)	A credible threat to engage in predatory pricing.
	(d)	Large set-up costs.
	(e)	All of the above.

23.	Economic profits can exist in an oligopolistic industry in the long run because of
	(a)	natural barriers to entry.
	(b)	barriers created by existing firms.
	(c)	barriers created by government policy.
	(d)	economies of scale and scope.
	(e)	All of the above.

24.	According to the theory of contestable markets,
	(a)	the mere threat of potential entry encourages oligopolists to hold profits near the competitive level.
	(b)	firms must actually enter an industry if prices and outputs are to be held near the competitive level.
	(c)	many firms in an industry make it contestable.
	(d)	high costs of entry make markets more contestable.
	(e)	Both (a) and (d) are correct.

25.	Economies of scope depend upon the size of the
	(a)	plants.	(b)	firm.
	(c)	industry.	(d)	economy.
	(e)	concentration ratio.

◆ **EXERCISES**

1.	The following graph describes a firm in a monopolistically competitive industry characterized by easy entry, product differentiation, and a large number of firms.

Figure 14-2

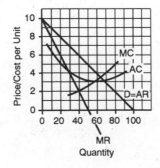

(a)   What price will a profit-maximizing firm set? _____

(b)   What economic profit will this firm receive? _____

(c)   Given that entry is relatively easy, is this a long-run equilibrium situation? Explain

(d)   Which curves will be affected and in which direction if the firm now increases its advertising expenditures by a fixed amount, causing increased sales?

(e)   If new firms were attracted to this industry, what curves in the graph would be affected the most? Why? What would be the *main* consequence for this firm?

(f)   Explain how the result in (e) illustrates the excess capacity theorem.

2.   A firm has the choice of constructing a plant with either of the average variable cost curves shown in the accompanying graph.

Figure 14-3

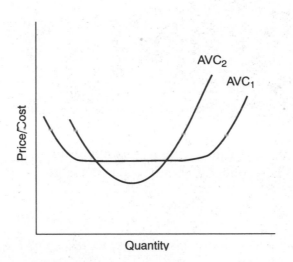

(a)   If there were considerable uncertainty about demand for the product, which plant would the firm choose to build? Why?

(b)   What does the shape of AVC_1 suggest about the nature of the fixed factors in this plant?

3. This exercise applies game theory to the choice of an advertising budget. Suppose two competitors, Pepsi and Coke, must each select its advertising expenditure. For simplicity assume there are only two sizes of advertising budgets: moderate and large. The relationship between advertising and profits for each firm is presented in the following payoff matrix which gives each firm's profits under each of its own budgets as well as that of the competitor's. Note that there are four possible combinations of budgets in the market; these are represented by the cells in the diagram. Coke's profits are presented in the left circle of each cell, while Pepsi's are in the right circle. [Note: Some students may wish to reread the caption to Figure 14-2 in the text to better understand the payoff matrix.]

Figure 14-4

Payoff matrix, profit in millions of dollars*

*Coke's profit is in the left shaded circle of each cell, Pepsi's is in the right circle

(a) If Pepsi and Coke colluded on their choices of advertising budgets, which would they select? Explain.

(b) Is the cooperative outcome in (a) likely to be stable? Explain.

(c) What is the noncooperative (i.e., Nash) equilibrium in this game? Explain.

194

4.   Use economic analysis to discuss each of the following events described in newspaper headlines. Use supply and demand diagrams to the extent possible.

   (a)   "Prices of Petroleum Products Rise As OPEC Restricts Oil Supplies" (1974)
          "Oil Prices Plummet with OPEC Price War" (1986)
          "OPEC Ministers unable to agree on New production Quotas." (1991)

   (b)   "GM Announces Price Hikes for 1992 Models; Ford and Chrysler Expected to Follow." (1991)

   (c)   "Personal Computer Price War Spurs Buying Spree" (1992)

   (d)   "Independent Gas Retailers Spur gas price wars in Southwestern Ontario." (1992)

◆ ANSWERS

Multiple-Choice Questions

1. (c) 2. (e) 3. (e) 4. (c) 5. (e) 6. (d) 7. (a) 8. (b) 9. (c) 10. (b) 11. (b) 12.(a) 13. (c) 14. (b) 15. (d) 16. (c) 17. (c) 18. (b) 19. (b) 20. (c) 21. (e) 22. (e) 23. (e) 24. (a) 25. (b)

Exercises

1.   (a) $6.00.
      (b)   ($6.00 - $3.50) x 40 = $100.00.
      (c)   No. The entry of new firms will reduce economic profits.
      (d)   The ATC curve rises; the D curve will shift rightward, with the MR curve shifting accordingly. The MC curve will be unchanged since, in this case, advertising is a fixed amount.
      (e)   The average revenue (demand) and marginal revenue curves for this firm would shift leftward, and economic profits would be reduced.
      (f)   The leftward shift of the downward-sloping demand curve produces tangency with the declining part of ATC. This must be at less than capacity, which is defined as output at which ATC is minimized.

2.   (a)   The firm would likely choose the plant with AVC_1. If demand were to vary considerably, the average cost of producing various quantities would not vary considerably, whereas with a plant characterized by AVC_2, costs, on average, could rise considerably if demand increased or decreased noticeably.
      (b)   It suggests that the fixed factors are such that their rate of utilization can be varied so as to keep the variable-to-fixed factor ratio constant or close to constant.

3. (a) Joint profits are maximized if both firms adopt moderate advertising budgets. In this case profits on each firm are $80 million, so that joint profits are $160 million.

   (b) No, the cooperative outcome of both firms adopting moderate budgets in unstable. Each firm can do better if it switches to a large budget while its competitor retains moderate expenditures. In the payoff matrix, a firm adopting a large budget would obtain profits of $90 million, while the competitor which remains with the moderate budget receives $50 million.

   (c) The noncooperative equilibrium obtains when each firm selects the large advertising budget. Note that this outcome results in the lowest possible joint profits. However, it is an equilibrium because no firm can do better given the choice of its competitor.

4. (a) OPEC drastically restricted supply in 1974, raising the price above $30 per barrel. A combination of factors including new entrants, innovative substitutes and cheating by cartel members caused the price to drop in the 1980's. In the early 1990's OPEC members have been unable to agree on enforceable output quotas, and the price of a barrel of oil is about $20.

   (b) This is a classic example of strategic pricing behavior by the "Big Three" U.S. automakers. It appears that Ford and Chrysler chose to follow the leader in setting their prices: a form of tacit collusion. However, increased competition from transnational producers has limited the ability of the Big Three to administer prices.

   (c) This particular price war was triggered by the develpoment of a 386 microprocessor by American Micro Devices that was compatible with Intel's which, until then, had a virtual monopoly on the production of 386 chips. Intel responded by slashing prices. This is a good example of innovative pressures in oligopoly.

   (d) The independent retailers have been attempting to increase their market share by offering lower prices. This is sometimes precipitated by entry or surplus production at the refinery. Brandname retailers respond by matching or even undercutting prices—a series of price decreases ensues, often resulting in tempory losses, until prices return to their normal levels.

Chapter 15

Public Policy Toward Monopoly and Competition

◆ LEARNING OBJECTIVES

After studying this chapter, you should be able to:

✔   distinguish between productive efficiency and allocative efficiency;

✔   identify the inefficiency of monopoly compared to perfect competition;

✔   understand the purposes of government competition policies;

✔   discuss the difficulties of regulating natural monopolies;

✔   understand that although the main thrust of anticombines and regulatory policies has been the protection of competitive forces, regulation has also been used to protect firms from competition;

✔   discuss the purposes and progress of the deregulation movement.

◆ HINTS AND TIPS

You might be guided by the fact that frequent errors on examinations are attributable to:

✔   failure to remember that allocative efficiency concerns the choice of relative quantities of goods to produce;

✔   forgetting that unless there are differences in costs, the supply curve of a competitive industry is equivalent to the marginal cost curve of a monopoly;

✔   confusion between marginal and average cost pricing regulations and their implications.

◆ MULTIPLE-CHOICE QUESTIONS

1. Resources are allocated efficiently when
    (a) there are no unemployed resources.
    (b) all firms are producing at the lowest attainable cost.
    (c) prices are as low as possible.
    (d) no alternative allocation of resources makes at least one household better off without making another household worse off.
    (e) profits are maximized.

2. If two firms are producing the same product with different marginal costs, then
    (a) a reallocation of output between the firms can lower the industry's total cost.
    (b) neither firm is producing its output at the lowest attainable cost.
    (c) some resources must be unemployed.
    (d) each firm is being wasteful.
    (e) one firm is not maximizing profits.

3. Allocative efficiency holds when
    (a) price equals marginal cost.
    (b) the consumer valuation of the last unit produced equals the value of resources used to produce this unit.
    (c) the sum of consumers' and producers' surplus is maximized.
    (d) it is impossible to reallocate resources in such a way as to make one individual better off, without making someone else worse off.
    (e) All of the above.

4. Productive efficiency holds
    (a) when $P = MC$ for perfect competition.
    (b) for perfect competition and monopolistic competition where long run profits are zero.
    (c) for natural monopolies where economies of scale are fully exploited.
    (d) throughout the market economy where the objective of firms is to maximize profits.
    (e) when firms produce that output where the ATC curve is at a minimum.

5. Producers' surplus is defined as
    (a) profits.
    (b) retained earnings.
    (c) total revenue less total costs.
    (d) total revenue less total variable costs.
    (e) total revenue less total fixed costs.

6. A major difference between equilibrium in a competitive industry and a monopoly is that
    (a) the monopoly produces where $MR = MC$, but the perfect competitor does not.
    (b) perfect competitors achieve productive efficiency, but monopolies do not.
    (c) the perfect competitor produces where $P = MC$, but the monopoly does not.
    (d) the monopoly achieves allocative efficiency but perfect competition does not.
    (e) All of the above.

7.   The deadweight loss of monopoly is
     (a)   its fixed cost.
     (b)   any negative profit due to cyclical decreases in demand.
     (c)   the forgone surplus due to the allocatively inefficient monopoly output level.
     (d)   the cost of maintaining effective barriers to entry.
     (e)   the extra administrative costs of operating a large firm.

Questions 8 to 11 refer to the following graph, in which the supply curve refers to a perfectly competitive industry and the marginal cost curve refers to a monopoly.

Figure 15-1

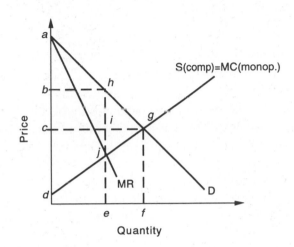

8.   The allocatively efficient levels of output and price are
     (a)   *e* and *b*, respectively.   (b)   *e* and *c*, respectively.
     (c)   *f* and *c*, respectively.   (d)   *f* and *a*, respectively.
     (e)   *e* and *d*, respectively.

9.   If this industry switches to monopoly from perfect competiton, the changes in price and quantity are
     (a)   +*cb* and -*fe*, respectively.   (b)   -*bc* and -*fe*, respectively.
     (c)   +*db* and +*ef*, respectively.   (d)   +*dc* and +*ef*, respectively.
     (e)   +*ca* and -*fe*, respectively.

10. Under monopoly, producers' surplus is area
     (a)   *bdjh*.   (b)   *bdgh*.
     (c)   *cdg*.   (d)   *adj*.
     (e)   *adg*.

11. If price increases from *c* to *b*, and therefore quantity demanded is reduced from *f* to *e*, consumers' surplus is reduced by area
     (a)   *hig*.   (b)   *bcih*.
     (c)   *hjg*.   (d)   *bcgh*.
     (e)   *efgh*.

12. The condition of allocative efficiency is satisfied only under perfect competition because only this market structure results in
    (a)   long run profits equal to zero.
    (b) $P = MC$.
    (c)   complete freedom of entry and exit.
    (d)   maximization of profits through cutthroat competition.
    (e)   productive efficiency.

13. Average cost pricing for a falling-cost natural monopoly results in
    (a)   zero profits.
    (b)   allocative efficiency.
    (c)   production at the optimal output.
    (d) $P = MC$.
    (e)   All of the above.

14. The larger the minimum efficient scale of firms, *ceteris paribus*,
    (a)   the more likely a concentrated market will improve productive efficiency.
    (b)   the greater the tendency toward natural monopoly.
    (c)   the greater the advantages of large-scale production.
    (d)   the fewer the number of firms comprising an industry.
    (e)   All of the above.

15. Productive efficiency requires that
    (a)   each firm produces its output at the lowest possible cost.
    (b)   each firm employ factors such that the ratio of their marginal products is equal to the ratio of their prices.
    (c)   the total cost of producing the industry's output is minimized.
    (d)   marginal cost of production be equalized across all firms in the industry.
    (e)   All of the above.

16. Cross-subsidization refers to
    (a)   the taxation of growing industries to subsidize declining ones.
    (b)   the use of profits from one of a firm's products to subsidize another of its products at a price below cost.
    (c)   transfers of profits between crown corporations and private firms in the same industry.
    (d)   transfers from rising-cost natural monopolies to falling-cost natural monopolies.
    (e)   taxation of private sector firms to subsidize public sector enterprises.

17. If a natural monopoly is regulated to charge a price that is equal to marginal cost where the marginal cost curve intersects the demand curve and is less than average cost, the resulting level of output is
    (a)   allocatively efficient, and a positive profit is earned.
    (b)   allocatively efficient, but the firm must be paid a subsidy or it will go out of business.
    (c)   less than the allocatively efficient level, and profits are zero.
    (d)   less than the allocatively efficient level, but negative profits are earned.
    (e)   greater than the allocatively efficient level, but negative profits are earned.

18. The original philosophy behind the regulation of natural monopolies such as public utilities
    (a) was to guarantee consumers a low price.
    (b) involved government ownership in key economic sectors.
    (c) was to achieve the advantages of large-scale production but prevent the monopoly from restricting output and raising price.
    (d) was to erect dependable and effective barriers to entry.
    (e) to protect domestic industries from foreign competition.

19. Which of the following is *not* one of the forces encouraging deregulation and privatization in advanced industrial nations?
    (a) The experience that many regulatory bodies serve to reduce competition rather than increase it.
    (b) The growing evidence that nationalized industries do not enhance productivity growth or allocative efficiency.
    (c) Increased pressures from world competition.
    (d) The conclusion that industrial performance improves when an oligopoly is replaced by a nationalized monopoly.
    (e) Concern over cross subsidization that is often required by regulatory agencies.

20. There is a growing consensus that natural monopoly regulation by public utility commissions
    (a) has served effectively to protect consumers from natural monopolies.
    (b) has led to allocative efficiency.
    (c) is concerned more with protecting firms from competition than with protecting consumers from natural monopoly.
    (d) has kept the sum of consumer and producer surplus at a maximum.
    (e) All of the above.

21. "Protectionist" policies by regulatory commissions
    (a) are aimed at protecting the consumer.
    (b) reflect a concern for existing firms and limiting the entry of potential competitors.
    (c) concern the trade-offs between domestic and foreign trade policy.
    (d) deal with work safety and environmental issues.
    (e) defend the market mechanism against monopoly control.

22. In the decision to privatize a crown corporation, government faces a trade-off between
    (a) deregulation and selling the crown corporation.
    (b) the selling price and future competition in the industry.
    (c) average cost pricing and rate of return regulation.
    (d) productive and allocative efficiency.
    (e) consumer and producer surplus.

23. The lack of effective combines enforcement in Canada prior to 1976 was partly due to
    (a) the inability of civil actions to cope with complex economic issues.
    (b) the passage of the Combines Investigation Act as criminal rather than civil legislation.
    (c) the fact that the fines were rather small.
    (d) the reluctance of Canadian courts to assess economic evidence.
    (e) Both (b) and (d) are correct.

24. Since 1976 *all but which* of the following has been introduced into Canadian competition policy?
    (a) The power to prohibit suppliers from refusing to supply.
    (b) Prohibiting producers from advertising a bargain price without reasonable quantities.
    (c) Prohibition of mergers.
    (d) Extension of the act to include service industries.
    (e) Allowance for civil as opposed to criminal actions.

25. A rising-cost firm that installs enough capacity to to meet demand when price is set equal to average cost
    (a) will invest in more capacity than is socially optimal.
    (b) will ultimately make profits.
    (c) must be subsidized to cover losses.
    (d) will produce an allocatively efficient output.
    (e) will produce that output where $P = MC$.

◆ **EXERCISES**

1. In the following graph *DD* is the market demand curve, and *DM* is the associated marginal revenue curve. *AN* is the long run supply curve for a competitive industry and also the marginal cost curve for a monopolist.

Figure 15-2

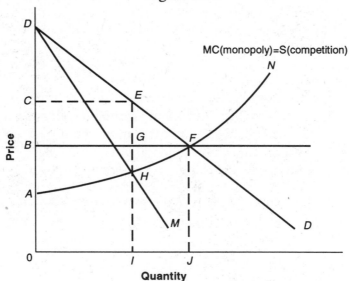

(a) For perfect competition, predict the following:
    (i) equilibrium price _____ and quantity _____.
    (ii) consumers' surplus _____.
    (iii) producers' surplus _____.
    (iv) the sum of producers' and consumers' surplus

(b) For monopoly, predict the following:
    (i) equilibrium price _____ and quantity _____.
    (ii) consumers' surplus _____.

(iii)   producers' surplus _____.

(iv)   the sum of producers' and consumers' surplus _____.

(c)   The surplus transferred from consumers to producers with monopolization of a competitive industry is _____.

(d)   The deadweight loss from monopoly is _____.

2.   A perfectly competitive market is illustrated in the first panel of the following graph, while a monopolistic market is presented in the second. Note that each market faces an identical demand curve.

Figure 15-3

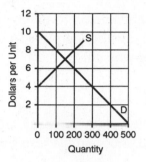 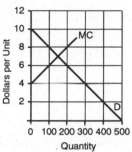

(a)   What are the equilibrium levels of price and output in the perfectly competitive market? In the monopoly market?

(b)   What shift in the monopolist's *MC* curve (relative to perfect competition) is required to have the levels of price and output the same in both market structures?

(c)   Starting from the equilibrium situations depicted in (a), illustrate that both price and quantity would change by less in the monopolistic market than in perfect competition in response to an increase in marginal costs by $2 per unit of output.

3.   This exercise explores the implications of regulatory pricing. The following graph depicts a market demand curve and a firm's cost structure characterized by constant marginal cost (*MC*) and a large set-up cost so that average cost (*AC*) is continuously declining over market demand. The firm is therefore a natural monopoly.

Figure 15-4

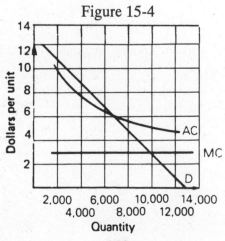

(a)   What is the allocatively efficient level of output? Why?

(b)   What are the unregulated monopolist's profit-maximizing price and quantity in this market and the associated profit level?

(c)   What is the resulting deadweight loss?

(d)   Suppose that a regulatory agency attempted to induce this monopolist to produce the allocatively efficient output by restricting price to equal marginal cost. Would the agency be successful? Why or why not?

(e)   As an alternative, suppose that the agency imposes "average cost pricing" on the monopolist. What is the regulated price and the resulting quantity?

(f)   Compare the level of profits and deadweight loss under "average cost pricing" with that under "marginal cost pricing" from (d).

4.   The demand curve for a product is $Q_d = 90,000 - 1,000P$ with P (price) expressed in dollars. In a competitive market, the supply curve is $2,000P - 45,000$ (with supply being zero at $P \le \$22.50$). Remember, the competitive supply curve is the horizontal summation of the firm's marginal cost curves above the minimum average variable cost (here, $22.50).

(a)   Determine the equilibrium price and quantity pf the product necessary for allocative efficiency. Use graph in (b) or solve algebraically.

(b)   Graph consumers' and producers' surpluses (total net benefits, in dollars) under allocative efficiency.

Figure 15-5

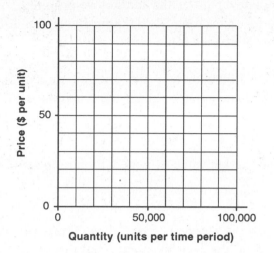

(c)   Assume that the product was supplied instead by a monopoly. Determine the quantity that will be supplied and the market price, and graph below the consumers' and producers' surpluses. The counterpart of the competitive supply curve is $MC = 22.5 + 0.0005Q$. [Note the graphic identity of MC in this graph to S in (b).]

Figure 15-6

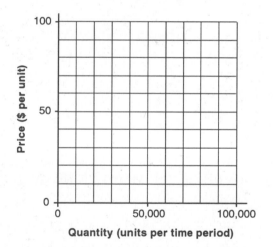

(d)   Compare producers' surplus, consumers' surplus, and total net benefits in (c) with those in (b).

5.   An interesting example of how government policies serve to promote monoploy power is provided by laws requiring licensing of taxicabs. New York City passed such a law in 1937, freezing the number of taxicab licenses (medallions) at 11,797—taxicabs without medallions are not suppose to pick up people who hail cabs from the street. Prior to the law, free entry had been allowed. In 1937 the price of taxicab medallions was near zero since existing cabs were "grandfathered": existing operators were granted a medallion by

205

virtue of already being in the industry. New entrants had to purchase a medallion from an existing owner at whatever price the market determined. As demand rose the market value of a medallion rose, reaching $100,000 in December 1985. About 1,600 medallions are traded each year, with banks often giving mortgages for their purchase.

(a)   Use a graph to illustrate why the price of medallions has increased over time. Why is the increase in market price likely to continue?

(b)   What does the market value of a medallion represent?

(c)   What effect has the emergence of "gypsy" cabs (illegal cabs without medallions) in the city had on the taxicab market and the market value of a medallion? How would unrestricted entry affect the market value of a medallion?

(d)   In April 1985, New York's Mayor Koch proposed increasing the number of medallions by 10 percent of the existing number. The new medallions were to be made available by auction. Earlier Koch had proposed giving each medallion owner a second one to use or sell. Contrast these two plans.

◆ ANSWERS

Multiple-Choice Questions

1. (d) 2. (a) 3. (e) 4. (d) 5. (d) 6. (c) 7. (c) 8. (c) 9. (a) 10. (a) 11. (d) 12.(b) 13. (a) 14. (e) 15. (e) 16. (b) 17. (b) 18. (c) 19. (d) 20. (c) 21. (b) 22. (b) 23. (e) 24. (c) 25. (a)

Exercises

1.   (a)   (i) *B,J*; (ii) area *BDF*; (iii) area *ABF*; (iv) area *ADF*.
       (b)   (i) *C, I*; (ii) area *CDE*; (iii) area *ACEH*; (iv) area *ADEH*.
       (c)   area *CBGE*.
       (d)   area *HEF*.

2. (a)

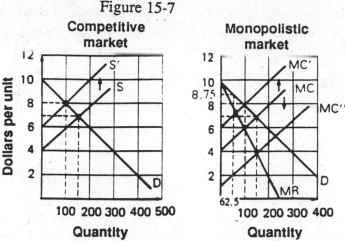

Figure 15-7

The initial equilibrium in perfect competition obtains at a price of $7 and a quantity of 150 units. The monopoly equilibrium is derived by first drawing the monopolist's marginal revenue curve (same price intercept and half the quantity intercept as the demand curve), which equals *MC* at an output of 100 units, implying a price of $8.

(b) The equilibrium in perfect competition obtains at a price of $7 and a quantity of 150 units. For these to be the profit-maximizing price and quantity of the monopolist, the market *MR* curve and the monopolist's *MC* curve must intersect at a quantity of 150. This requires (for a uniform shift) that *MC* be $3 lower per unit of output—for illustration, *MC"*.

(c) In panel (i), shift the supply curve a vertical distance of $2 to *S'*; the new equilibrium price is $8 and quantity is 100. In panel (ii), shift the *MC* curve a vertical distance of $2 to *MC'*; equate *MR* and *MC'* to obtain the new profit-maximizing price of $8.75 and quantity of 62.5 (approximately). Thus both price and quantity change less in the monopoly situation.

3.

Figure 15-8

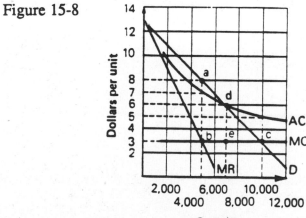

(a) 10,000. Because the value of the resources used to produce the 10,000th unit (i.e., *MC*) equals the value that households place on the consumption of this unit.

(b) $8, 5,000 units, and $5,000.

(c) area *abc* = ($8 - $3) (10,000 - 5,000)/2 = $12,500.

(d)   If the market price were \$3 and the firm produced 10,000 units, *TR* would be \$30,000. But *AC* would be \$5, which implies a *TC* of \$50,000. Therefore, the firm would be making a loss of \$20,000; it would eventually go out of business unless the loss was offset by a subsidy from the government.

(e)   Price could be regulated at \$6, which would yield a market quantity of 7,000 units.

(f)   Under average cost pricing in (e), profits are zero but the deadweight loss is area *dec* = (\$6 - \$3) (10,000 - 7,000)/2 = \$4,500. Marginal cost pricing in (d) does not yield any deadweight loss, but the firm is forced to incur an operating loss.

4.   (a)   Set demand equal to supply and solve for price (45) and output (45,000). (See panel (i) of the graph.)

(b)   Consumers' surplus is area (a) and producers' surplus is area (b) in panel (i) below.

(c)   Price is *h* and quantity is 27,000. In panel (ii), consumers' surplus is shown by the triangle *ehg*; producers' surplus is the quadrangle 22.5 *hgf*.

(d)   Under competitive conditions, consumers' surplus (*CS*) is more and producers' surplus (*PS*) is less than under monopoly. For example, *CS* in (c) is the area *ehg* in panel (ii), which is less than triangle (a) in panel (i). Net benefits (consumers' surplus plus producers' surplus) are less under monopoly. The amount of the reduction (the so-called deadweight allocative loss) is shown by the triangle *ifg* in panel (ii).

Figure 15-9

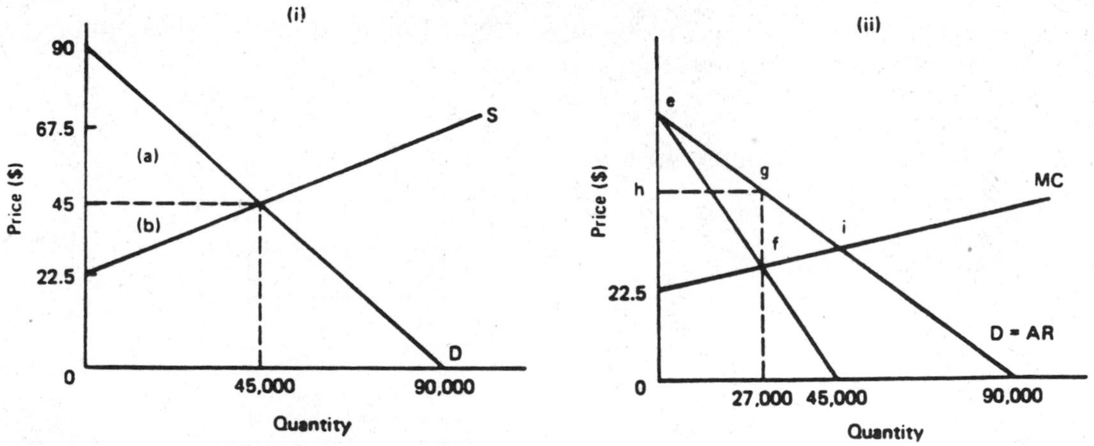

5.   (a)   Supply is fixed, or perfectly inelastic. As demand increases over time, the price will be driven up.

Figure 15-10

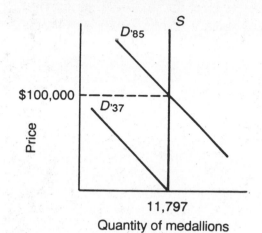

Quantity of medallions

(b) It represents the present value of the stream of future profits obtainable from owning and operating a cab in New York City.

(c) Entry is characterized by a rightward shift in the supply curve, thereby eroding the price of a medallion. While gypsy cabs operate illegally, authorities in New York have for the most part ignored them in recent years: they have therefore reduced the market value of a medallion. With free entry, the supply curve will shift to the right until it intersects current demand at a medallion price of zero.

(d) A ten precent increase in the quantity of medallions would lower their price, but not by as much as a doubling of their number. Thus, current owners would suffer less of a capital loss with the first plan. On the other hand, current owners gain nothing with the first plan since the medallions are auctioned off, while under the second plan they would receive a second medallion free. The relative magnitudes of these offsetting effects would determine their preferred plan.

Chapter 16

Takeovers, Mergers and Foreign Direct Investment

◆ LEARNING OBJECTIVES

After studying this chapter, you should be able to:

✔ understand that if a firm does not realize its profit potential, it is vulnerable to a takeover bid;

✔ evaluate who primarily benefits from corporate takeover activity and to what extent any costs are imposed on the economy as a whole;

✔ explain how the separation of ownership from control creates divergent interests in operating a firm;

✔ apply principal-agent analysis to indicate why managers may not pursue stockholders' interests;

✔ distinguish key predictions of firm behavior based on theories of profit maximization, sales maximization, full-cost pricing, and nonmaximization;

✔ discuss the costs and benefits of transnational corporations to the host country; and

✔ outline the debate on the costs and benefits of foreign investment in Canada.

◆ HINTS AND TIPS

You might be guided by the fact that frequent errors on examinations are attributable to an:

✔ inadequate appreciation of the role of profits in nonmaximizing theories of the firm.

◆ MULTIPLE-CHOICE QUESTIONS

1. A merger between a publisher and a printing company is an example of a
   (a) conglomerate merger.
   (b) vertical merger.
   (c) horizontal merger.
   (d) leveraged buyout.
   (e) a tender offer.

2. New management in a takeover may make more efficient use of a target firm's assets by
   (a) operating the target firm more efficiently.
   (b) providing funds that the target firm could not obtain.
   (c) providing access to markets that the target firm could not obtain independently.
   (d) better exploiting economies of scale.
   (e) All of the above.

3. Most economists believe that the threat of a takeover
   (a) induces an inefficient resource allocation.
   (b) will eventually drive the economy into another recession.
   (c) restricts managers from pursuing objectives other than profit maximization.
   (d) has no effect on the current managers of firms.
   (e) is disruptive to the efficient operation of a firm.

4. Hostile takeovers have tended to benefit most the
   (a) workers of the acquired firms.
   (b) stockholders of the acquired firms.
   (c) managers of the acquired firms.
   (d) stockholders of the acquiring firms.
   (e) consumers of the acquired firm's output.

5. Junk bonds are
   (a) viewed as inferior investments that offer lower interest rates.
   (b) sold to finance leveraged buyouts.
   (c) any bonds with an interest yield below the market rate.
   (d) a form of debt held by scrap dealers.
   (e) debt issued by municipalities.

6. Leveraged buyouts
   (a) are a means of dismantling unprofitable conglomerates.
   (b) can provide current management with a defense against hostile takeover bids.
   (c) are takeovers financed with borrowed funds.
   (d) are often financed with junk bonds.
   (e) All of the above.

7. One economic rationale for a conglomerate merger is
   (a) economies of scale.
   (b) the division of labor at the management level.
   (c) the principal-agent problem.
   (d) the spreading of risk across different industries.
   (e) to acquire more monopoly power in a given industry.

8. Which of the following is viewed in Canada as a potential benefit associated with transnational corporations?
   (a) Extraterritoriality.
   (b) Arbitrage of country-specific economic policies.
   (c) Centralized relocation of research and development activities.
   (d) A more rapid rise in capital per worker than could be provided by domestic savings.
   (e) Shifting to jurisdictions with tax advantages.

9. Government attempts to limit leveraged buyouts are most warranted on economic grounds if
   (a) risks to the economy exceed the risks borne by acquiring firms.
   (b) managers of acquired firms lose their jobs.
   (c) the acquiring firm goes bankrupt and bondholders lose money.
   (d) the government is also able to reduce the severity of the business cycle.
   (e) it protects stock prices from falling.

10. Principal-agent problems are more likely to arise when
   (a) managers are protected from hostile takeovers by poison pills.
   (b) managers' performance can be easily evaluated relative to competitors'.
   (c) owners manage the firm.
   (d) a few stockholders own most of the shares outstanding.
   (e) All of the above.

11. The hypothesis of minority control
   (a) refers to programs that have encouraged stock ownership by visible minorities.
   (b) recognizes that a group holding much less than 51 percent of total shares may effectively select directors and management.
   (c) holds that a minority of employees, the top managers, control the firm.
   (d) maintains that a minority of corporations, those in the military-industrial complex, control our economy.
   (e) suggests that most firms are contrlled through proxy votes.

12. The fact that a well-organized minority may exercise control of a corporation does not in itself deny the predictions derived from the theory of the firm because
   (a) their control may require the proxy votes of a majority.
   (b) management is generally unresponsive to shareholders, whether they are a minority or a majority.
   (c) the overriding objective may still be profit maximization with disputes centering on the means of maximizing profits.
   (d) of the theory of the principal-agent problem.
   (e) All of the above.

13. The theory of sales maximization subject to a minimum profit constraint is based on the premise that
   (a) a controlling management derives personal benefits from the size of a firm as well as its profit level.

(b) the firm's objectives are always decided at the annual shareholders' meeting.

(c) a minority of shareholders, who have goals different from those of the majority of shareholders, can form a majority of actual votes.

(d) firms only desire a normal return to their investments.

(e) All of the above.

14. A firm that practices full-cost pricing
(a) sets price equal to marginal cost.
(b) sets price equal to average cost at the profit-maximizing output.
(c) equates marginal revenue with marginal cost.
(d) sets price equal to average cost at normal capacity output plus some markup.
(e) will always make zero economic profits.

15. Full-cost pricing
(a) can never be consistent with profit maximization, even if it is costly to change prices.
(b) is consistent with slow response, in terms of price, to any change in cost or demand.
(c) if followed by the firm, leads to more frequent price changing than profit maximization.
(d) implies that firms, when setting prices, seek merely to break even.
(e) All of the above.

16. Satisficing theory argues that
(a) the majority of shareholders are satisfied with their management.
(b) the firm's objective is not profit maximization but simply to attain some minimally acceptable profit level.
(c) the firm will produce the output corresponding to maximum market share.
(d) the most successful firms are those that produce goods that best satisfy consumers.
(e) firms deliberately keep profits low to satisfy governments.

17. A basic difference between satisficing theory and the theories of profit maximization and sales maximization is that
(a) satisficing is based on the goals of management, whereas the others are based on the goals of shareholders.
(b) satisficing predicts the largest level of output among the three theories.
(c) satisficing predicts that the firm will never produce the output level corresponding to either maximum profits or maximum sales.
(d) satisficing predicts a range of outputs; the others predict unique output levels.
(e) shareholders are satisfied with management so long as profits are positive.

18. Which of the following is *not* true of Transnational corporations (TNC's)?
(a) They are characterized by a centralized production facility that exports to many countries in the world.
(b) They have the ability to shift costs and profits to countries with the most advantageous tax laws.
(c) They account for the majority of international trade and investment.

214

(d)   Much international trade is between different units of the same TNC.
(e)   They pose a problem of extraterritoriality.

19.   Which of the following is viewed as a benefit of foreign investment in Canada?
(a)   A higher rate of economic growth.
(b)   A greater total investment than what would have been achieved through domestic savings.
(c)   Participation in the global division of labor as brought about by TNC's.
(d)   A more rapid rise in capital per worker.
(e)   All of the above.

20.   A difference between maximizing and nonmaximizing theories of firm behavior is
(a)   the speed and magnitude, but not the general direction, of the response to changes in demand or cost conditions.
(b)   that firms are nonmaximizers because they have inadequate information to maximize profits.
(c)   that maximizing and nonmaximizing firms respond entirely differently to changes in economic conditions.
(d)   that maximizing firms display a great deal of inertia.
(e)   All of the above.

21.   The sales-maximizing hypothesis implies that a firm
(a)   sells as many units as it can at a fixed price.
(b)   attempts to maximize its market share without regard to profits.
(c)   cuts price in order to sell the level of output where $MR = MC$.
(d)   seeks to maximize sales revenue, subject to a profit constraint.
(e)   will produce that output where $MC = ATC$.

◆ EXERCISES

1.   The following graph represents demand and cost conditions for a firm.

Figure 16-1

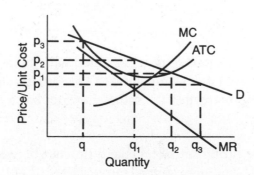

(a)   What would be the choice of price and output for a profit maximizer? _____
(b)   What would be the range of price and output for a profit satisficer who is content to cover opportunity costs as a minimum? _____

(c)   What could be the price and output of a sales maximizer who is willing to accept losses for short periods (assume sufficient economies of scale so that *LRAC* will be less than p at q_3)? _____

2.   Assume that a firm is capable of making a reasonable projection of its profits ($\prod$) as it expands output (Q) and that this relationship is

$$\prod = 7Q - Q^2 - 6$$

(a)   For values of $Q = 1, 2, 3, 3.5, 4, 5,$ and 6, plot the profit function on the graph.
(b)   If a satisficing firm has a profit target of 4, what ranges of output will that firm accept?

(c)   What output is consistent with profit maximization?

Figure 16-2

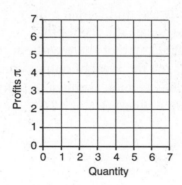

(d)   If the firm is a sales maximizer and the only constraint was to have profits of a least 2, approximately what output will it choose?

*3.   To suggest why economists tend to be dissatisfied with nonmaximizing models for price-output decisions, this problem extends the analysis of Exercise 2. In doing that exercise, you should already have noted that the satisficing firm has a rather wide range of outputs to choose from.

Note the following: the profit function is the difference between $TR = 17Q - Q^2$ and $TC = 10Q + 6$; $MR = 17 - 2Q$, and; the demand curve is $P = 17 - Q$.

(a)   Confirm that the profit-maximizing output is 3.5, at which the price is 13.5.

(b)   Now allow fixed costs to increase by 1 so that $TC = 10Q + 7$. How are the decisions for satisficer, profit maximizer, and sales maximizer altered? You may use the graph to help derive your answers.

(c)   Now change the cost function to $11Q + 6$ to test the effect of a change in marginal costs. You should get straightforward answers for the maximizers, but what about the satisficer?

Figure 16-3

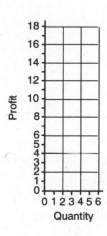

Quantity

(d)   Now assume the original cost conditions but with a favorable demand shift to $P = 17 - 0.5Q$ (which also increases the demand elasticity at every price). Work out the decisions for the maximizers. How might the profit satisficer deal with the wide range of choices that meet the criterion that profits be at least 4?

◆ ANSWERS

Multiple-Choice Questions

1. (b) 2. (e) 3. (c) 4. (b) 5. (b) 6. (e) 7. (d) 8. (d) 9. (a) 10. (a) 11. (b) 12. (c) 13. (a) 14. (d) 15. (b) 16. (b) 17. (d) 18. (a) 19. (e) 20. (a) 21. (d)

Exercises

1.   (a) p_2 and q_1;
       (b)   from p_3 and q to p_1 and q_2;
       (c)   p and q_3.

2. (a)

Figure 16-4

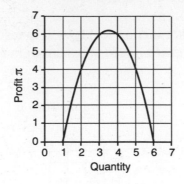

(b) From $Q = 2$ to $Q = 5$.
(c) $Q = 3.5$.
(d) $Q = 5.5$ (approximately).

*3. (a) In this case, marginal cost is constant at 10. Setting $MC = MR$ yields $10 = 17 - 2Q$, which solves for $Q = 3.5$; $P = 17 - Q$, or 13.5.

(b) This has the effect of shifting the profit curve down a vertical distance of $1 at each level of output. The resulting profit curve is labeled *b* in the following graph. The output of the profit maximizer is unaffected. The output of the satisficer with a profit target of $4 now ranges from 2.5 to 4.5, approximately. The sales maximizer who has a profit target of $2 reduces output to approximately 5.25.

(c) The resulting profit curve is labeled *c* in the graph. The profit maximizer produces three units, and the sales maximizer produces four units. The satisficer can no longer attain the minimum profit level of $4. The closest it can come is $3, which is achieved when the profit-maximizing output of three units is produced.

Figure 16-5

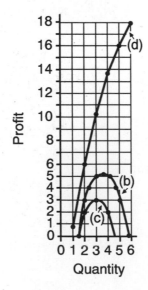

218

(d)   The resulting profit curve is labeled d in the graph. As requested in Exercise 2, the profit curve is plotted only up to an output level of six units, which is the output of both the profit maximizer and the sales maximizer (actually, each would like to increase output beyond six units). The satisficer produces anywhere between (approximately) 1.25 and 6 units, despite the substantial difference in profits over this range.

PART FIVE

THE DISTRIBUTION OF INCOME

Chapter 17

Factor Price and Factor Mobility

◆ LEARNING OBJECTIVES

After studying this chapter, you should be able to:

✔ comprehend how Canadian income is distributed by factors (functional distribution of income) and across households (size distribution of income);

✔ understand why the demand for factors of production is regarded as a derived demand;

✔ demonstrate why firms will continue to hire factors only as long as the added revenue from their output is greater than or equal to the added cost;

✔ explain the factors that determine the elasticity of factor demand;

✔ appreciate the key role of factor mobility, across firms and across industries, in determining (1) how a market system allocates resources, (2) the proportions of a factor's total pay, which are transfer earnings and rents, and (3) how disequilibrium differentials in earnings are eliminated;

✔ recognize the special conditions that affect the supply of various factors, particularly nonmonetary considerations and distinguish equilibrium and disequilibrium differentials in net advantage;

✔ grasp the concept of economic rent and understand how the proportion of a factor's earnings that is rent depends on the alternatives that are open to the factor of production.

◆ HINTS AND TIPS

You might be guided by the fact that some of the most common errors made on examinations are:

✔ the inability to apply correctly the formula, $w = MRP$, in order to determine a perfectly competitive firm's profit-maximizing employment of a factor of production;

✔   confusing the effects of a change in product price versus a change in factor price on a perfectly competitive firm's labor demand curve; the former shifts the labor demand curve while the latter causes a movement along a labor demand curve;

✔   the inability to explain why a part of a factor's earnings may consist of an economic rent.

◆ MULTIPLE-CHOICE QUESTIONS

1.   The functional distribution of income
      (a)   emphasizes the function of income in attracting workers.
      (b)   is concerned with distribution by income class.
      (c)   can be graphically shown by a Lorenz curve.
      (d)   shows income shares of factors of production.
      (e)   deals with the transfer earnings portion of total factor incomes.

2.   Complete equality of income distribution would appear on a Lorenz curve as a
      (a)   diagonal line.
      (b)   convex line.
      (c)   concave curve.
      (d)   single point.
      (e)   series of points below the diagonal.

Use the following graph to answer questions 3 and 4:

Figure 17-1

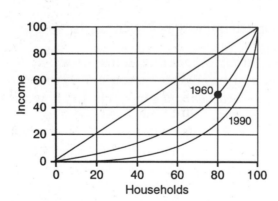

3.   The Lorenz curve for a hypothetical economy is given for two different years. Between 1960 and 1990,
      (a)   the income distribution became less equal.
      (b)   the income distribution became more equal.
      (c)   the poverty rate rose.
      (d)   the poverty rate fell.
      (e)   the employment-income share of total income increased.

224

4. In 1960, the richest 20 percent of households received
   (a) twice as much income as the poorest 20 percent of households.
   (b) as much income as the other 80 percent of households.
   (c) twice as much income as the other 80 percent of households.
   (d) half as much income as the other 80 percent of households.
   (e) None of the above.

5. The total demand for an input is the
   (a) mirror image of the supply.
   (b) sum of the derived demands for it in all of its various uses.
   (c) sum of the demands for all of the goods the input produces.
   (d) sole determinant of that factor's price.
   (e) sole determinant of economic rents.

6. The marginal revenue product of a factor is
   (a) the change in revenue from selling the extra output produced by an additional unit of a factor.
   (b) average physical productivity of the factor multiplied by product price.
   (c) the change in revenue from selling one more unit of output.
   (d) equal to the market price of the product that is produced by the factor.
   (e) its marginal physical product times the factor's price.

7. The marginal physical product of labor is
   (a) total output divided by total labor in use.
   (b) the change in output divided by the change in labor use.
   (c) total labor in use divided by total output.
   (d) the change in labor use divided by the change in output.
   (e) None of the above.

8. A perfectly competitive, profit-maximizing firm that is a price taker in factor markets hires a factor up to the point at which
   (a) the factor's price equals its marginal revenue product.
   (b) the marginal cost of hiring the factor equals the additional revenue obtained from that factor's marginal contribution to output.
   (c) the factor's price equals its marginal physical product times the product's price.
   (d) All of the above.
   (e) None of the above.

9. Perfectly competitive, profit-maximizing firms that employ any factor until marginal revenue product equals its price will hire
   (a) additional units of the factor if its price falls, other things equal.
   (b) more of the factor if the price of the product it produces falls, other things equal.
   (c) less of the factor if technology changes such that factor productivity rises, other things equal.
   (d) additional units of the factor if the factor's price exceeds its marginal revenue product.
   (e) the same quantities of all factors.

10. Which of the following explains why a price-taking, profit-maximizing firm's demand curve for labor slopes downward? As the quantity of labor employed rises,
    (a) the marginal physical product of labor eventually falls.
    (b) the firm's marginal revenue declines as output increases.
    (c) the marginal cost of hiring another unit of labor increases.
    (d) All of the above.
    (e) None of the above.

11. If the quantity demanded for a factor of production decreases by 10 percent when its price increases by 8 percent, the elasticity of demand for the factor is
    (a) -18.0.   (b) 1.25 percent.
    (c) -0.80.   (d) -2.00.
    (e) -1.25.

12. Which of the following is *not* true about the demand for a factor of production?
    (a) It is more elastic the greater the elasticity of demand for the final product.
    (b) It is more elastic in cases where technology dictates its use in fixed proportions with other factors.
    (c) It is less elastic the smaller its share of the total cost of the product.
    (d) It is more elastic the longer the time period considered.
    (e) It is more elastic the greater its substitutability with alternative inputs.

13. A perfectly competitive industry's demand curve for a factor
    (a) is likely to be more elastic than a firm's demand curve for the same factor.
    (b) is always perfectly inelastic.
    (c) has the same elasticity as every firm in that industry.
    (d) the mirror image of the industry's supply curve for the factor.
    (e) None of the above.

14. Suppose that a worker's wage rate increases. If we observe total work effort to increase, then
    (a) the substitution effect must have been greater than the income effect.
    (b) the worker's labor supply curve must be downward sloping.
    (c) the income effect must have been greater than the substitution effect.
    (d) all employment earnings must be economic rents.
    (e) the worker's marginal physical productivity has increased.

15. A highly mobile factor of production
    (a) is one that shifts easily between uses in response to small changes in incentives.
    (b) displays supply inelasticity in most uses.
    (c) is a particularly applicable concept for the short run.
    (d) will tend to have a large proportion of its earnings made up of economic rents.
    (e) Both (a) and (d).

Questions 16 to 19 refer to the following graph. The demand and supply curves apply to a competitive market for a factor of production. Point A is the initial market equilibrium situation; other points represent alternative equilibria caused by parallel shifts in either the demand curve or the supply curve, both *not* both.

Figure 17-2

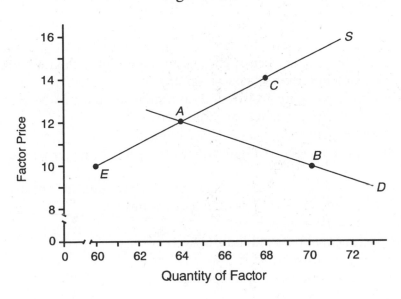

16. At the initial equilibrium situation at point A,
   (a)   total income paid to the factor is $12.
   (b)   total factor earnings are $768.
   (c)   the economic rent of the sixty-fourth unit is zero.
   (d)   Both (b) and (c).
   (e)   None of the above.

17. If the equilibrium in this factor market changed from point A to point B, then
   (a)   the supply curve for the factor has shifted to the right.
   (b)   total factor earnings are $700.
   (c)   the economic rent of the sixty-fourth unit is now positive.
   (d)   All of the above.
   (e)   None of the above.

18. If the equilibrium in this factor market changed from point A to point C, then
   (a)   the new equilibrium unit price of the factor is $14.
   (b)   total factor earnings are lower at C than those associated with point A.
   (c)   the total demand for the factor decreased.
   (d)   Both (a) and (b).
   (e)   All of the above.

19. Assuming an equilibrium factor price of $12,
   (a)   the sixtieth unit of the factor makes no economic rents.
   (b)   the price of the sixtieth unit of the factor is comprised totally of economic rents.
   (c)   the transfer earning to the sixtieth unit of the factor is $10.
   (d)   the economic rent to the sixtieth unit of the factor is $10.
   (e)   None of the above.

20. Equilibrium differentials in factor prices may reflect
    (a) intrinsic differences in factor characteristics.
    (b) acquired differences in factor characteristics.
    (c) nonmonetary advantages in uses of the factor.
    (d) All of the above.
    (e) None of the above.

21. Which of the following is not an example of an equilibrium differential in a factor price?
    (a) Land in downtown Toronto is more expensive than land in the suburbs.
    (b) Wages in the Quebec construction trades are higher than elsewhere in the country because of a booming Quebec economy.
    (c) Individuals working in isolated communities tend to be paid more than their counterparts in the more accessible cities.
    (d) A dentist is paid more than a dental hygienist.
    (e) Certain workers receive higher wages because of greater working hazards.

22. One would expect which of the following to view most of the payment to Roberto Alomar of the Toronto Blue Jays as transfer earnings?
    (a) The Toronto Blue Jays.
    (b) The professional baseball industry.
    (c) University professors.
    (d) National transfer payment recipients.
    (e) None of the above.

23. Economic rent
    (a) refers exclusively to the income of landowners.
    (b) is taxable under the income tax law, whereas transfer earnings are not.
    (c) is earned only by completely immobile factors.
    (d) is the excess of income over transfer earnings.
    (e) refers exclusively to the income of capital.

24. As a factor of production, agricultural land
    (a) is considered to be highly immobile in both a physical and an economic sense.
    (b) is the only factor that is paid economic rents
    (c) is mobile in an economic sense because it has many alternative uses as a factor of production.
    (d) is completely immobile because it cannot be moved.
    (e) ceases to be considered a factor of production if it is used for purposes other than farming.

25. Assume that a disequilibrium differential exists such that wages in occupation A are higher than those in occupation B. According to the hypothesis of equal net advantage, we would expect
    (a) nonmonetary advantages to be equalized between the two occupations.
    (b) the demand curve for labor in occupation B to shift to the right, since its cost of labor is cheaper.
    (c) the supply curve of labor in occupation A to shift to the left, since more workers want to enter occupation A.
    (d) the supply curve of labor in occupation B to shift to the left, since more workers wish to enter occupation A.
    (e) the wage differential to be long-lasting.

228

26. Which of the following is likely to shift the demand curve for carpenters to the right?
    (a) A decrease in carpenters' wages.
    (b) An increase in carpenters' wages.
    (c) A decrease in the demand for residential construction.
    (d) A decrease in carpenters' productivity.
    (e) None of the above.

27. Which of the following will unambiguously increase the wage rate of economists?
    (a) The demand curve for economists shifts to the left.
    (b) Both the demand and supply curves for economists shift to the right.
    (c) Both the demand and supply curves for economists shift to the left.
    (d) The supply curve for economists shifts to the left.
    (e) None of the above.

Answer questions 28 through 34 by referring to the schedule below which indicates output at various levels of labor use as well as the firm's product price per unit.

Labor	Output	Marginal physical product	Price/Unit
0	0	0	$2
1	16	16	2
2	36	20	2
3	54	18	2
4	68	14	2
5	80	___	2
6	90	10	2
7	98	8	2
8	104	6	2

28. What is the magnitude of the marginal physical product of the fifth worker?
    (a) 80.   (b) 16.
    (c) 12.   (d) 2.
    (e) 40.

29. The marginal revenue product of the fourth worker is
    (a) $108.   (b) $2.
    (c) $14.   (d) $68.
    (e) $28.

229

30. The marginal revenue product of the seventh worker is
    (a)   greater than the *MRP* of the fourth worker.
    (b)   equal to the *MRP* of the second worker.
    (c)   less than the *MRP* of the eighth worker.
    (d)   equal to $16.
    (e)   None of the above.

31. Over the range of the second to the eighth worker, the value of the *MRP*
    (a)   decreases due to diminishing marginal physical productivity.
    (b)   remains constant at $2.
    (c)   decreases because marginal revenue declines as more output is sold.
    (d)   Both (a) and (c) are correct.
    (e)   increases because total revenue product increases as more output is sold.

32. If the current wage rate per worker were $16, what is the profit-maximizing level of labor use?
    (a)   Five workers because *MRP* is greater than $16.
    (b)   Eight workers because *MRP* is less than $16.
    (c)   Seven workers because *MRP* is equal to $16.
    (d)   Six workers because *MRP* is equal to $16.
    (e)   None of the above.

33. If the firm's product price increased from $2 to $3, then
    (a)   the *MRP* curve would shift to the right.
    (b)   at every level of employment, the value of *MRP* would decrease.
    (c)   the firm would hire more workers, assuming the wage paid to workers did not change.
    (d)   the wage rate must also increase by 50 percent.
    (e)   Both (a) and (c).

34. An increase in the wage rate would
    (a)   shift the *MRP* curve to the right.
    (b)   trigger the firm to hire more workers.
    (c)   shift the *MRP* curve to the left.
    (d)   necessarily lead to a decrease in the firm's product price.
    (e)   None of the above.

◆ EXERCISES

This exercise demonstrates that the "law" of diminishing returns yields a downward-sloping factor demand curve for a profit-maximizing firm that sells its product in a perfectly competitive market. It also shows what causes shifts in the demand curve for the factor. The following table is partly completed to assist you. Three cases are illustrated: Case B reflects a lower product price than for case A. Case C assumes that labor productivity is different from that in cases A and B. The marginal physical productivity of labor is noted as *MPP*, and the product price per unit is *P*.

Units of Labor	Output	MPP	Case A P	Case A MRP	Case B P	Case B MRP	Case C MPP	Case C P	Case C MRP
1	50	50	$30	$1,500	$27	$1,350	60	$30	$1,800
2	63	13	30	390	27	351	15	30	450
3	75	12	30	360	27	324	14	30	420
4	85	10	30	300	27	270	12	30	360
5	94	—	30	—	27	—	11	30	—
6	99	—	30	—	27	—	7	30	—

(a) Complete the table and plot all three *MRP* curves in the graph on the next page.

(b) Explain why the *MRP* curve slopes downward in all three cases.

(c) For case A, what is the firm's demand for workers if the wage is $360? Explain your answer.

(d) For case A, explain why the firm's hiring would increase if the wage fell from $360 to $270. What is the new profit-maximizing amount of labor?

(e) For case B, what is the firm's demand for workers if the weekly wage is $270? How does this value compare with that for case A in part (d)?

(f) For every wage rate, explain why the firm's demand for labor is less in case B than in case A.

(g) What effect did the lower product price in case B have on the position and the slope of the demand curve for labor?

(h) For case C, what is the firm's demand for labor when the weekly wage is $360? How does this value compare with that of case A, in part (c)?

(i) Explain why the firm's demand for labor at every wage is greater for case C than for case A.

Figure 17-3

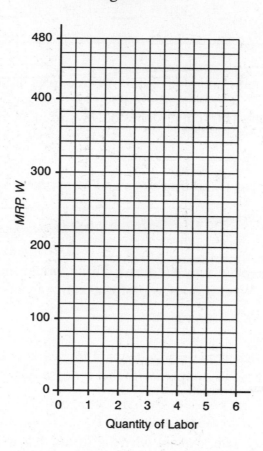

2. Given that *DD* is the demand curve for commercial airplane pilots and *W* is equilibrium monthly salary, draw in supply curves consistent with
(a) none of earnings being economic rent.
(b) all earnings being economic rents.
(c) half of earnings being economic rent.

Figure 17-4

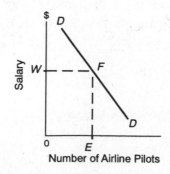

3. Consider the diagram below which represents a labor market for a specific type of worker. The initial demand curve is L^D, but there are two possible supply curves: L^S_A and L^S_B.

Figure 17-5

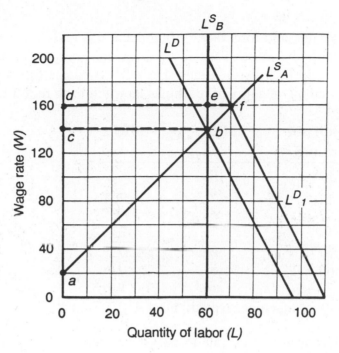

(a) What are the equilibrium values of W and L and the total payment to this factor in each case?

(b) What is the division of total payment to this factor between economic rent and transfer earnings in each case?

(c) For case A, what is the division between transfer earnings and economic rent for the sixtieth unit of labor? The fortieth?

(d) Assuming that case A holds, now suppose that the government attempts to increase employment in this industry by shifting the labor demand curve to the right (the new labor demand curve is L^D_1). What are the new equilibrium wage and quantity of labor demanded?

(e) By how much does the government policy increase economic rents in this market?

(f)   How much of the increase in economic rents goes to labor that was employed before the policy was introduced?

4.   (a)   A firm's demand for a factor of production is given by its marginal revenue product, and if the price of the factor is given, the quantity demanded can be determined as in Exercise 1. Using the *MRP* schedules for Firms A and B given here, determine the quantity of machines they will each rent if the rental price is $8.

Quantity of machines	MRP_A	MRP_B
10	10	8
20	9	6
30	8	4
40	7	2
50	6	0
60	5	0

Quantity of machines rented: Firm A ___; Firm B ___

(b)   A single firm may be able to take the rental price as given, but if A and B represent the *MRP* in two different industries and if the total number of machines available to these two industries is fixed, industry A can acquire more machines only by bidding them away from industry B. Assuming that the stock of machines available is 70, how should they be most efficiently allocated between the two industries?

Quantity of machines rented: Industry A ___; Industry B ___.

(c)   You can show the result from (b) graphically by plotting the two *MRP* curves in the machine market represented by the graph below. The horizontal axis represents the total number of machines available. The *MRP* of machines in A is measured from the left-hand origin, and the *MRP* of machines in B is measured from the right-hand origin. The *MRP* for B is plotted for you. Plot the *MRP* for A, and determine the rental price where these two curves intersect. What is this price, and how are the machines allocated between the two industries?

234

Figure 17-6

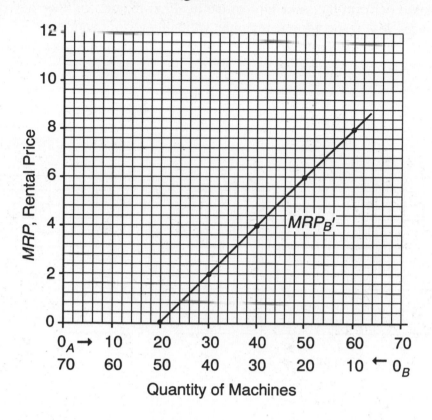

(d) Suppose that the productivity of machines in industry *B* rises because of technological improvements, and the new *MRP* schedule in *B* is as shown below. Plot this curve, and determine the new equilibrium rental price and allocation of machines between the two industries.

Quantity	MRP_B
10	11
20	9
30	7
40	5
50	3

(e) By how many machines did the *MRP* curve shift horizontally to the left, and how many additional machines did industry *B* end up renting? Explain why the number of machines *B* rents does not rise by as much as the *MRP* curve shifts to the left.

235

*5.   There are two regional labor markets within a country, X and Y. Workers are equally qualified to perform the same type of job in either region, and they have no nonmonetary preferences with respect to the region in which they work and live. The initial situation in each labor market is portrayed in the following graph, point *a* for market X and point *h* for market Y.

Figure 17-7

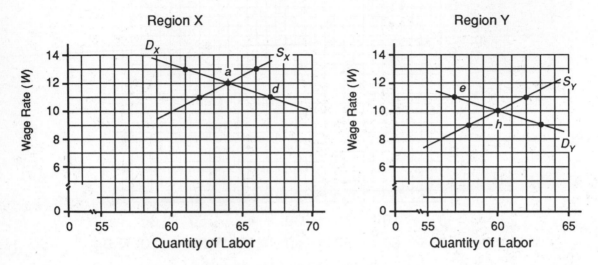

(a)   In terms of the information provided, what type of differential exists between the two markets?

(b)   In terms of the principle of net advantage, explain why labor flows will cause shifts in the labor supply curves such that new equilibria might occur at points *d* and *e*.

(c)   Prove that the labor flows have increased economic efficiency by increasing the country's value of total output. (*Hint*:: The change in the value of output for either market is the area under its labor demand curve evaluated from the initial equilibrium wage to the new one, $W = \$11$.)

6.   The demand and supply conditions in a competitive factor market are portrayed in the graph below. Two possible demand scenarios are labeled D_1 and D_2. The current equilibrium values of price and employment are 8 and 40, respectively.

Figure 17-8

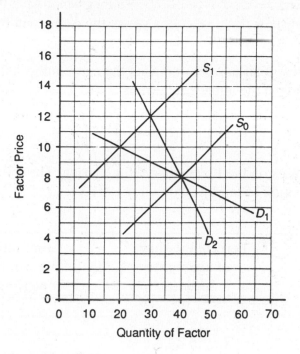

(a)   If S_0 holds, what are current total factor earnings? What is the value of economic rents for the thirtieth unit?

(b)   Suppose that the supply curve for the factor shifts up to the line labeled S_1. What are the new equilibrium values of price and employment for the two demand scenarios?

(c)   Using midpoints between the new and old equilibrium values, calculate the elasticity of demand for both demand curves. Which demand curve has the higher elasticity?

(d)   In terms of the elasticity values you have calculated, which demand curve implies, (all else equal),

(i)   a lower elasticity of demand for the product that this factor produces?

(ii)   a higher degree of substitutability of other factors for this factor when its price increases?

(iii)   larger increases in the factor's marginal productivity as less of the factor is used?

(iv)   lower total factor earnings at the new equilibrium situation compared with those at the initial equilibrium?

7.   This exercise focuses on the Lorenz curve for Canada. The following table provides data on the size distribution of family income for 1991.

Family income rank	Percentage share of aggregate income	Cumulative percentage of aggregate
Lowest fifth	6.4	
Second fifth	12.2	
Middle fifth	17.6	
Fourth fifth	23.9	
Highest fifth	40.0	

Source: *Statistics Canada*, 13-207

(a)   Calculate the cumulative income-population distribution for Canada in 1991.

(b)   Plot the 1991 Lorenz curve for Canada on the following grid.

Figure 17-9

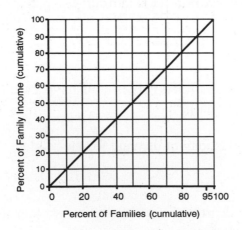

(c)   By visual inspection of your Lorenz curve, can you conclude that income in Canada was equally distributed?

◆ ANSWERS

Multiple-Choice Questions

1. (d) 2. (a) 3. (a) 4. (b) 5. (b) 6. (a) 7. (b) 8. (d) 9. (a) 10. (a) 11. (e) 12. (b) 13. (e) 14. (a) 15. (a) 16. (d) 17. (d) 18. (a) 19. (c) 20. (d) 21. (b) 22. (a) 23. (d) 24. (c) 25. (d) 26. (e) 27. (d) 28. (c) 29. (e) 30. (d) 31. (a) 32. (c) 33. (e) 34. (e)

Exercises

1.　(a)　Marginal physical product: 9, 5; case A, MRP = $270, $150; case B, MRP = $243, $135; case C, MRP = $330, $210

Figure 17-10

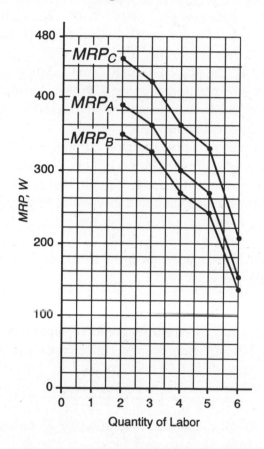

(b)　As more labor is employed, marginal physical productivity falls; this is the "law" of diminishing returns.

(c)　The firm demands three units of labor. The firm's profits will be maximized if it equates the marginal cost of obtaining labor ($360) to the marginal revenue product.

(d)　Three units of labor no longer represents a profit-maximizing situation since the MRP of the third unit of labor is $360 while the wage rate is $270. The firm will hire two more units of labor (a total of five), at which point MRP = $270.

(e)   For case B, the firm will hire four units of labor, at which point *MRP* = $270. This is one less unit of labor than in case A.

(f)   The price (marginal revenue) per unit is less; compare $27 with $30.

(g)   The demand curve for labor in case B lies to the left of the demand curve in case A. The shift is not parallel.

(h)   For case C, the firm will hire four units of labor, which is one more than in case A, part (c).

(i)   The demand for labor in case C will be greater than for case A since the marginal productivity of each unit of labor has increased.

2. (a)   Horizontal supply curve at *W*.
    (b)   Vertical supply curve at *E*.
    (c)   Any of a number of supply curves dividing rectangle *OWFE* into two equal areas; a diagonal straight line from *O* to *F* would be one example.

3. (a)   In each case, *W* = $140 and *L* = 60, so total factor payment is $8,400.
    (b)   In case A, economic rent is the area below the wage line and above the supply curve (area *abc* in the graph), which equals $3,600 (=(120 x 60) divided by 2). Transfer earnings equal total factor payments minus economic rent or, in this case, $4,800. In case B, there is a perfectly inelastic supply curve, so all $8,400 of factor payments are economic rent.
    (c)   For the sixtieth unit of labor, transfer earnings equal the wage rate of $140. The fortieth unit is willing to work for $100 but is paid $140. Therefore, for this unit transfer earnings equal $100 and economic rent is $40.
    (d)   The new equilibrium wage and quantity are $160 and 70 units, respectively.
    (e)   Economic rents now equal area *adf* in the graph. Thus the increase in economic rent is area *bcdf*, which equals $1,300.
    (f)   The 60 units of labor employed prior to the policy change receive area *bcde* in additional rents; this equals $1,200.

4. (a)   Firm *A*, 30; Firm *B*, 10
    (b)   The 70 machines must have the same *MRP* regardless of the industry where they are used. Hence if 50 machines are allocated to industry *A* and 20 to industry *B*, *MRP* will be equalized at 6.
    (c)   The two curves intersect at a rental price of $6, where industry *A* rents 50 machines and industry *B* rents 20. See the next page for the plotted relationships.
    (d)   Industry *A* rents 40 machines, and industry *B* rents 30. The equilibrium rental price increases from $6 to about $7.

Figure 17-11

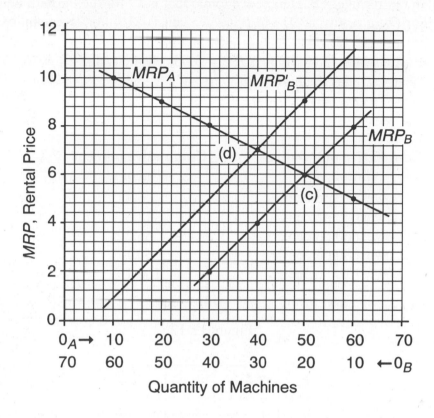

(e)   The *MRP* curve shifts to the left by about 15 machines, and industry *B* rents 10 more machines than initially. *B* does not rent 15 more machines because *A* is willing to pay a higher rental price to avoid losing that many machines (rather than $6). If *B* is to match that higher rental price, it would rent only 10 more machines.

*5.   (a)   There is a disequilibrium differential of $2 per unit of labor since there are no nonmonetary considerations, no differences in labor productivity, and no difference in the types of jobs.

(b)   There are net advantages between the two regions; workers by moving from *Y* to *X* will increase their wage rate. As this flow occurs, the supply curve for labor in region *Y* will shift to the left and the supply curve in region *X* will shift to the right. Wages will rise in *Y* and fall in *X*. Migration from *Y* to *X* will continue until the wage differential is eliminated (wage = $11 in both regions).

(c)   The decrease in the value of output in region *Y* is the area under the demand curve between wage rates of $10 and $11. This value is given by (-3 x 10) + 0.5(3 x 1) = -$31.50. The increase in the value of output in region *X* is given by (3 x 11) + 0.5(3 x 1) = +$34.50. Hence the total value of output has increased by this reallocation of labor.

241

6.   (a)   Total factor earnings are $320. The thirtieth unit is prepared to supply services for $6 but receives $8. Hence, economic rent is $2 for the thirtieth unit.

    (b)   For D_1, quantity is 20 and price per unit is $10. For D_2, quantity is 30 and price per unit is $12.

    (c)   Elasticity for D_1 = 20/30 x 9/2 = 3.00; elasticity for D_2 = 10/35 x 10/4 = 0.71. Clearly, D_1 has the higher elasticity.

    (d)   (i) D_2 (ii) D_1 (iii) D_2 (iv) D_1

7.   (a)

Cumulative population (families)	Cumulative percent of income
Lowest 20 percent	6.4
Lowest 40 percent	18.6
Lowest 60 percent	36.2
Lowest 80 percent	60.1
Lowest 100 percent	100.1

    (b)

Figure 17-12

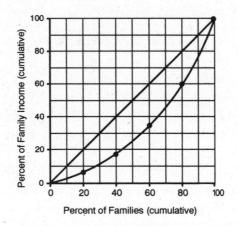

    (c)   No; the Lorenz curve for 1991 lies below the diagonal line.

Chapter 18

Labor Markets, Unions, and Discrimination

◆ LEARNING OBJECTIVES

After studying this chapter, you should be able to:

✔   understand the reasons why different labor groups earn different incomes;

✔   demonstrate the effects of labor market structure (competitive, seller's monopoly, and buyer's monopsony) on wages and employment levels;

✔   recognize the potential conflicts that unions face between the goals of raising wages and preserving employment opportunities for their members;

✔   comprehend the effects of minimum wage laws on employment under different market structures;

✔   explain the direct effects of labor market discrimination on wage levels, unemployment, and employment opportunities of those who suffer from discrimination and the indirect effects of discrimination on other labor markets;

✔   understand the features of pay equity legislation and discuss the advantages and disadvantages of it.

◆ HINTS AND TIPS

You might be guided by the fact that some of the most common errors on examinations are:

✔   confusing the supply curve of labor facing a monopsonist with the monopsonist's marginal cost curve of labor;

✔   knowing that a monopsonist's profit-maximizing employment level obtains when the marginal cost of labor (not the wage rate!) is equal to marginal revenue product.

1. Which of the following, by itself, would tend to generate a higher wage for worker *A* compared to worker *B*?
   (a) Worker *A* has a job that is safer in terms of the chances of injury.
   (b) Worker *A*, of a particular ethnic heritage, has encountered more labor market discrimination.
   (c) Worker *B* has more years of formal education.
   (d) Worker *B* is employed by a monopsonist firm.
   (e) Both workers are accountants, but worker *B* has more knowledge of computer software than A.

2. Which of the following would tend to increase the willingness of eligible high school graduates to seek admission at a university or college?
   (a) Employers' demand for university graduates is expected to decline.
   (b) Governments increase funding for scholarships, bursaries, and student loans.
   (c) High school graduates face expanding job opportunities.
   (d) Tuition and residence fees continue to rise at a rate greater than the overall inflation rate in the economy.
   (e) A large supply of university and college graduates has flooded the labor market in the past few years.

3. The short-run labor demand curve for a monopolist firm is downward sloping because
   (a) marginal physical product falls as more labor is employed.
   (b) marginal revenue falls as the monopolist sells more output.
   (c) the marginal cost of labor rises as the firm hires more workers.
   (d) the price of the monopolist's product increases with additional sales.
   (e) Both (a) and (b).

4. A firm that currently pays $8 per hour to each of its ten workers discovers that it must pay $9 to get an eleventh worker. What are the marginal costs to the firm of obtaining the eleventh worker?
   (a) $1.   (b) $9.
   (c) $17.   (d) $19.
   (e) $10.

5. If a union negotiates a wage above the competitive level in a competitive industry, all but which of the following will occur?
   (a) Employment in the industry will normally fall.
   (b) Those employed will earn a higher wage rate than before.
   (c) A pool of unemployed workers will be created.
   (d) The supply curve of labor will shift to the right.
   (e) None of the above.

6. Where the supply curve of labor is upward-sloping, the marginal cost curve of labor to the monopsonist
   (a) is the same as the supply curve of labor.
   (b) is the same as the average cost curve of labor.

(c)   lies above the supply curve of labor.
(d)   lies below and parallel to the supply curve.
(e)   intersects the supply curve at the equilibrium wage.

7. A labor union entering a competitive labor market can achieve higher wages for some workers by
(a)   restricting entry into the industry.
(b)   negotiating a higher wage through collective bargaining.
(c)   increasing the supply of labor into the occupation.
(d)   Both (a) and (b).
(e)   All of the above.

8. A monopsonist in a nonunion labor market
(a)   lowers both the wage rate and employment below their competitive levels.
(b)   lowers the wage rate but not employment below their competitive levels.
(c)   has the same employment level and the same wage as a competitive firm.
(d)   raises the wage rate but decreases employment with respect to their competitive levels.
(e)   raises both the wage rate and employment above their competitive levels.

9. A union negotiating a higher wage in a monopsonistic labor market
(a)   will cause increased unemployment in the industry.
(b)   can raise the wage rate, but not employment, over the monopsonistic outcome.
(c)   can raise both the wage rate and employment over the monopsonistic outcome.
(d)   has the same effect on employment as a minimum wage set above the competitive level.
(e)   None of the above.

10. A minimum wage is said to be *binding* or *effective* if
(a)   it has been set by a union.
(b)   the minimum is below the market wage that would otherwise prevail.
(c)   it is the lowest wage that allows a level of income above the poverty line.
(d)   all workers who desire employment at that wage are in fact employed.
(e)   None of the above.

11. Which of the following statements concerning the likely consequences of a comprehensive minimum wage is correct?
(a)   In competitive labor markets, an effective minimum wage has no adverse employment effects.
(b)   In monopsonistic labor markets, a minimum wage set equal to the competitive wage will increase wages but not employment.
(c)   The employment effects of a minimum wage in competitive labor markets will be the same as in monopsonistic labor markets.
(d)   In monopsonistic labor markets, a binding minimum wage may decrease wage rates but increase employment.
(e)   In competitive labor markets, an effective minimum wage may increase wages but decrease employment.

Questions 12 to 18 refer to the following graph, which depicts a labor market for unskilled workers.

Figure 18-1

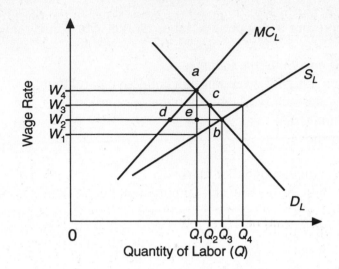

12. If perfect competition existed in this market, the wage and quantity of employment would be
    (a) W_4 and Q_1.　　　　　　　　(b) W_3 and Q_2.
    (c) W_1 and Q_1.　　　　　　　　(d) W_2 and Q_3.
    (e) W_2 and Q_4.

13. If this market were monopsonistic, the firm would hire
    (a) Q_1 workers.　　　　　　　　(b) Q_3 workers.
    (c) Q_2 workers.　　　　　　　　(d) Q_4 workers.
    (e) somewhere between Q_3 and Q_4 workers.

14. A profit-maximizing monopsony would pay a wage of
    (a) W_1.　　　　　　　　　　　　(b) W_3.
    (c) W_2.　　　　　　　　　　　　(d) W_4.
    (e) somewhere between one half of $(W_1 + W_4)$.

15. If a minimum wage of W_2 is imposed on the monopsony, the supply curve of labor becomes
    (a) $MC_L - S_L$.　　　　　　　　(b) acb.
    (c) W_2bS_L.　　　　　　　　　　(d) W_2daMC_L.
    (e) W_2dea.

16. In this case, the minimum wage of W_2 would generate employment of
    (a) Q_1.　　　　　　　　　　　　(b) Q_3.
    (c) Q_2.　　　　　　　　　　　　(d) Q_4.
    (e) less than Q_1.

246

17. If a minimum wage of W_3 were imposed on the market, the monopsonist would hire
    (a) Q_2 workers.
    (b) more than Q_3 workers since the marginal cost of labor would fall.
    (c) Q_4 workers because the demand for labor shifts to the right.
    (d) Q_1 workers.
    (e) no workers.

18. With a minimum wage of W_3, total unemployment in this market would be
    (a) $Q_3 - Q_2$.   (b) $Q_4 - Q_3$.
    (c) $Q_4 - Q_2$.   (d) $Q_4 - Q_1$.
    (e) zero.

19. If discrimination prevented a certain group of people from entering labor market E but not labor market O,
    (a) the wage rate would be lower than the competitive level in both markets.
    (b) the labor supply curve is farther to the left than it would otherwise be in both markets.
    (c) wage rates will tend to be higher in market E and lower in market O than they would be with no discrimination.
    (d) individuals in labor market E would benefit only if the demand curve for labor is elastic.
    (e) None of the above.

20. Which of the following has *not* been a cause of the male-female wage differentials?
    (a) Women have been underrepresented in high-paying occuptions.
    (b) Proportionately fewer women than men have reached higher-paying jobs in the occupations in which they both work.
    (c) Because women have had greater labor force attachment than men, they are paid less for comparable work.
    (d) Women who reached higher-paying jobs did so more slowly than men.
    (e) In the past, women have had less on-the-job training than men.

21. Pay equity policies require that
    (a) occupations with the same intrinsic value should receive the same rate of pay.
    (b) only supply and demand factors should determine relative wages.
    (c) returns to labor and capital should be comparable across the country.
    (d) wages must be the same among jobs even though jobs differ in terms of initiative, skills, training, etc.
    (e) None of the above.

22. Suppose that women are discouraged from becoming engineers, but face no barriers in becoming schoolteachers. Then, it follows
    (a) men will earn higher salaries as engineers than they would with free access of engineering jobs by women.
    (b) salaries of women engineers will be higher than they would otherwise be.
    (c) women will earn higher salaries than men as schoolteachers.
    (d) the gap between salaries earned by men and women will narrow.
    (e) the gap between salaries earned by men and women will be unaffected.

Answer questions 23 through 25 by refering to the diagrams and information below.

An economy consists of two competitive industries, X and Y, and a total labor force of 120 workers. Industry X requires more highly skilled workers relative to industry Y. Workers, although equally productive *within* each industry, differ by the color of their eyes. Nine of the workers in each industry have green eyes, the rest have blue eyes. Now, new owners take over industry X. They don't trust any worker with green eyes.

23.   Before the new owners took possession of industry X, the differential in the wage rate between the two industries
        (a)   represented "discrimination" by employers in Y, since the wage was $2 lower.
        (b)   was a short-run differential of $2.
        (c)   was an equilibrium differential of $2.
        (d)   was $2, because employers in industry X must have been monopsonists.
        (e)   was $2, because of the "mix" of green-eyed and blue-eyed workers in each industry.

Figure 18-2

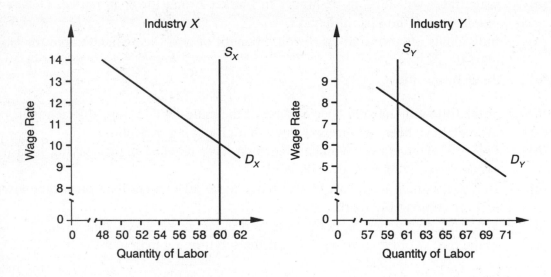

24.   Now, the new owners fire every green-eyed worker in X, but do not replace them with blue-eyed workers. If all green-eyed workers find jobs in Y, then
        (a)   51 workers in X are paid $13 each.
        (b)   69 workers in Y are paid $5 each.
        (c)   total income of all blue-eyed workers in X increases from $600 to $663.
        (d)   total income of all workers in Y falls from $480 to $345.
        (e)   All of the above.

25.   If the workers in Y had pressured the government to impose a minimum wage of $8 before the green-eyed workers in X were fired, then we would
        (a)   predict an excess supply in Y if all displaced green-eyed workers moved to Y.
        (b)   observe the creation of a $8 wage differential.
        (c)   anticipate that all displaced green-eyed workers in X might leave the labor market.
        (d)   Both (a) and (c).
        (e)   None of the above.

248

1. Suppose that there is a competitive market for workers in a particular industry. The equilibrium level of employment is 200, and the wage rate is $50. The labor demand and supply curves are given by $Q_D = 300 - 2W$ and $Q_S = 4W$, respectively.

   (a) A union now successfully organizes workers and obtains a wage rate of $60. Assuming that unionization does not affect the industry's demand curve, calculate the number of unionized members who are employed in this industry. How many workers lost their jobs? How many workers would like to work in this industry?

   (b) A union could have achieved the same levels of the wage rate and employment by restricting the supply of workers using required apprenticeship programs and/or reduced openings for trainees. Show that a new, restricted labor supply curve of $Q_S = -60 + 4W$ would yield the same wage and employment levels as in (a).

   (c) The reduction in employment caused by a union wage that is above the competitive level depends on the elasticity of labor demand. If the industry's demand curve for labor had been given by $Q_D = 200$, what is the implied elasticity of labor demand? How many workers would have lost their jobs due to unionization? (Assume that the labor supply curve is $Q_S = 4W$.)

2. Columns 1 and 2 represent the supply-of-labor relationship for a monopsonistic employer. Fill in the values for total cost in column 3 and then calculate the marginal cost values in column 4. This exercise should demonstrate to you that the marginal cost of labor (MC_L) lies above the supply curve of labor in a nonparallel fashion.

(1) Quantity of labor	(2) Wage rate	(3) Total cost	(4) Marginal labor cost
8	$10.00	$80.00	
9	10.50	_____	_____
10	11.00	_____	_____
11	11.50	_____	_____
12	12.00	_____	_____
13	12.50	_____	_____
14	13.00	_____	_____

3. Referring to the graph, which represents the labor market in an industry, answer the following questions.

Figure 18-3

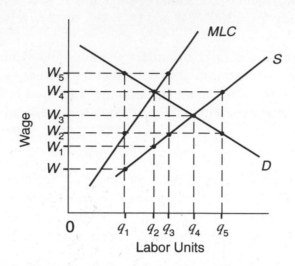

(a) If a competitive market prevailed, the equilibrium wage would be _____ and the amount of employment would be _____.

(b) If a wage-setting union enters this (competitive) market and tries to establish a higher wage at, for example, w_4, the amount of employment would be _____, and the amount of surplus labor unemployed would be _____. How would the labor supply curve look?

(c) Assume that this market consists of a single large firm hiring labor in a local market. If the firm hired q_1 workers, it would have to pay all workers the wage_____, but the marginal labor cost of the last person hired would be _____. Because the marginal revenue product of the last person (q_1) hired is equal to the amount _____, _____there is an incentive for the firm to continue hiring up to the amount _____, at which the wage will be _____, the marginal labor cost will be _____, and the marginal revenue product will be _____. Compare this with the result in (a).

(d) Suppose that a union now organizes in the monopsonist market and sets a wage at w_3. The amount of employment will be _____.

(e) Draw a new labor supply curve showing what happens when a union organizes this labor market but instead of setting a high wage excludes workers by stiff apprenticeship rules. Predict the effects.

4. There are two competitive labor markets in the economy of Arcadia. Market X has a labor demand function given by $W = 360 - 3Q$ and a labor supply function $W = 40 + 2Q$. The wage rate is denoted as W, and the quantity of labor is Q. Market Z has the same labor demand function as X but a labor supply function $W = 20 + 2Q$.

250

(a)   Calculate the competitive equilibrium levels of W and Q in each labor market.

(b)   Suppose that a minimum wage of 162 had been imposed in market Z. At the minimum wage, what is the quantity of labor demanded? The quantity of labor supplied? How many workers are displaced in this market?

(c)   If all of the unemployed persons in (b) entered labor market X, the supply curve of labor in X becomes $W = 30 + 2Q$. How many will obtain employment in market X? What will happen to the wage in market X?

5.   This exercise focuses on the concept pay equity. The following diagrams depict the markets in a small town for two types of labor: production line workers and office employees (e.g., clerks, secretaries, receptionists). The initial equilibria in these markets are determined by perfectly competitive forces and are characterized by 500 employees in each market, but production workers are paid an hourly wage of $8, while office employees receive a wage of $4. Although everyone (regardless of gender) is paid the same wage *within* each market, a majority of production workers are male and a majority of office employees are female; therefore, the *average* female wage is lower than the *average* male wage. These average statistics suggest that indirect discrimination due to historical occupational restrictions on women may be present. Assume that the government sends its experts (the "pay police") to investigate. After the experts rate these occupations with respect to required skills and education, working conditions, accountability, and mental demands, they conclude that these occupations are indeed of comparable worth or equal value and should be paid the same hourly wage. The firms in this town are therefore in violation of the pay equity legislation and must rectify the situation immediately.

Figure 18-4

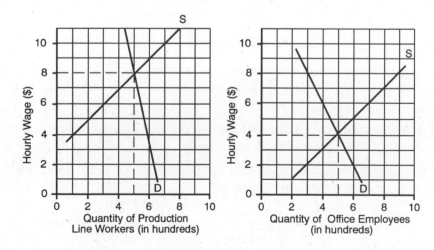

(a)   Suppose that firms comply with the legislation by paying the average wage of $6 in each market. Discuss the implications for employment and unemployment in each market (be sure to indicate how many people lose their jobs and how many join the labor force).

(b)   Suppose that the firms comply instead by paying everyone in each market $8 an hour. Discuss the implications for employment and unemployment in each market.

(c)   Who decides the "worth" of the "experts"?

(d)   Indicate in the diagrams what happens to the competitive wage structure over time as more women move into production-line work.

6.   The last chapter focused on the demand for labor for a perfectly competitive firm. This exercise illustrates the demand curve for labor for a monopolist in the product market. Information for the competitive firm (case A) is already entered in the table. Case B represents a monopolist firm that faces a downward-sloping demand curve for its product; its *MR* declines as more output is produced and sold. The marginal physical product of labor is denoted as *MPP*.

Total labor employed	Units of output per week	*MPP*	Case A		Case B	
			MR	*MRP*	*MR*	*MRP*
1	50	50	30	1,500	40	2,000
2	63	13	30	390	34	___
3	75	12	30	360	30	___
4	85	10	30	300	27	___
5	94	9	30	270	21	___
6	99	5	30	150	20	___

(a)   Fill in the missing values for *MRP* for the monopolist case.

(b)   What is the perfect competitor's demand for labor if the weekly wage were $360? For the monopolist firm?

(c)   Suppose that the weekly wage fell from $360 to $270. Compute the new demand for labor in both cases.

(d)   For the perfect competitor, why did *MRP* decrease as it hired more labor? For the monopolist firm, why did *MRP* decrease as it hired more labor?

(e)   Using midpoints of intervals between wages of $360 and $270, calculate the elasticity of demand for labor in each case. Which case implies the more elastic demand curve for labor?

◆ ANSWERS

Multiple-Choice Questions

1. (d) 2. (b) 3. (e) 4. (d) 5. (d) 6. (c) 7. (d) 8. (a) 9. (c) 10. (e) 11. (e) 12. (d) 13. (a)
14. (a) 15. (c) 16. (b) 17. (a) 18. (c) 19. (c) 20. (c) 21. (a) 22. (a) 23. (c) 24. (e) 25. (d)

Exercises

1.   (a)   Substituting $W = 60$ into the demand equation, we obtain an employment level of 180. Twenty workers lost their jobs. At $W = 60$, 240 individuals wish to work in this industry.

(b)   Equating the new supply equation with the demand equation, we obtain $W = 60$ and employment of 180, which is the same result as in (a).

(c)   The new demand curve is perfectly inelastic; changes in the wage rate have no effect on the quantity of labor demanded. As a result, the union could increase the wage by any amount without loss of jobs.

2.   Total cost: $80.00; $94.50; $110.00; $126.50; $144.00; $162.50; $182.00. Marginal cost: $14.50; $15.50; $16.50; $17.50; $18.50; $19.50

3.   (a) w_3; q_4

(b) q_2; $q_5 - q_2$; horizontal at w_4 to q_5 on supply curve and thereafter the supply curve for wages greater than w_4.

(c) w; w_2, w_5; q_2; w_1; w_4; w_4; employment is less and the amount of wages is lower than in (a).

(d) q_4

(e)   The supply curve shifts leftward. All wage predictions are raised, and employment levels are lowered.

4.   (a)   For market X, equilibrium Q is found by equating $360 - 3Q$ to $40 + 2Q$. Hence $Q = 64$ and $W = 168$. For market Z, $Q = 68$ and $W = 156$.

(b)   At the minimum wage, the quantity of labor demanded is 66 while the quantity of labor supplied is 71. Unemployment is therefore 5, and employment in market Z would be 2 fewer than under competitive conditions.

(c) The supply curve in X now becomes $W = 30 + 2Q$ (or $Q = 0.5W - 15$ instead of $Q = 0.5W - 10$). Setting $D = S$ and solving, $Q = 66$ and $W = 162$. Thus, two of the unemployed workers from Z are now employed in X, and the wage in X falls to 162 from 168.

5. (a) At \$6 per hour the quantity supplied of production-line workers is 300, and the quantity demanded is 550. Hence, there are 250 vacant jobs in this market (50 new jobs and 200 vacated jobs). At the same wage the quantity demanded for office employees is 400, but the quantity supplied is 700. Therefore, there are 300 unemployed in this market. Of this number, 100 had jobs before the wage increase, and 200 entered the labor force because of the more attractive wage.

(b) At the \$8 wage rate, the market for production-line workers is in equilibrium. However, in the market for office employees there are now only 300 employed and 600 unemployed, 200 of who had jobs prior to the wage increase from \$4.

(c) Your guess is as good as ours.

(d) Over time, as women acquire new skills and change occupations, or as new female workers make different unrestricted career choices, the supply of production workers shifts to the right as women enter this occupation, and the supply of office employees shifts to the left as women exit. The wage gap therefore decreases. As it is impossible to account for and calibrate all of the differences in non-monetary advantages and disadvantages between these occupations (to both women and men), it is impossible to say if the wage gap will completely close. However, we can say that the net advantage of either occupation to gender will tend to be eliminated by either over time or by market forces.

6. (a) MRP = \$442, \$360, \$270, \$189, \$100.

(b) The perfect competitor would hire three units of labor since MRP = \$360. The monopolist would also hire three units.

(c) The monopolist would now hire four units while the competitive firm would hire five units.

(d) MRP decreased as more labor units were employed because of diminishing marginal productivity. This is also true for a monopolist firm. However, the monopolist's MRP also decreased as output increased because its marginal revenue fell.

(e) Elasticity for the perfect competitor is 1.75 (= 2/4 x 315/90). The monopoly firm has an elasticity of 1.00 (= 1/3.5 x 315/90). Thus, the perfect competitor has the more elastic demand curve for labor.

Chapter 19

Nonrenewable Natural Resources and Capital

◆ LEARNING OBJECTIVES

After studying this chapter, you should be able to:

✔ understand that the socially optimal rate of exploitation for a completely nonrenewable resource is determined by the current and future price of the resource, the interest rate, and the elasticity of demand for the resource;

✔ explain why rising prices of resources act as a conservation device and as a stimulus to encourage the discovery of new supplies;

✔ identify the possible failures of the price system to produce optimal results and to discuss the role of government to deal with them;

✔ distinguish between the two prices of capital, the *purchase price* and the *rental price* and to understand that in competitive markets the rental price is equal to the capital's marginal revenue product in each period,

✔ demonstate, by using the concept of present value, how the maximum purchase price of capital is related to the discounted stream over time of expected marginal revenue products of the capital;

✔ comprehend why an individual firm will invest in capital goods as long as the present value of the stream of future net incomes that are provided by another unit of capital exceeds its purchase price.

◆ HINTS AND TIPS

You might be guided by the fact that some of the most common errors on examinations are:

✔ confusing a stock concept (capital) with a flow concept (investment);

✔ forgetting that, as long as there are opportunity costs of funds, current dollar values cannot be compared equally with future dollar values;

✔ incorrectly applying the formula for present value.

◆ MULTIPLE-CHOICE QUESTIONS

1. If the current price of oil is $2.00 per barrel and the annual interest rate is 7%, it pays to
   (a) produce less now if next year's price is less than $2.14.
   (b) have the same extraction rate every year regardless of what happens to oil prices in the future.
   (c) produce more now if next year's price is less than $2.14.
   (d) produce more next year if oil prices rise less than 7% from today's prices.
   (e) None of the above.

2. With perfect competition, the price of an exhaustible resource with a known stock whose cost of extraction and transportation are negligible should rise by
   (a) a constant percentage amount from year to year until the stock is depleted.
   (b) 10 percent if the rate of interest is 10%.
   (c) the rate at which the resource is extracted.
   (d) the rate of growth of national output.
   (e) the overall inflation rate in the economy.

3. The actual rate at which an exhaustible resource is extracted will be more even through time when
   (a) the demand curve for the resource is perfectly elastic.
   (b) there are many substitutes for this resource.
   (c) the demand curve for the resource is relatively steep.
   (d) the final products that have a high input content of this resource have a high elasticity of demand.
   (e) Both (b) and (d).

4. Which of the following would *not* be a likely consequence of an expected increase in the price of a nonrenewable resource like oil?
   (a) Substitute products (such as solar energy) would be developed.
   (b) Current rates of extraction by owners would be moderated.
   (c) Discovery of new sources of supply would be encouraged.
   (d) The necessity to conserve on oil use would be reduced.
   (e) Firms extracting would be encouraged to invest more in capital equipment required in oil extraction and refining.

5. According to *Hotelling's Rule*, the rate of extraction of any nonrenewable resource should be such that its price increases at a rate equal to
   (a) the overall rate of inflation.
   (b) the growth in national income.
   (c) the rate at which new supplies of the resource are found.
   (d) the interest rate.
   (e) the growth rate in national debt.

6. Which of the following is likely to be a consequence of a government imposed constant-price policy for a nonrenewable resource?
   (a) The resource will be exhausted much slower.
   (b) Conservation and innovation will be encouraged.
   (c) Oil companies will have less incentives to explore for new supplies.
   (d) The adjustments to a depleting resource will have been spread more evenly over time.
   (e) All of the above.

7. Which of the following constitutes a potential failure of the price system to produce the optimal rate of resource extraction?
    (a) Private owners have better information than government agencies to determine the optimal extraction rate.
    (b) The interest rate is different from the social rate of discount.
    (c) The current extraction rate is increased when the interest rate (equal to the social rate of discount) rises.
    (d) Proper extraction management is applied by private owners of resources.
    (e) All of the above.

8. The present value of $100 received one year from now is
    (a) $100 if the interest rate is positive.
    (b) more than $107 if the interest rate is more than 7%.
    (c) $106 if the interest rate is 6%.
    (d) Both (b) and (c).
    (e) None of the above.

9. The rental price of capital for a given period
    (a) is always equal to its purchase price.
    (b) will be equated with the capital's marginal revenue product in that period as a result of profit maximization.
    (c) is zero if the firm owns its capital.
    (d) is the rate of return on capital for each dollar invested in that capital.
    (e) is always equal to the interest rate.

10. If the interest rate is i, the present value of R dollars received a year from now is
    (a) Ri.   (b) $R/(1 + i)$.
    (c) R/i.   (d) $i/(1 + R)$.
    (e) i/R.

11. If the interest rate is 5%, the present value of $500 received two years from now is
    (a) $453.51.   (b) $525.
    (c) $467.19.   (d) $551.25.
    (e) $510.

12. The formula for the present value of $10 received three years from now and an interest rate of 10% is
    (a) $\$10/(.1)^3$.   (b) $\$10/3(1.1)$.
    (c) $(1.1)^3/\$10$.   (d) $\$10/(1.1)^3$.
    (e) $\$10^3/(1.1)^3$.

13. If the interest rate is 4%, the present value of $100 received each year forever is
    (a) $2,500.   (b) $250.
    (c) $25.   (d) $96.15.
    (e) $104.

14. If R equals the annual stream of receipts from a machine into the indefinite future, PP equals its purchase price, and i equals the interest rate, then a capital good should be purchased if
    (a) $R \times i < PP$.   (b) $R/PP < i$.
    (c) $R/i > PP$.   (d) $R < i \times PP$.
    (e)   None of the above.

15. Suppose that a capital asset whose purchase price is $10,000 is expected to produce a perpetual stream of net receipts per period of $700. It follows that
    (a)   this asset should be purchased when the cost of borrowed funds is 10%.
    (b)   this asset should be purchased irrespective of the interest rate since it generates net revenues in perpetuity.
    (c)   the present value of this asset is greater than $10,000 for all interest rates above 7%.
    (d)   the present value of this asset is greater than $10,000 for all interest rates below 9%.
    (e)   None of the above.

16. The present value of a capital asset will increase if
    (a)   the MRP values per period decrease.
    (b) MRP values are received farther into the future.
    (c)   the interest rate decreases.
    (d)   the purchase price of the capital asset decreases.
    (e)   None of the above.

17. The cost of constructing a proposed dam is $10,000,000 and its annual maintenance costs are $100,000. The dam is expected to last forever. If the interest rate is 5%, the present value of the total cost of the dam is
    (a) $10,000,000.   (b) $12,000,000.
    (c) $2,000,00.   (d) $10,100,000.
    (e)   impossible to estimate with the information provided.

18. The demand curve for capital (or the *marginal efficiency of capital* curve) shifts to the right as
    (a)   capital is accumulated.
    (b)   the interest rate decreases.
    (c)   technology improves capital productivity.
    (d)   diminishing returns to capital occur.
    (e)   Both (a) and (c).

19. The higher the interest rate, *all other things equal*
    (a)   firms will find capital expansion to be more profitable.
    (b)   the lower a firm's equilibrium capital stock.
    (c)   the higher the present value of the income stream produced by a capital good.
    (d)   the greater the shift in the firm's demand for capital curve.
    (e)   None of the above.

Answer questions 20 through 24 using the following data concerning a machine. You will find it useful to refer to Table 19-1 at the end of this chapter.

A business can buy a machine that yields net revenue of $1,000 at the end of the first year and $2,000 at the end of the second year, after which the machine falls apart and thus has no scrap value.

20. If the rate of interest is 10 percent, the present value of the $1,000 received one year hence is equal to
   (a) $900.   (b) $990.
   (c) $909.   (d) $100.
   (e) $1,100.

21. If the rate of interest in both years is 10 percent, the *total* present value of the machine over the two-year period is
   (a) $2,561.   (b) $3,000.
   (c) $2,727.   (d) $3,520.
   (e) $3,300.

22. Assuming an interest rate of 10 percent, the firm will buy this machine if its purchase price is
   (a) less than or equal to $2,561.
   (b) greater than $2,561 but less than $2,727.
   (c) equal to $2,727.
   (d) somewhere in the range $3,000 to $3,520.
   (e) None of the above.

23. If the interest rate were 12 percent and the purchase price were $3,000, what would the first year's net revenue (before discounting) have to be to warrant purchasing this machine? Continue to assume that the net revenue in the second year remains at $2,000.
   (a) $893.   (b) $1,256.
   (c) $1,406.   (d) $1,574.
   (e) None of the above.

24. The interest rate that generates a total present value of net revenue flows for this machine of $2,487 is
   (a) 15 percent.   (b) 12 percent.
   (c) 8 percent.   (d) 14 percent.
   (e) None of the above.

◆ EXERCISES

1. (a) Just for practice, fill in the following blanks using the present value (PV) table 19-1 at the end of this chapter.

This many dollars	in t years	has this PV	at i
10	5	_____	6%
100	50	$60.80	_____
1,000	_____	3.00	12%
_____	6	4.56	14%

259

(b)   More practice, this time with the annuity table, Table 19-2.

This many dollars	in t years	has this PV	at i
10	5	——————	6%
100	50	$3,919.60	——————
1,000	——————	8,304.00	12%
——————	6	38.89	14%

2.   This exercise demonstrates the relationship between changes in various components of the present value formula (equation [2] in the text) and the desired capital stock.

The Base Case

At a current interest rate of 10 percent, *Acme Machine Shop*, maximizes profits with 20 machines. It is considering buying one more machine that costs $500. The financial manager estimates that the machine will generate $545 in additional net income one year from now.

(a)   By making the appropriate substitutions, write the algebraic expression for the present value of this incremental capital good.

(b)   Using either Table 19-1 or your calculator, calculate the magnitude of the present value. Should the financial manager recommend that *Acme* expand its capital stock (invest) by one?

The investment decision in part (b) may change if economic conditions change or if the financial manager revises her forecasts. We outline three cases below.
Case 1: Variations in the interest rate, *i*

(c)   If the interest rate had been 8 percent rather than 10 percent, would the financial manager have made a different recommendation? Explain.

(d)   What have you concluded about the effect of an interest rate decrease on the present value of a capital asset? About the relationship between interest rates and the desired capital stock?

Case 2: An change in expected net receipts, R

Suppose *Acme's* financial manager forecast of net revenues had been $555 rather than $545.

(e)   Assuming an interest rate of 10 percent, would the financial manager have recommended a capital stock of 21?

(f)   What have you concluded about the effect of an increase in R and the present value of a capital good? About the relationship between net expected receipts and the desired capital stock?

Case 3: A change in the timing of receipts, t

Similar to case 2, the financial manager is convinced that net revenues will be $555. However, they will not be received after one year, but rather after two years! Hence, the company will receive no net receipts after one year.

(g)   If the interest rate were 10 percent two years from now, would the financial manager recommend the purchase of the machine? What have you concluded about the relationship between present value and the timing of net receipts?

3.   **Jackson Tanner, A *Griffen*?**

This problem deals with the application of the present value concept to human capital theory that was introduced in Chapter 18. Although some readers might find it offensive to treat individuals as "capital," it is true that firms are willing to "invest" in their workers in order to increase future productivity and profits. In this case a baseball team is considering hiring a player, Jackson Tanner.

Jackson Tanner, an ageing catcher with the *Mudville Mustangs* has had a illustrious career in professional baseball. Although he has a .286 lifetime batting average and holds the all-time record for catching no-hit games, the *Mustangs* gave him his unconditional release at the end of the 1993 season because of his lacklustre performance during the last two baseball seasons.

Jay Hubert, the wily general manager of the *Grover Griffens*, believes that Tanner has two good seasons left in the big leagues. With the proper coaching and sports therapy, Hubert believes than Tanner can make the *Griffens* a pennant contender and increase the team's revenue through large TV royalties, fan attendance, and sales of beer, nachos, and hot dogs at home games.

Tanner wants a $500,000 signing bonus at the beginning of the 1994 season, and a two-year contract that guarantees a salary of $1,000,000 at the end of the 1994 season and $1,500,000 at the end of the 1995 season. He also wants a no-trade and no-release clause during the contract.

Hubert knows that Tanner will need extra therapeutic care and coaching. He estimates that these costs are $100,000 per year of the contract. Moreover, he estimates that the team's stream of net receipts of having Tanner as a starting catcher with the current complement of players as being $1,800,000 at the end of the 1994 season and $1,7000,000 at the end of the 1995 season. The annual interest rate over the two seasons is expected to be 6 percent.

(a) Using Table 19-1, calculate the present value of the total costs associated with hiring Tanner.

(b) Providing that Hubert's estimates of the stream of net receipts are based on the best possible information, should the *Griffens* offer Tanner the two-year contract that he seeks? Explain.

4. *Moosejay Printing Company* is analyzing a proposal to purchase labor-saving equipment estimated to save $15,000 less $1,000 maintenance costs a year. It calculates a 10-year economic life of the equipment and $10,000 salvage at the end of the tenth year. If the purchase price of the equipment is $75,000, should it expand its current capital stock if the firm wishes a minimum rate of return of 14%? [*Hint*: If the present value of the revenue flows calculated at an interest rate of 14% is greater than the purchase price, then the rate of return on the equipment must be greater than 14%.]

5. The mythical nonrenewable natural resource, zube oil, is produced and sold in a perfectly competitive market. The reserves of zube oil are known with certainty, and demand is constant. The entire stock is of identical quality and can be extracted and delivered to market with negligible extraction and transportation costs. Its price in 1993 is $100 per barrel. The rate of interest is 10 percent.

(a) Explain why, under these assumption, the price of zube oil in 1994 will be $110 per barrel.

(b) Predict the consequences of the following in the market for zube oil:

(i) Demand for zube oil increases as the economy grows and population and per-capita incomes increase.

(ii) Additional reserves of zube oil are unexpectedly discovered.

(iii) The government passes a law prohibiting the sale of zube oil at a price higher than the current competitive equilibrium price.

◆ ANSWERS

Multiple-Choice Questions

1. (c) 2. (b) 3. (c) 4. (d) 5. (d) 6. (c) 7. (b) 8. (e) 9. (b) 10. (b) 11. (a) 12. (d) 13. (a)
14. (c) 15. (e) 16. (c) 17. (b) 18. (c) 19. (b) 20. (c) 21. (a) 22. (a) 23. (d) 24. (b)

Exercises

1.   (a) $7.47, 1 percent, 50, $10.
       (b) $42.12, 1 percent, 50, $10.

2.   (a) $PV = \$545/(1.1)$.
       (b) PV is equal to $495.41. Since this value is less than the machine's purchase price, the financial manager would not recommend its purchase.
       (c)   Yes, the present value of the net income flows is now $504.67. Since present value of the income stream is greater than the purchase price of $500, *Acme's* profits would increase if it expanded its capital stock by one machine.
       (d)   There is a negative relationship between PV and i. In the example above, when the interest rate fell from 10 to 8 percent, present value increased. The decrease in the interest rate increased the desired capital stock from 20 to 21.
       (e)   Yes, since the PV of expected net revenue ($504.50) is greater than the machine's purchase price ($500).
       (f)   There is a positive relationship between PV and R. The increase in R makes capital expansion profitable.
       (g)   No, since the present value $\{\$555/(1.1)^2 = \$458.43\}$ is less than the purchase price. Comparing the answers to part (e) and (g), we clearly see that the present value of receiving $555 one year from now is greater than the present value of receiving $555 two years from now. Thus, the more distant in time the revenue is received, the lower its present value today.

3.   (a)   The present value of total costs are consists of the signing bonus, wages in both the of the two years and the $100,000 training costs per year. Hence, $PV =$ $500,000 + \$1,100,000/(1.06) + \$1,600,000/(1.06)^2$ or $2,961,300.
       (b)   Yes, since the present value of the expected net receipts are greater than the present value of the total costs. In this case, the PV of receipts are given by $\$1,800,000/(1.06) + \$1,700,000/(1.06)^2$ or $3,205,000.

4.   Yes, since the present value of the savings and the salvage value are greater than the purchase price. At 14%, PV of the net savings plus the salvage value is ($15,000 - $1,000) times 5.216 (according to Table 19-2) **plus** $\$10,000/(1.14)^{10}$. This sum is equal to $75,724 (= $73,024 + $2,700). Since the PV is greater than $75,000, *Moosejay* should invest in this machine. Note also, that since the present value of net savings is *greater than* the purchase price, the rate of return must be greater than 14 percent. [In fact, the rate of return is 14.3 percent.]

5.   (a)   Firms with inventories must earn exactly as much per dollar of investment as they would be investing elsewhere at 10 percent. If zube oil prices were expected to rise faster than 10 percent, investors would hold more zube oil as an investment rather than release it for current consumption, driving its current price up. As the same time, the stock held for the future would increase, and future prices would

fall. The same process would work in reverse if zube oil prices were rising at a rate less than 10 percent.

(b) (i) The demand curve shifts outward, causing the price to increase. Because the shift is not just a one-time increase in demand, but rather a process that continues over time, the rate of extraction of the resource will be affected: with progressively greater market demand, price will be driven up at a rate equal to the interest rate through successfully smaller increments in output.

(ii) Supply increases, causing price to fall.

(iii) If an illegal black market in zube oil does not emerge, quantity demanded will be greater and quantity supplied will be less than the free-market level. Thus, a shortage of zube oil will emerge. If the controls are believed to be permanent, the rate of extraction of zube oil will remain constant, rather than declining over time as the price rises. Thus, the deposit will be exhausted more rapidly than under a market solution, and the current generation of zube oil customers benefits at the expense of future generations where no zube oil will be available.

Table 19.2 Present value of $1.00 received annually for n years

$$PV = \left(\frac{1}{1+i}\right)^1 + \left(\frac{1}{1+i}\right)^2 + \cdots + \left(\frac{1}{1+i}\right)^n$$

Years (n)	1%	2%	4%	5%	6%	8%	10%	12%	14%	15%
1	0.990	0.980	0.962	0.952	0.943	0.926	0.909	0.893	0.877	0.870
2	1.970	1.942	1.886	1.859	1.833	1.783	1.736	1.690	1.647	1.626
3	2.941	2.884	2.775	2.723	2.673	2.577	2.487	2.402	2.322	2.283
4	3.902	3.808	3.630	3.546	3.465	3.312	3.170	3.037	2.914	2.855
5	4.853	4.713	4.452	4.329	4.212	3.993	3.791	3.605	3.433	3.352
6	5.795	5.601	5.242	5.076	4.917	4.623	4.355	4.111	3.889	3.784
7	6.728	6.472	6.002	5.786	5.582	5.206	4.868	4.565	4.288	4.160
8	7.652	7.325	6.733	6.463	6.210	5.747	5.335	4.968	4.639	4.487
9	8.566	8.162	7.435	7.108	6.802	6.247	5.759	5.328	4.946	4.772
10	9.714	8.983	8.111	7.722	7.360	6.710	6.145	5.650	5.216	5.019
11	10.368	9.787	8.760	8.306	7.877	7.139	6.495	5.988	5.453	5.234
12	11.255	10.575	9.385	8.863	8.384	7.536	6.814	6.194	5.660	5.421
13	12.134	11.343	9.986	9.394	8.853	7.904	7.103	6.424	5.842	5.583
14	13.004	12.106	10.563	9.899	9.295	8.244	7.367	6.628	6.002	5.724
15	13.865	12.849	11.118	10.380	9.712	8.559	7.606	6.811	6.142	5.847
16	14.718	13.578	11.652	10.838	10.106	8.851	7.824	6.974	6.265	5.954
17	15.562	14.292	12.166	11.274	10.477	9.122	8.022	7.120	6.373	6.047
18	16.398	14.992	12.659	11.690	10.828	9.372	8.201	7.250	6.467	6.128
19	17.226	15.678	13.134	12.085	11.158	9.604	8.365	7.466	6.550	6.198
20	18.046	16.351	13.590	12.462	11.470	9.818	8.514	7.469	6.623	6.259
21	18.857	17.011	14.029	12.821	11.764	10.017	8.649	7.562	6.687	6.312
22	19.660	17.658	14.451	13.163	12.042	10.201	8.772	7.645	6.743	6.359
23	20.456	18.292	14.857	13.489	12.303	10.371	8.883	7.718	6.792	6.399
24	21.234	18.914	15.247	13.799	12.550	10.529	8.985	7.784	6.835	6.434
25	22.023	19.523	15.622	14.094	12.783	10.675	9.077	7.843	6.873	6.464
26	22.795	20.121	15.983	14.375	13.003	10.810	9.161	7.896	6.906	6.591
27	23.560	20.707	16.330	14.643	13.211	10.935	9.237	7.943	6.935	6.514
28	24.316	21.281	16.663	14.898	13.406	11.051	9.307	7.984	6.961	6.534
29	25.066	21.844	16.984	15.141	13.591	11.158	9.370	8.022	6.983	6.551
30	25.808	27.306	17.292	15.373	13.765	11.258	9.247	8.055	7.003	6.566
40	32.835	27.355	19.793	17.159	15.046	11.925	9.779	8.244	7.105	6.642
50	39.196	31.424	21.482	18.256	15.762	12.234	9.915	8.304	7.133	6.661

Table 19.1 Present value of $1.00

$$PV = \left(\frac{1}{1+i}\right)^n$$

Years hence (n)	1%	2%	4%	5%	6%	8%	10%	12%	14%	15%
1	0.990	0.980	0.962	0.952	0.943	0.926	0.909	0.893	0.877	0.870
2	0.980	0.961	0.925	0.907	0.890	0.857	0.826	0.797	0.769	0.756
3	0.971	0.942	0.889	0.864	0.840	0.794	0.751	0.712	0.675	0.658
4	0.961	0.924	0.855	0.823	0.792	0.735	0.683	0.636	0.592	0.572
5	0.951	0.906	0.822	0.784	0.747	0.681	0.621	0.567	0.519	0.497
6	0.942	0.888	0.790	0.746	0.705	0.630	0.564	0.507	0.456	0.432
7	0.933	0.871	0.760	0.711	0.665	0.583	0.513	0.452	0.400	0.376
8	0.923	0.853	0.731	0.677	0.627	0.540	0.467	0.404	0.351	0.327
9	0.914	0.837	0.703	0.645	0.592	0.500	0.424	0.351	0.308	0.284
10	0.905	0.820	0.676	0.614	0.558	0.463	0.386	0.322	0.270	0.247
11	0.896	0.804	0.650	0.585	0.527	0.429	0.350	0.287	0.237	0.215
12	0.887	0.788	0.625	0.557	0.497	0.397	0.319	0.257	0.208	0.187
13	0.879	0.773	0.601	0.530	0.469	0.368	0.290	0.229	0.182	0.163
14	0.870	0.758	0.577	0.505	0.442	0.340	0.263	0.205	0.160	0.141
15	0.861	0.743	0.555	0.481	0.417	0.315	0.239	0.183	0.140	0.123
16	0.853	0.728	0.534	0.458	0.394	0.292	0.218	0.163	0.123	0.107
17	0.844	0.714	0.513	0.436	0.371	0.270	0.198	0.146	0.108	0.093
18	0.836	0.700	0.494	0.416	0.350	0.250	0.180	0.130	0.095	0.081
19	0.828	0.686	0.475	0.396	0.331	0.232	0.164	0.116	0.083	0.070
20	0.820	0.673	0.456	0.377	0.312	0.215	0.149	0.104	0.073	0.061
21	0.811	0.660	0.439	0.359	0.294	0.199	0.135	0.093	0.064	0.053
22	0.803	0.647	0.422	0.342	0.278	0.184	0.123	0.083	0.056	0.046
23	0.795	0.634	0.406	0.326	0.262	0.170	0.112	0.074	0.049	0.040
24	0.788	0.622	0.390	0.310	0.247	0.158	0.102	0.066	0.043	0.035
25	0.780	0.610	0.375	0.295	0.233	0.146	0.092	0.059	0.038	0.030
26	0.772	0.598	0.361	0.281	0.220	0.135	0.084	0.053	0.033	0.026
27	0.764	0.586	0.347	0.268	0.207	0.125	0.076	0.047	0.029	0.023
28	0.757	0.574	0.333	0.255	0.196	0.116	0.069	0.042	0.026	0.020
29	0.749	0.563	0.321	0.243	0.185	0.107	0.063	0.037	0.022	0.017
30	0.742	0.552	0.308	0.231	0.174	0.099	0.057	0.033	0.020	0.015
40	0.672	0.453	0.208	0.142	0.097	0.046	0.022	0.011	0.005	0.004
50	0.608	0.372	0.141	0.087	0.054	0.021	0.009	0.003	0.001	0.001

PART SIX

THE MARKET ECONOMY: PROBLEMS AND POLICIES

Chapter 20

Benefits and Costs of Government Internvention

◆ LEARNING OBJECTIVES

After studying this chapter, you should be able to:

✔   explain how the market system coordinates the allocation of resources;

✔   explain the role of windfall profits and losses;

✔   distinguish between private valuations and social valuations of benefits and costs;

✔   identify the major causes of market failure and of government failure;

✔   define *externalities* and identify methods for internalizing them;

✔   understand that society's goals for government involvement include activities beyond those concerned with economic efficiency;

✔   explain why it is neither possible nor efficient to correct all market failures, nor is it always efficient to do nothing.

◆ HINTS AND TIPS

You might be guided by the fact that frequent errors on examinations are attributable to:

✔   a failure to remember that social cost equals the sum of private and external costs.

◆ MULTIPLE-CHOICE QUESTIONS

1. The likely result in a market economy if the government taxed away all profits would be
    (a) a more rapid shift of resources to expanding industries.
    (b) the removal of the most important incentive for resource allocation.
    (c) improved market signals and responses.
    (d) improved information about temporary shortages and surpluses.
    (e) enhanced efficiency in resource allocation.

2. Which of the following is *not* an argument for increased reliance on markets for allocating resources?
    (a) The market system coordinates millions of independent economic decisions automatically.
    (b) Profits in a market economy provide a stimulus for innovation and growth..
    (c) Markets function best when external benefits are associated with consumption or production.
    (d) Market forces provide an effective means of adapting to changing economic conditions.
    (e) In a market system relative prices reflect relative costs.

3. The appearance of windfall profits in one industry in a market economy indicates
    (a) unexpected changes in supply and/or demand in the industry.
    (b) a disequilibrium phenomenon.
    (c) an unanticipated benefit to producers in that industry.
    (d) signal that too few resources are allocated to this industry.
    (e) All of the above

4. One of the most important features of the price system is
    (a) long-term stability of prices and output.
    (b) its ability to respond quickly and automatically to changing demand and supply conditions.
    (c) the assurance that consumers will pay for collective consumption goods.
    (d) that it solves the problem of scarcity and provides abundance for all.
    (e) that it provides an equitable distribution of income.

5. If a ton of newspaper costs $350 to produce and in the process causes $10 worth of pollution damage to the environment,
    (a) the private cost is $360 per ton.
    (b) the social cost is $10 per ton and the private cost is $350 per ton.
    (c) the private cost is $350 per ton and the social cost is $340 per ton.
    (d) the social cost is $360 per ton and the private cost is $350 per ton.
    (e) the social cost is $10 per ton and the private cost is $360 per ton.

6. Which of the following is the best example of a collective consumption good in a classroom?
    (a) A pencil.   (b) A student's notes.
    (c) A copy of the textbook.   (d) The temperature in the room.
    (e) The instructor's desk.

7.   Adverse selection refers to a situation where
     (a)   the managers of corporations pursue goals other than profits.
     (b)   the values of consumers and producers differ.
     (c)   one party to a transaction has more information about, say, the quality of the product than the other party.
     (d)   the government selects the wrong form of intervention for correcting a market failure.
     (e)   the management of a firm differs from its owners.

8.   If there are costly externalities associated with an economic activity and that activity is carried out until the private marginal benefit equals the private marginal cost,
     (a)   this activity should be subsidized.
     (b)   the social marginal net benefit is positive.
     (c)   private costs exceed social costs.
     (d)   too many resources are being allocated to this activity.
     (e)   output of this activity should increase.

9.   The presence of external benefits associated with production implies that
     (a)   private output exceeds the socially optimal output.
     (b)   private output is less than the socially optimal output.
     (c)   private output corresponds to the socially optimal output.
     (d)   Any of the above, depending on the relative magnitude of social and private benefits.
     (e)   Any of the above, depending upon whether social benefits exceeds external benefits.

10. A positive externality would probably result from
     (a)   a discharge of a toxic waste into the St. Lawrence River.
     (b)   a newly painted house.
     (c)   the dumping garbage on a seldom-used country road.
     (d)   cigarette smoking.
     (e)   a loud radio at a public beach.

11. A market economy is unlikely to provide a sufficient amount of a collective consumption good like national defense because
     (a)   national defense does not benefit everyone to the same degree.
     (b)   private firms produce national defense less efficiently than does the government.
     (c)   consumers are poorly informed about the benefits of national defense.
     (d)   it is impossible to withhold national defense from people who don't pay for it.
     (e)   Both (a) and (b) are correct.

12. Which one of the following would not be a source of inefficient market outcomes?
     (a)   Externalities.   (b)   Collective consumption goods.
     (c)   Windfall profits and losses.   (d)   Information asymmetries.
     (e)   Moral hazard.

13. A Toronto resident who drives a car to work rather than taking public transportation
    (a) is reducing the free-rider problem.
    (b) is likely to be creating a negative externality.
    (c) creates a situation in which private cost is likely to exceed social cost.
    (d) is contributing to efficient resource allocation.
    (e) All of the above.

14. Efficient government intervention requires that
    (a) the costs of government enforcement be zero.
    (b) the marginal benefits of intervention be just equal to the marginal costs of intervention.
    (c) intervention should continue until all negative externalities have been eliminated.
    (d) there be no productivity losses in the private sector as a result of government intervention.
    (e) all intervention be self-financing.

15. Which of the following can the government use to correct market failure?
    (a) Taxes and/or subsidies.
    (b) Rules and regulations restricting market activity.
    (c) Public provision of goods and services.
    (d) Restructuring incentives.
    (e) All of the above.

16. Principal-agent problems that government agencies confront are similar to those that private firms face, but they
    (a) are less serious because stockholders of a firm almost never agree on the objectives of the firm.
    (b) are more serious because managers of firms can be more easily replaced than government bureaucrats.
    (c) should not be considered a form of government "imperfection".
    (d) should be considered a benefit rather than a cost of government intervention.
    (e) are less serious because of governments' unlimited ability to tax.

17. Arrow's impossibility theorem
    (a) shows that in some cases the majority-rule voting procedure results in inconsistent social decisions.
    (b) proves that efficient government intervention is impossible.
    (c) concerns the inability of governments to make sound social decisions.
    (d) suggests that it is impossible for markets to achieve efficient outcomes because of various market imperfections.
    (e) establishes that efficient resource allocation can never be obtained by governments.

18. The economically efficient quantity of a public good is the level of output at which
    (a) the sum of everyone's individual valuations of the good is just equal to its marginal cost.
    (b) the marginal cost of additional output of the public good is zero.
    (c) the sum of individual valuations is maximized.
    (d) the valuations of all individuals are equal.
    (e) each individual's marginal valuation is zero.

19. In practice, assessing the benefits and costs of a proposed government program is difficult because
    (a) the effects of the program may be difficult to determine.
    (b) many benefits and costs occur in the distant future.
    (c) some costs and benefits are difficult, perhaps impossible, to quantify.
    (d) All of the above.
    (e) Both (a) and (b) are correct, but not (c).

20. Rent-seeking behavior refers to
    (a) the conversion of owner-occupied housing to rental housing.
    (b) activities by individuals seeking favorable government actions.
    (c) consumers seeking low rent housing.
    (d) actions in former socialist countries to convert public housing to private owner-
        ship.
    (e) firms that avoid the fixed costs of plant and equipment by leasing instead of buy-
        ing.

21. Which of the following is *not* a cost of government intervention?
    (a) Direct resource costs.   (b) Compliance costs.
    (c) Change in production costs.   (d) Rent-seeking.
    (e) Externalities.

◆ **EXERCISES**

1. The following graph below illustrates the situation for a firm that is producing a good
   that imposes external costs on neighboring residences. Marginal revenues to the firm are
   shown by the line *AB*; *PMC* represents the private marginal costs to the firm; *MD* represents the external costs or marginal damage resulting from production. Label the graph as
   needed to answer the questions.

Figure 20-1

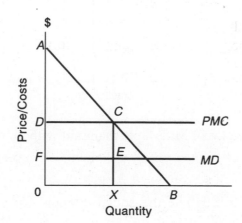

273

(a)   Explain why output X is the private optimum (profit-maximizing) output for the firm.

(b)   Draw the social marginal cost curve on the graph.
(c)   The total external cost of producing quantity X is indicated by area _____.
(d)   Indicate on the graph the socially optimal output level as Z.
(e)   The additional external costs from producing X instead of Z is equal to the area _____.
(f)   The additional private costs from producing X instead of Z is equal to the area _____.
(g)   Explain why there will be a net gain in welfare (that is, net social benefits will be positive) in reducing output from X to Z.

2.   Assume that Mr. Maple has access to his wooded retreat by way of a 2-kilometer road that he and another individual, Mr. Oak, must maintain. The demands for quality on the part of Mr. Oak and Mr. Maple are shown in the graphs, where the quality of the road can be measured as the number of times the road is graded or tons of gravel added. The cost of increasing quality is shown as $S = MC$. (We assume that "zero" quality implies that the road is barely passable.)

Figure 20-2

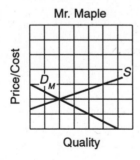
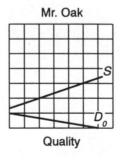
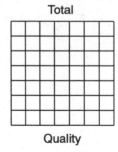

(a)   What quality level will Mr. Maple maintain without considering Mr. Oak?

(b)   How would you illustrate the social demand for road quality? Use the graph. (*Hint:* Recall the discussions in the text on external benefits and collective consumption goods.)

274

(c)   Given the costs of quality improvements as shown, would the socially optimal quality level represent an improved road quality compared to the level maintained by Mr. Maple alone?

(d)   If the level of road quality given by (c) were produced and the costs were shared, would Mr. Maple pay more or less than in (a)?

3.   For each of the government programs or regulations cited, identify what types of market failure might be used as a rationale for government intervention.

(a)   National defense.

(b)   Pollution control regulations.

(c)   Public health insurance programs.

(d)   Environment Canada Weather Service.

(e)   Student loan programs.

(f)   Government support for scientific research.

(g)   Truth-in-lending laws, requiring lenders to disclose to borrowers the true rate of interest.

(h)   Minimum wage legislation.

(i)   Quotas limiting the number of fish that can be caught.

(j)   Zoning regulations.

4. In the accompanying graph, the marginal damage (*MD*) schedule refers to *incremental* pollution costs associated with a unit increase in production activity. The marginal private benefit (*MPB*) schedule is the *incremental* private gain (*MR* - *MC*) to the producer as output is increased.

Figure 20-3

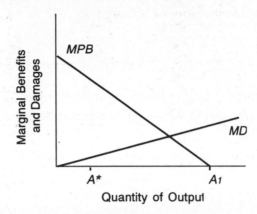

(a) With no government intervention, what level of output would the producer choose? Why?

(b) From society's point of view, what is the optimal output level? Explain.

(c) Suppose that the government, unaware of the precise shape of the *MD* schedule, limits the producer to A^* of output. At A^*, is society better off or worse off than in a no-intervention situation? Explain.

5. A small community is in the process of repainting city hall. The citizens have narrowed the potential colors down to a choice of either red, white, or blue and have also agreed that combinations of the three are undesirable. To choose one color from among the three, a committee of three individuals has been selected. Each of the committee members has a personal preference ranking of the alternatives as indicated in the following schedule (1 is most preferred, 3 is least preferred).

Individual Preference Rankings

Committee member

Color	A	B	C
Red	1	3	2
White	2	1	3
Blue	3	2	1

276

Since a vote over the entire field of three colors results in a three-way tie (each committee member has a different most preferred color), the committee has agreed to select the winning color by elimination through majority voting in pairwise matches (i.e., the color with the most votes in the first contest between any two colors proceeds to a second contest with the remaining color).

(a)   If the agenda calls for red versus white in the first contest, what will ultimately be the color of city hall?

(b)   If the first round had pitted white against blue, what color would have been chosen from the three?

(c)   Alternatively, if the first round had matched red against blue, what color would city hall have been painted?

◆ **ANSWERS**

Multiple-Choice Questions

1. (b) 2. (c) 3. (e) 4. (b) 5. (d) 6. (d) 7. (c) 8. (d) 9. (b) 10. (b) 11. (d) 12. (c) 13. (b) 14. (b) 15. (e) 16. (b) 17. (a) 18. (a) 19. (d) 20. (b) 21. (e)

Exercises

1.   (a)

Figure 20 4

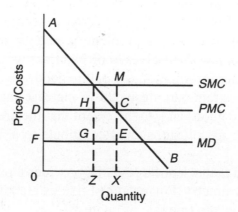

Output X maximizes net private benefit (i.e., profits) where $MR = PMC$.
(b)   See graph: $SMC = PMC + MD$.
(c) $OFEX$.
(d)   See graph.

(e)   *ZGEX.*

(f)   *ZHCX.*

(g)   Reducing output from *X* to *Z* will decrease social costs by *ZIMX* (*ZHCX* + *ZGEX*) but will decrease revenues to the firm by a lesser amount, *ZICX*. The triangle *IMC* represents the net social gain.

2.   (a)   The point where the demand and *S* (= *MC*) curves intersect for Mr. Maple.

        (b)   Add the demand schedules vertically; that is, find the total willingness to pay for each level of quality from 0 to Q^*.

Figure 20-5

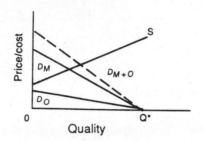

        (c)   Yes. The line *S* = *MC* would intersect D_{M+0} to the right of the D_M intersection with *S*, indicating an improvement in road quality.

        (d)   It depends on how the costs are shared. If both Mr. Oak and Mr. Maple pay one-half, Mr. Maple would pay less than in (a). The new cost would be only slightly above what Mr. Maple paid before, but half the cost would be borne by Mr. Oak. Other cost-sharing arrangements are certainly possible.

3.   (a)   National defense is a collective consumption good. Adding to the population of a country does not diminish the extent to which each citizen is defended by a given size and quality of the armed forces.

        (b)   Pollution is an external cost.

        (c)   Asymmetric information. Until the advent of publicly provided health insurance, it was difficult for the elderly to purchase health insurance because insurance companies were aware of the problem of adverse selection (i.e., they feared that only those who knew themselves to be bad risks would buy health insurance).

        (d)   Providing weather information is a public good.

        (e)   Student loan programs are designed to increase the general educational level in society (a public good) and, to the extent that they reduce the immediate financial burden of going to college, should contribute to a more equitable distribution of income.

        (f)   It can be argued that scientific research provides a public good.

        (g)   Information asymmetry. Financial institutions are far more likely than the average borrower to know the true rate of interest.

        (h)   Minimum wage legislation is a form of price floor. Proponents usually argue that it will achieve a more equitable distribution of income.

        (i)   External cost. Fish are a common-property resource. An individual taking more fish reduces the catch of others but does not count this as a cost, though it is to society.

(j)   Zoning laws regulating such things as lot size, signage and certain types of activities (such as fraternities in a residential area) are meant to reduce external costs.

4.   (a)   The producer would choose output A_1 since this output corresponds to $MPB - 0$, which implies that total private benefits are at a maximum. Each unit less than A_1 adds to private benefits because $MPB > 0$; similarly, each unit greater than A_1 deceases private benefits.

    (b)   Where the MPB and MD curves intersect at output A_0. Beyond this, the incremental costs to society exceed the incremental benefits.

    (c)   Worse off. By restricting output to A^*, the net benefit forgone by society (compared to the optimal output A_0) is area ZTQ (that is, the loss in total benefits to the producer, A^*TQA_0, minus the reduction in marginal damages, A^*ZQA_0).

Figure 20-6

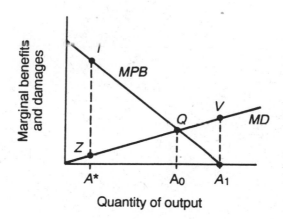

5.   (a)   Blue. Both A and C prefer red to white, so red proceeds to the second contest against blue. Both B and C prefer blue to red, so blue is the ultimate winner.

    (b)   Red. White wins the first round, and red wins over white in the second round.

    (c)   White.

Chapter 21

Social and Environmental Regulation

◆ LEARNING OBJECTIVES

After studying this chapter, you should be able to:

✔ understand the economic basis for many types of social and environmental regulation;

✔ explain why the economically efficient level of pollution is generally not zero;

✔ compare the different policy instruments that can be used to control pollution;

✔ understand the economic basis for health and safety regulation;

✔ distinguish cost-effectiveness from benefit-cost analysis and their role in evaluating government regulations.

◆ HINTS AND TIPS

You might be guided by the fact that frequent errors on examinations are attributable to:

✔ confusion between production of pollution and production of pollution abatement;

✔ a lack of understanding that efficiency is concerned with the cost of pollution as well as the cost of pollution abatement.

◆ MULTIPLE-CHOICE QUESTIONS

1. A profit-maximizing competitive firm
   (a) always produces in excess of the output that is allocatively efficient.
   (b) always generates pollution as a by-product of production.
   (c) produces more than the allocatively efficient output when it ignores external costs associated with its production.
   (d) automatically considers external costs in making production decisions.
   (e) internalizes all external costs.

2. The socially optimal level of a good's output is that quantity where
   (a) all marginal costs, private plus external, equal all marginal benefits, private plus external.
   (b) external costs are minimized.
   (c) the social benefit of the last unit of output is just equal to its external cost.
   (d) all externalities are eliminated.
   (e) All of the above.

3. If incremental costs of pollution abatement increase with increasing levels of abatement, the optimal
   (a) pollution level is the minimum attainable.
   (b) level of pollution reduction is the amount where the marginal benefits of prevention equal the marginal costs.
   (c) pollution level is necessarily zero
   (d) amount of abatement is zero.
   (e) pollution level is that where all external costs have been eliminated.

4. A firm currently emitting pollutants would have an incentive to reduce emissions if
   (a) an emissions tax per unit of discharge were imposed.
   (b) private citizens were able to sue for pollution damages.
   (c) it were forced to purchase emissions permits.
   (d) a tax on output were designed to internalize the externality.
   (e) Any of the above actions were taken.

5. A common problem with the successful use of emissions taxes is that
   (a) information on external costs is not always available for setting tax rates.
   (b) they do not provide appropriate incentives for pollution reduction.
   (c) firms will generally not reduce emissions to zero.
   (d) the government must also specify the means by which firms are to abate pollution.
   (e) some firms will still pollute more than others.

6. Tradable emissions permits
   (a) are, in effect, equivalent to creating a market for "bads".
   (b) can achieve the same resource allocation as emissions taxes.
   (c) are cost-effective in that for a given amount of pollution, the total cost of abatement is minimized.
   (d) is an example in which markets themselves can be used to correct market failures.
   (e) All of the above.

Questions 7 to 10 refer to the following graph which depicts the marginal benefit (*MB*) and marginal cost (*MC*) of pollution abatement.

Figure 21-1

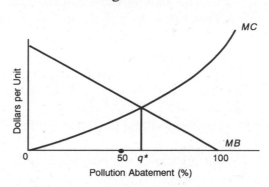

7.   The marginal benefits of pollution abatement
      (a)   are the value of reducing pollution damages.
      (b)   increase as *MB* shifts rightward.
      (c)   decline as the level of abatement increases.
      (d)   are equivalent to a demand curve for pollution control.
      (e)   All of the above.

8.   The economically efficient amount of pollution abatement is
      (a)   the output at which marginal benefits equal marginal costs.
      (b)   100 percent, since that maximizes the gains from pollution control.
      (c)   zero.
      (d)   dependent upon the external costs of pollution which are not given in the graph.
      (e)   impossible to determine without additional information about the type of pollution.

9.   New findings of adverse health effects or other damages from this pollutant will
      (a)   shift the marginal cost curve rightward.
      (b)   shift the marginal benefit curve rightward.
      (c)   shift both the marginal benefit curve and the marginal cost curve rightward.
      (d)   have no effect on either the marginal benefit curve or the marginal cost curve.
      (e)   decrease the optimal abatement level.

10.   Other things being equal, an improvement in pollution control technology
      (a)   shifts *MC* rightward, increasing the optimal level of pollution control.
      (b)   shifts *MC* leftward, decreasing the optimal level of pollution control.
      (c)   shifts both the *MC* and *MB* curves rightward.
      (d)   shifts *MB* rightward, increasing the optimal level of pollution control.
      (e)   will not affect either of the curves in this diagram.

11.   With multiple firms emitting pollutants, economic efficiency requires that
      (a)   all emitters reduce pollution by the same percentage.
      (b)   marginal costs of abatement be equal for all emitters.
      (c)   all emitters reduce pollution by the same absolute amount.
      (d)   there be zero emissions.
      (e)   firms reduce emissions in proportion to their size.

12. The requirement that all pollution sources adopt a specific pollution control technique when there are many methods for controlling a certain type of pollution
    (a) is likely to be the most efficient way to achieve a certain amount of pollution abatement.
    (b) is likely to be less efficient than either emissions taxes or tradable emissions permits in achieving a given amount of abatement.
    (c) is more efficient the more divergent the abatement costs of different firms.
    (d) eliminates the need for monitoring and enforcement by the regulatory agency.
    (e) is likely to minimize total costs of achieving a given level of abatement in the industry.

13. Which of the following is *not* true of direct pollution controls?
    (a) They are cost-effective.
    (b) They are slow to adopt improved abatement technology.
    (c) They are costly to monitor and enforce.
    (d) They require the government to direct firms on *how* to abate.
    (e) All of the above are true.

14. Government regulation of health and safety issues are desirable because
    (a) health and safety information is a public good.
    (b) information about product safety may be impossible to obtain or to evaluate.
    (c) when information is costly, health and safety standards can enhance efficiency.
    (d) with full information, private markets produce efficient levels of safety.
    (e) All of the above.

15. Comparing different life-saving options by computing the cost per life saved by each is an example of
    (a) cost-effectiveness analysis.
    (b) benefit-cost analysis.
    (c) the engineering approach to public decision making.
    (d) paternalism as the basis of regulatory policy.
    (e) financial accounting.

16. If the plastics industry has been disposing of its wastes free of charge, government regulation to ensure a more efficient use of resources would affect the industry's output and product price in which of the following ways?
    (a) Both output and price would decrease.
    (b) Output would decrease, but there would be no change in price.
    (c) Output would be unchanged, but price would increase.
    (d) Price would increase and output would decrease.
    (e) There would be no change in either price or output.

17. If the production of steel generates external costs, profit maximization in steel production will result in
    (a) too much steel at too high a price.
    (b) too little steel at too low a price.
    (c) too much steel at too low a price.
    (d) too little steel at too high a price.
    (e) the socially efficient output of steel, but at too low a price.

18. Internalizing an externality will
    (a)   shift the demand curve to the left.
    (b)   shift the supply curve (MC for a monopoly) to the left.
    (c)   shift both the demand and supply curves to the left.
    (d)   increase the size of external costs.
    (e)   have no effect on either demand or supply.

◆ **EXERCISES**

1. Suppose that installation of an air bag adds $100 to the cost of making each automobile at every level of output. Other things being equal and assuming a downward-sloping demand curve,
    (a)   marginal cost will _____.
    (b)   average cost will _____.
    (c)   the supply curve will _____.
    (d)   short-run equilibrium price will _____, but by less than _____.
    (e)   short-run equilibrium output will _____.

2. The following schedule shows (a) how the cost of production increases as a pulp and paper firm expands output and (b) the effect of pollution from the firm on commercial fishing in the area.

Output (tons per week)	Total private cost	Value of fishing loss due to pollution
0	$ 0	$ 0
1	500	100
2	550	225
3	620	365
4	710	515
5	820	675
6	1,050	845
7	1,350	1,025

(a)   Complete the following table, and graph your results in the grid that follows.

Output (tons per week)	Average private cost (APC)	Marginal private cost (MPC)	Average social cost (ASC)	Marginal social cost (MSC)
1	_____	_____	_____	_____
2	_____	_____	_____	_____
3	_____	_____	_____	_____
4	_____	_____	_____	_____
5	_____	_____	_____	_____
6	_____	_____	_____	_____
7	_____	_____	_____	_____

285

Figure 21-2

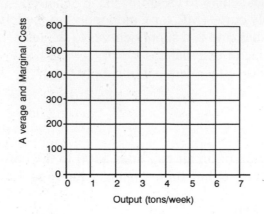

(b) If the firm were producing 4 tons of output per week, how much revenue would be required to cover its private costs? How much revenue would be required to cover the social costs?

(c) Assume that the market for this firm's product (paper) is perfectly competitive and that the firm's private costs of production are typical for the industry. Predict the long-run equilibrium price and the output for this firm in the absence of pollution controls.

(d) Assume now that firms in this industry are required either to pay compensation for the negative externalities or incur abatement costs. The industry price would be (higher, the same, lower) and the output (less, the same, greater). This firm's ability to survive would depend on the long run equilibrium price for paper being at least _____ or on its being able to keep the total of negative externalities and costs of abatement at levels as (low, high) as those of its competitors.

3. A policy analyst in a government agency has been told to choose among the following programs designed to save lives. Assume that all of the programs produce the same outcome over the same time period except in the expected number of lives saved.

Program	Total number of lives saved	Program costs (billions)	Cost per life saved(millions)
A	10	$1.2	_____
B	20	3.1	_____
C	20	2.8	_____
D	40	6.8	_____

(a) Complete the table to compute the program that is most cost-effective in saving lives.

(b)   If you had to choose among these four programs, what additional information would you need to make the choice using benefit-cost analysis?

*4.   The graphs present the marginal cost curves for pollution abatement for two firms in a given industry (for simplicity, assume that there is no fixed cost associated with abatement). The regulatory agency has determined that the level of pollution emissions must decrease by a total of eight units. Assume that the type of pollution in this industry is readily measurable.

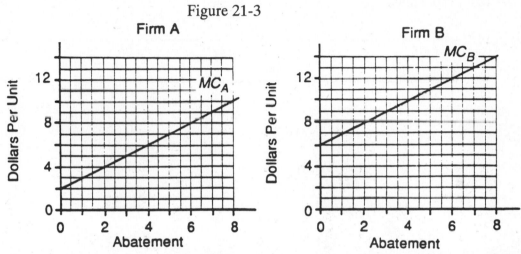

Figure 21-3

(a)   Suppose that the regulatory agency directly controls these firms by ruling that each firm must decrease emissions by four units. What is the total industry cost of abating the eight units of pollution?

(b)   Instead of direct controls, suppose that the regulatory agency imposes a tax on emissions of $8 per unit. What is the level of abatement by each firm?

(c)   What is the total cost of abatement for the industry when the emissions tax is imposed?

(d)   Now consider the effect of the introduction of a system of tradable emissions permits. Specifically, suppose that the agency rules that each firm must abate emissions by four units but that either firm can reduce this by any amount so long as it can induce the other firm to increase its abatement by an offsetting amount. What would be the resulting levels of abatement by these firms? Explain.

(e)   What is the total abatement cost to the industry under the system of tradable emissions permits?

◆ ANSWERS

Multiple-Choice Questions

1. (c) 2. (a) 3. (b) 4. (e) 5. (a) 6. (e) 7. (e) 8. (a) 9. (b) 10. (a) 11. (b) 12. (b) 13. (a) 14. (e) 15. (a) 16. (d) 17. (c) 18. (b)

Exercises

1.   (a)   rise by $100.   (b)   rise by $100.
       (c)   shift to the left.   (d)   rise; less than $100.
       (e)   decline.

2.   (a)

Output (tons/week)	APC	MPC	ASC	MSC
0	$ 0.00		$ 0.00	
		$500		600.00
1	500.00		600.00	
		50		175
2	275.00		387.50	
		70		210
3	206.67		328.33	
		90		240
4	177.50		306.25	
		110		270
5	164.00		299.00	
		230		400
6	175.00		315.83	
		300		480
7	192.86		339.29	

Figure 21-4

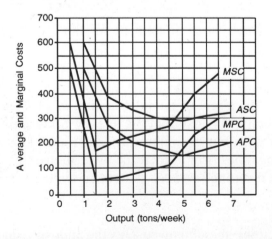

(b) $710 (per ton price of $177.50); $1,225 (per ton price of $306.25).
(c) $164; 5 tons per week (this is the output where average costs are at a minimum).
(d)   higher; less; $299 (the lowest average social cost); low.

288

3. (a) $120; $155; $140; $170. Program A is the most cost-effective program.

(b) You would need information regarding the value of the additional lives saved. For example, only programs B and C produce an identical outcome (20 lives saved). The others produce different outcomes. A related ethical issue is whether the value of a life varies across individuals; court decisions awarding compensation to victims of accidents, negligence, and other torts indicate that our society does make such distinctions.

*4. (a) Each firm abates four units, so the marginal abatement costs for Firms A and B are $6 and $10, respectively. Since there are no fixed costs to abatement, total abatement cost for each firm is given by the area under its abatement marginal cost curve measured up to its level of abatement. Thus for Firm A, total abatement cost is $16 = ($2 x 4) + [($6 - $2) x 4]/2; for Firm B, it is $32 = ($6 x 4) + [($10 - $6) x 4]/2. Therefore, industry abatement cost is $48 = $16 + $32.

(b) A tax of $8 imposed on each unit of emissions represents a savings of $8 for each unit of abatement. Thus each firm abates until the savings from an additional unit of abatement equals the marginal cost of abatement. For Firm A this occurs at a level of abatement equal to six units, while for Firm B it occurs at two units of abatement.

(c) Given the levels of abatement determined in (b), abatement cost for Firm A is $30 = ($2 x 6) + [($8 - $2) x 6]/2, while for Firm B it is $14 = ($6 x 2) + [($8 - $6) x 2]/2. Thus industry abatement cost is $44.

(d) Abatement of the fourth unit costs Firm A $6 but costs Firm B $10; thus the potential for gains from trade exists. For example, Firm B would pay up to $10 to avoid having to abate the fourth unit of emission, and Firm A would accept anything over $6 to induce it to increase slightly its level of abatement ($7 for the fifth unit). Thus these firms will negotiate to buy and sell emissions permits until no further gains from trade are achievable. This occurs when the firms face equal marginal abatement costs; Firm B will have reduced its level of abatement by two units to a total of two, and Firm A will have increased its level by an offsetting two units to a total of six.

(e) Since the level of abatement for each firm is the same as that under the emissions tax discussed earlier, the total abatement cost for the industry is the same at $44.

Chapter 22

Taxation and Public Expenditure

◆ LEARNING OBJECTIVES

After studying this chapter, you should be able to:

✔   understand the roles of the tax system in raising revenue, redistributing income and affecting resource allocation;

✔   explain progressive and regressive taxes;

✔   discuss different concepts of equity and principals of taxation;

✔   understand that tax incidence does not depend on who pays the tax bill;

✔   explain the economic logic for the distribution of government responsibilities in fiscal federalism;

✔   understand the operation and economic implications of the Goods and Services Tax (GST).

◆ HINTS AND TIPS

You might be guided by the fact that frequent errors on examinations are attributable to:

✔   confusion between average and marginal tax rates;

✔   the erroneous belief that an increasing marginal tax rate is a necessary and sufficient condition for progressivity of the tax system.

◆ MULTIPLE-CHOICE QUESTIONS

1. Horizontal equity refers to
   (a) the East-West distribution of income.
   (b) the treatment of individuals with identical incomes but different circumstances.
   (c) the treatment of households of similar composition but with different incomes.
   (d) the flat-rate tax scheme.
   (e) changes in the marginal tax rate across income levels.

2. If the amount of tax paid increases as income rises, the tax
   (a) is proportional.
   (b) is progressive.
   (c) is regressive.
   (d) is a flat-rate tax.
   (e) may be any of the above.

3. If rich people and poor people smoke the same amount, a sales tax on cigarettes is regressive because
   (a) everyone spends the same proportion of income on cigarettes.
   (b) the demand for cigarettes is inelastic.
   (c) the tax paid per person represents a larger proportion of a poor person's income.
   (d) the rich are better informed about the health hazards of smoking.
   (e) the poor pay more taxes.

4. If a tax takes the same amount of money from everyone regardless of individual income, the tax is
   (a) a flat-rate tax.   (b) proportional.
   (c) regressive.   (d) horizontally inequitable.
   (e) All of the above.

5. If the income tax is progressive, the marginal tax rate must be
   (a) less than the average tax rate.
   (b) the same as the average tax rate.
   (c) greater than the average tax rate.
   (d) continuously increasing with income.
   (e) constant.

6. If an individual's average tax rate is 30 percent and marginal tax rate is 50 percent, an additional $100 income would imply additional tax payments of
   (a) $50.   (b) $30.
   (c) $80.   (d) $20.
   (e) Indeterminable without income level.

7. Tax expenditures refer to
   (a) how the government spends its tax revenues.
   (b) an individual's annual tax payments.
   (c) tax concessions that are made to influence the behavior of taxpaying units.
   (d) intergovernmental transfers.
   (e) expenditures of future tax revenues.

8. The central idea behind the Laffer curve is that as tax rates increase,
   (a) the tax base will increase.
   (b) a tax revolt by taxpayers will be ignited.
   (c) more economic activity will go unreported so as to evade income taxation.
   (d) tax revenue will reach a maximum and then decline as tax rates continue to increase.
   (e) the size of the government increases.

9. Tax incidence indicates
   (a) who actually bears the final burden of the tax.
   (b) who pays the tax to the government.
   (c) the degree of progressivity in the tax.
   (d) the degree of vertical equity in the tax.
   (e) the frequency with which taxpaying units must submit taxes to the government.

10. The incidence of a sales tax
   (a) is borne entirely by consumers, who must pay the tax in addition to the good's price.
   (b) is borne entirely by producers, who lower prices by the amount of the tax in order to sell.
   (c) is generally shared by consumers and producers, depending on the elasticities of demand and supply.
   (d) is shared equally between consumers and producers in competitive markets.
   (e) None of the above.

11. Which of the following is *not* an example of a government transfer payment to individuals?
   (a) Salaries of government employees.
   (b) Canada Pension Plan.
   (c) Unemployment insurance benefits.
   (d) Child tax credits.
   (e) Workers' compensation.

12. Under the equalization payments program, the federal government
   (a) equalizes the tax revenue of each province.
   (b) transfers money from its general revenue to provinces with below average tax capacity.
   (c) transfers tax revenue to provinces to ensure a reasonably equal educational expenditure per student across the country.
   (d) ensures that each province taxes income at the same rate (except Quebec, which collects its own income tax).
   (e) provides equal unconditional grants to each province.

13. According to the benefit principle of taxation,
    (a)   the amount of taxes paid should be equal across income groups.
    (b)   taxes should be paid according to the benefits that taxpayers derive from public expenditure.
    (c)   there should be no user charges for government services.
    (d)   the greater one's income, the greater the benefit generally received from public expenditures.
    (e)   the economy benefits the most when the government maximizes its tax revenue.

14. Decentralization of government economic activity can be justified by all but which of the following?
    (a)   Regional preferences.
    (b)   Income redistribution efforts.
    (c)   Particular local needs for public expenditure.
    (d)   Internalization of spillovers of services across jurisdictions.
    (e)   Responsiveness to changing preferences.

15. Increasing amounts of tax revenue have been transferred to the provincial and municipal governments for all *but* which of the following reasons?
    (a)   There is a high income elasticity of demand for municipal services.
    (b)   Municipal services tend to use labor whose productivity growth has been below the national average, so relative costs of these services have risen.
    (c)   Inclusion of equalization payments in the Canadian Constitution.
    (d)   The 1977 Fiscal Arrangements Act which introduced Established Program Finanacing.
    (e)   Neither (c) nor (d) are reasons.

16. Which of the following is *not* a feature of the Goods and Services Tax (GST)?
    (a)   The GST eliminates tax cascading.
    (b)   It taxes exports but exempts imports.
    (c)   It is a value added tax.
    (d)   It replaced the 13.5 percent Manufacturers' Sales Tax.
    (e)   Relative to the old Federal sales Tax, the GST applies to a broader base.

17. The judgment concerning whether a tax is regressive, proportional, or progressive is based on a comparison of the amount of tax with the
    (a)   tax base.   (b)   value of the item being taxed.
    (c)   taxpayer's income.   (d)   distribution of income.
    (e)   level of government expenditures.

18. The more elastic the demand for a commodity on which a specific excise tax is levied, other things being equal, the
    (a)   greater the after-tax price increase.
    (b)   less the reduction in the quantity produced.
    (c)   more elastic the associated supply curve.
    (d)   less the after-tax price increase and the greater the reduction in quantity.
    (e)   more progressive the tax.

19. Vertical equity in a tax system
    (a)   concerns equity across income groups.
    (b)   focuses on comparisons of taxes paid by taxpayers with different incomes.
    (c)   is often used to support regressive taxation.
    (d)   attempts to tax monopoly power by a surtax on firms that have undergone vertical mergers.
    (e)   Both (a) and (b) are correct.

20. A marginal tax rate of 58 percent on taxable income of $200,000 implies
    (a)   that a person with $200,000 of taxable income pays $116,000 in taxes.
    (b)   that the tax system is progressive.
    (c)   that the tax system is vertically equitable.
    (d)   that a dollar of income above $200,000 increases one's tax liability by $0.58.
    (e)   All of the above.

21. In 1991 total taxes from all levels of government represented what proportion (approximately) of total Canadian income?
    (a)   A tenth.   (b)   A fifth.
    (c)   A quarter.   (d)   A third.
    (e)   A half.

22. Since the proportion of income spent on commodities such as alcohol and gasoline declines as incomes increase, the taxes on these commodities are
    (a)   regressive.   (b)   proportional.
    (c)   progressive.   (d)   vertically equitable.
    (e)   horizontally equitable.

23. In Canada the burden of the property tax is
    (a)   borne by landlords only.
    (b)   borne by tenants only.
    (c)   shared by landlords and tenants.
    (d)   borne by the mortgage lender.
    (d)   shared by the landlord and the mortgage lender.

24. Which of the following is *not* a reason for intergovernmental transfers in Canada?
    (a)   Spillover effects.
    (b)   Use of the federal government's spending power.
    (c)   Not all jurisdictions have access to revenue that matches the division of responsibilities.
    (d)   The federal government is constitutionally obliged to share responsibility with the provinces for the pursuit of interpersonal equity.
    (e)   Under Established Programs Financing (EPF's) federal contributions to hosipital insurance, medicare and postsecondary education are dependent upon the costs of these programs.

1.   (a)   The table that follows shows the amount of tax paid by four individuals in four different income categories under each of three tax regimes: A, B, and C. Indicate whether the tax is proportional, regressive, or progressive.

        (b)   Taking all taxes together (A + B + C), is the tax system progressive, regressive, or proportional?

2.   (a)   Suppose that a negative income tax provides $5,000 guaranteed income for a family and a 50 percent marginal tax rate on earnings. Complete the table.

(b)   The following version of the negative income tax was part of a 1970 experiment. A family of five earns $96 a week in income and receives $10.75 a week in cash from the government (1970 dollars); if earnings fall to $50, the family will receive $43 a week from the government, and if there are no earnings, the family will receive $78 a week from the government. Calculate the implicit marginal rate of taxation.

3.   The three graphs represent three different market situations with respect to the supply and demand for rental accommodation in the short run. Assume that a property tax equal to a fixed amount per rental unit is imposed in all three situations.

Figure 22-1

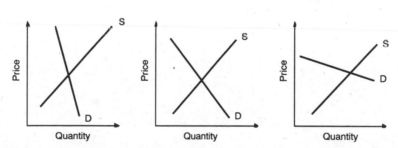

(a)   In which market situation would the landlord bear most of the tax burden? Explain.

(b)   The following graph reproduces the situation in the center graph. Draw a possible long-run supply curve, and compare the long-run shifting of the property tax burden with your answer to (a). (*Hint:* Draw the long-run supply curve through the initial short-run equilibrium.)

Figure 22-2

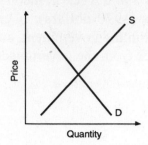

(c)   In which of these market situations is the change in the quantity of rental accommodation due to the tax, the smallest? Why? (Restrict your answer to the short run.)

(d)   Suppose that in the second market situation, rent controls had fixed the rent or
price at the original equilibrium. Is the tax burden shouldered by landlords altered
because of rent control?

4.   The following graph depicts market demand and supply curves for a commodity prior to
any government intervention; the equilibrium price and quantity are therefore $3 and 30
units, respectively. A tax of $2 per unit is now imposed on this commodity.

Figure 22-3

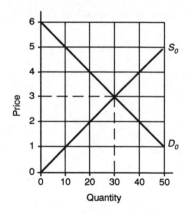

(a)   Suppose that the tax is levied on (i.e., paid by) producers.
    (i)   Characterize the introduction of the tax by drawing the effective supply
        curve that consumers face. Label it S_1.
    (ii)   What price will consumers pay per unit?

    (iii) What is the after-tax "net price" paid to firms?

    (iv)   Tax incidence per unit can be defined for firms as the difference between
        the initial price and the after-tax net price. What is the incidence per unit
        borne by firms?

298

(v)   What is the incidence per unit borne by consumers?

(vi)   What is government tax revenue?

(b)   Suppose now that the tax is levied on consumers.
    (i)   Characterize the introduction of the tax by drawing the effective demand curve that producers face. Label it D_1.
    (ii)   What price will consumers pay per unit (inclusive of the tax)?

    (iii)   What is the net-of-tax price that firms retain?

    (iv)   What is the incidence per unit borne by firms?

    (v)   What is the incidence per unit borne by consumers?

    (vi)   What is government tax revenue?

(c)   Does tax incidence depend on who pays the tax?

5.   This exercise compares the Retail Sales Tax (RST), the Goods and Services Tax (GST), and the Manufacturers' Sales Tax (MST) when applied to a commodity that has four stages of production. The following schedule presents the purchases and sales at each stage.

(a)   Suppose that an RST of 7 percent is introduced. At which stage in the production process is it imposed, and what is total tax revenue?

(b)   Instead, suppose that a GST of 7 percent is imposed such that at each stage a 7 percent tax is paid on sales, but all taxes paid on purchases from other firms are credited. What is the net tax paid at each stage, and what is total tax revenue?

(c)   Suppose that a value added tax of 7 percent is imposed. What is the tax liability at each stage, and what is total tax revenue?

(d)   What is the difference between the value added tax and the GST?

(e)   An alternative scheme is the MST. Suppose that this program must guarantee the same total tax yield ($700) as those in parts (a), (b), and (c). What is the required tax rate for the MST?

◆ ANSWERS

Multiple-Choice Questions

1. (b) 2. (e) 3. (c) 4. (c) 5. (c) 6. (a) 7. (c) 8. (d) 9. (a) 10. (c) 11. (a) 12. (b) 13. (b) 14. (d) 15. (e) 16. (b) 17. (c) 18. (d) 19. (e) 20. (d) 21. (d) 22. (a) 23. (c) 24. (e)

Exercises

1.   (a)   Tax A is proportional; tax B is regressive; tax C is progressive.
      (b)   The tax rates are 22 percent for $10,000, 23 percent for $20,000, 24 percent for $40,000, and 25.3 percent for $60,000. The tax system is slightly progressive.

2.   (a)   Column B: -$5,000; -$4,000; -$2,500; -$1,500; 0.
            Column C: $5,000; $6,000; $7,500; $8,500; $10,000.
      (b)   Marginal tax rate $= \dfrac{\Delta T}{\Delta Y} = \dfrac{43-15}{40}$ or $\dfrac{35}{50} = 0.70$.

3. (a) Situation (iii). Demand is very elastic, and the quantity demanded of accommodation would decline significantly with a small change in price.

    (b) The long-run supply curve is more elastic than the short-run supply curve. In the following graph, it is represented by the flatter curve S_L going through the initial equilibrium point. The tax shifts each supply curve uniformly upward by the same distance (e.g., t). The short-run equilibrium is E_S, and the long-run equilibrium is E_L. The price paid by consumers is therefore higher in the long run, and the quantity of accommodation is smaller. Thus in the long run when supply is more elastic, landlords can shift a greater share of the tax burden onto the shoulders of consumers.

Figure 22-4

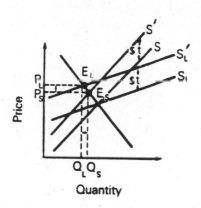

    (c) The first market situation. Demand is inelastic and does not respond significantly to the higher price.

    (d) In the short run, the landlord would shoulder all of the tax burden.

4. (a) (i) see graph; (ii) $4; (iii) $2; (iv) $1 = $3 - $2; (v) $1 = $4 - $3; (vi) $40.

    (b) (i) see graph; (ii) $4, (iii) $2; (iv) $1 – $3 - $2; (v) $1 = $4 - $3; (vi) $40.

    (c) No; in both cases firms and consumers share the burden of the tax equally.

Figure 22-5

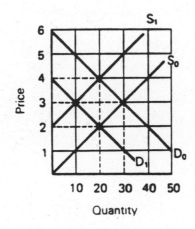

301

5. (a) It is imposed on sales of $10,000 at the retail level. Thus total tax revenue is $700.

   (b) Primary pays $70 = 0.07 x $1,000. Manufacturing pays $210 = (0.07 x $4,000) - $70. Wholesale pays $140 = (0.07 x $6,000) - $210 - $70. Finally, retail pays $280 = (0.07 x $10,000) - $140 - $210 - $70. Total tax revenue is $700 = $70 + $210 + $140 + $280.

   (c) Value added at the primary stage is $1,000, so tax payments are $70. At the manufacturing stage, value added is $3,000 (= $4,000 - $1,000), so taxes here are $210. The value added of wholesalers is $2,000, implying a tax liability of $140. Finally, the value added of retailers is $4,000, so tax payments at the retail level are $280. The total is $700.

   (d) There is no difference.

   (e) Sales of manufactured goods are $4,000, and the government must collect $700 in tax revenue. Thus the required MST rate is 17.5 percent [($700/$4,000) x 100 percent].

Chapter 23

Canadian Social Policy

◆ LEARNING OBJECTIVES

After studying this chapter, you should be able to:

✔   understand Canada's various social programs;

✔   appreciate the economic inefficiencies that are created by many well-intended policies;

✔   understand the relative impacts of tax credits and tax exemptions or deductions;

✔   be more conversant with the current debate surrounding reform of the unemployment insurance program;

✔   understand the issues regarding pensions and the expected economic effects of an aging population.

◆ HINTS AND TIPS

You might be guided by the fact that frequent errors on examinations are attributable to:

✔   an inadequate appreciation of the differences between a tax exemption and a tax credit.

◆ MULTIPLE-CHOICE QUESTIONS

1.   A demogrant is a social policy with
     (a)   an income-related eligibility criterion.
     (b)   an age or residence eligibility requirement.
     (c)   a specified length of employment as a qualifying criterion.
     (d)   eligibility conditional upon the demographics of the population.
     (e)   no eligibility requirement, in that it is given to all Canadians.

2.   A program such as the child tax exemption
      (a)   is an income-tested benefit.
      (b)   is known as a tax expenditure.
      (c)   is most beneficial to people with no taxable income.
      (d)   provides the same benefit to all similarly structured households, regardless of
             income.
      (e)   Both (b) and (c) are correct.

3.   Which of the following is *not* one of the major challenges that must be addressed by
      Canadian social policy in the upcoming decades?
      (a)   An increasing burden of child-related tax concessions as the average age of the
             population decreases.
      (b)   The burden of the deficit and debt on government expenditures.
      (c)   The requisite adjustments that must be made in Canada to an ever-changing inter-
             national market.
      (d)   The impact of an aging population on the health and pension systems.
      (e)   Both (a) and (b).

4.   Any effective reform of Canada's social programs necessitates federal-provincial coordi-
      nation for which for the following reasons?
      (a)   Many social policies have different regional impacts.
      (b)   Many federal and provincial programs overlap.
      (c)   Much of federal expenditure on social programs is in the form of transfers to the
             provinces.
      (d)   All of the above.
      (e)   None of the above.

5.   Among industrial nations, Canada allocates a below average share of its national income
      to social spending. One reason why this statistic may be misleading is that
      (a)   Canada has a smaller than average population.
      (b)   Canada has a relatively larger proportion of retirees who do not contribute to
             national income.
      (c)   it does not include tax expenditures, which play an important role in Canadian
             social programs.
      (d)   Canada's national income is small relative to that of most industrial nations, so
             we are less able to afford social programs.
      (e)   the relative costs of social program delivery in Canada are less than other indus-
             trialized nations.

6.   The implicit tax-back rate refers to the
      (a)   rate at which individuals must pay their taxes to the government.
      (b)   reduction in earned income due to income taxation.
      (c)   rate at which social benefits are reduced due to earned income.
      (d)   speed with which the government processes refunds on individuals' annual
             income tax statements.
      (e)   frequency with which employers must forward all employee tax withholdings to
             the government.

7. Because of "stacking," a low-income individual who is currently receiving social benefits and is considering earning additional income through part-time employment *may* face an effective marginal tax rate on the earned income
   (a) no higher than the explicit income tax rate.
   (b) no higher than the highest explicit marginal tax bracket in the country.
   (c) no higher than the value of social benefits received.
   (d) no higher than 100 percent, or all of earned income.
   (e) higher than 100 percent.

8. Which of the following is *not* a feature of universality in social programs?
   (a) Benefits are provided without a means test.
   (b) Recipients are made to feel demeaned.
   (c) Because the benefits are taxable, the net benefits are not universal.
   (d) Because a large number of people benefit from these programs, they are politically more difficult to dismantle.
   (e) They are not targeted at the poor.

9. Which of the following statements is a reasonable economic argument for some subsidization of postsecondary education?
   (a) All of the benefits of a university education accrue to the student in the form of a higher lifetime income.
   (b) It is vertically equitable that all taxpayers pay to educate individuals who will earn above average incomes.
   (c) Charging the full cost of education would deter many children from low income families from continuing their education.
   (d) There are external benefits to the entire nation from a better-educated population.
   (e) Both (c) and (d) are correct.

10. Which of the following is likely to occur if the qualification period for unemployment insurance were shortened to 10 weeks in some regions?
   (a) The scheme would tend to become a subsidy for seasonal employment.
   (b) Provincial and municipal governments would create make-work schemes that provide employment for 10 weeks.
   (c) The rate of labor turnover would increase.
   (d) Labor mobility towards occupations and locations with more stable employment prospects would be discouraged.
   (e) All of the above.

11. *All but which* of the following is a feature of Canada's unemployment insurance program?
   (a) It provides more extended benefits (i.e., shorter qualifying periods and longer weeks of benefits) in regions with above average unemployment rates.
   (b) It is one of the few programs in the world that provides benefits to those who voluntarily quit their jobs.
   (c) It provides incentives to relocate to areas with better employment prospects.
   (d) It provides extended coverage for individuals attending approved training courses.
   (e) It has been reformed to provide expanded parental and sickness benefits.

12. Which of the following has gained attention as a proposal for altering the financing of universities?
    (a) To substantially increase tuition fees for those programs that promise relatively higher private returns.
    (b) To introduce a voucher system.
    (c) To introduce a system of contingent student loans.
    (d) To charge relatively lower fees for those programs with greater external benefits.
    (e) All of the above.

13. An individual with a marginal tax rate of 25 percent would prefer a child tax credit of $200 to a child tax exemption up to
    (a) $25.   (b) $50.
    (c) $200.   (d) $800.
    (e) $1000.

14. Many of the proposals for reform of the family benefits program recommend an increasing role for child tax credits. One of the central problems with an increased reliance on the child tax credit is that
    (a) everyone receives the same after-tax benefit, regardless of income.
    (b) relative to other transfer mechanisms, it is very costly to administer.
    (c) it is paid once a year and based on last year's income, not current needs.
    (d) it does not contribute to horizontal equity.
    (e) it reduces a rich person's tax liability more than a poor person's.

15. The next few decades promise to be a time of difficulty for retirement schemes in Canada because
    (a) private pension plans are being replaced by government plans.
    (b) a greater proportion of the population will be retired, and a smaller proportion will be working.
    (c) more people are refusing to accept mandatory retirement at age 65.
    (d) the popularity of RRSPs has meant that there is less saving for retirement years.
    (e) Both (b) and (d) are correct.

16. "Vestibility" in a pension scheme means that
    (a) the pension contributions made by the employer belong to the employee.
    (b) the employee can change jobs without losing any benefits.
    (c) there is a minimum qualifying period of employment before an employee can join a pension plan.
    (d) the pension plan is fully indexed and protected from inflation.
    (e) the funds are invested in riskless, low-yield government bonds.

17. Which of the following is *not* true of Canadian benefit programs for the elderly?
    (a) Registered Retirement savings Plans are a means of deferring taxes to the retirement years when one's marginal tax rate may be lower.
    (b) The Canada Pension Plan is only paid to individuals who contributed to it during their working lives.
    (c) Old Age Security is paid to individuals over 65 years of age and making less than $25,000 per year.

(d)   The Guaranteed Income Supplement is paid to all Canadians over 65 years of age.

(e)   Both (c) and (d).

18.   The argument that medical doctors induce patient demand for their own services is based on

(a)   a system of per capitation payments.
(b)   a fee-for-service system.
(c)   the growing popularity of health maintenance organizations (HMOs).
(d)   intrinsic dishonesty on the part of many doctors.
(e)   the privatization of the health sector.

◆ EXERCISES

1.   (a)   Classify each of the following Canadian social programs as a demogrant (D) or income-tested (I).

	Class
Family allowance	_____
Unemployment insurance	_____
Old age security	_____
Pension income exemption	_____
Child tax exemption	_____
Canada Assistance Plan	_____
Child tax credit	_____
Age exemption	_____

(b)   Identify three of these social programs that contribute to horizontal equity.

2.   This exercise is designed to highlight the relative impacts on the distribution of income from child tax credits and child tax exemptions. Consider five families, each of which has two children of similar ages. The incomes of these families are listed in the following table, with the associated marginal tax rates.

Assume that each marginal tax rate applies to income brackets of $10,000, so that the first $10,000 earned is subject to a 10 percent tax, the next $10,000 earned is subject to a 20 percent tax, and so on. Thus, someone earning $20,000 must pay $3,000 in tax: $1,000 on the first $10,000 and $2,000 on the next $10,000.

Gross family income	Marginal tax rate (per $10,000 bracket)
$10,000	0.1
20,000	0.2
30,000	0.3
40,000	0.4
50,000	0.5

(a) Determine the after-tax income of each household prior to the introduction of any benefit program for families with children.

(b) Suppose the government introduces a child tax credit (CTC) equal to $1,000 per child. Suppose further that this credit is subject to a tax-back rate that depends on family income according to the following schedule:

Gross family income	Tax-back rate applied to CTC
up to $10,000	0.00
$10,001-$20,000	0.25
$20,001-$30,000	0.50
$30,001-$40,000	0.75
$40,001 and above	1.00

Determine the after-tax income of each of the five families.

(c) Instead of a child tax credit, suppose that government introduces a child tax exemption equal to $1,667 per child. Determine the after-tax income of each family.

(d) Contrast the effect of these two benefit programs on the distribution of income. Which better satisfies the objective of vertical equity?

(e) Compare the costs of these programs to the government in terms of forgone tax revenue.

◆ ANSWERS

Multiple-Choice Questions

1. (e) 2. (b) 3. (a) 4. (d) 5. (c) 6. (c) 7. (e) 8. (b) 9. (e) 10. (e) 11. (c) 12.(e) 13. (d) 14. (c) 15. (b) 16. (a) 17. (e) 18. (b)

Exercises

1. (a)

Family allowance	D
Unemployment insurance	I
Old age security	D
Pension income exemption	D
Child tax exemption	D
Canada Assistance Plan	I
Child tax credit	D
Age exemption	D

(b)   Family allowance, child tax exemption, and child tax credit.

2. (a) $9,000, $17,000, $24,000, $30,000, and $35,000.

(b)   Calculate: gross income - taxes + (2 x $1,000) (1 - tax-back rate), which yields $11,000, $18,500, $25,000, $30,500, and $35,000.

(c)   Each household's taxable income is now its gross income minus $3,334 (i.e., the exemption for two children). The resulting taxes payable are calculated by applying the marginal tax rates to the tax brackets for taxable income. Stated otherwise, relative to (a), each household's after-tax income increases by its marginal tax rate multiplied by $3,334. This yields $9,333, $17,667, $25,000, $31,334, and $36,667.

(d)   In going from a child tax credit in (b) to a child tax exemption in (c), the after-tax incomes of the two low-income households decrease, while those of the two higher-income households increase. Thus the child tax credit provides more vertical equity than the child tax exemption.

(e)   Each scheme costs $5,000 (ignoring the rounding error of $1).

PART SEVEN

INTERNATIONAL TRADE

Chapter 24

The Gains from Trade

◆ **LEARNING OBJECTIVES**

After studying this chapter, you should be able to:

✔ recognize that international trade among countries involves basically the same principles of exchange that apply to trade among individuals;

✔ realize that although gains from trade occur even when production is fixed, further gains arise when nations increase output of goods in which they have a comparative advantage;

✔ understand that comparative advantage arises from differences in the opportunity costs of producing particular goods;

✔ acknowledge that comparative advantage may be determined by natural resource endowments and climate but may also be determined dynamically by changing human skills and experience in production;

✔ explain that the terms of trade, defined as the ratio of export prices to import prices, indicate how the gains from trade are divided between buyers and sellers.

◆ **HINTS AND TIPS**

You might be guided by the fact that frequent errors on examinations are attributable to:

✔ confusion between absolute advantage and comparative advantage;

✔ the erroneous belief that absolute advantage is necessary for gains from trade.

◆ MULTIPLE-CHOICE QUESTIONS

1. Country X has an absolute advantage over country Y in the production of widgets if
    (a)   fewer resources are required in X to produce a given quantity of widgets than in Y.
    (b)   a given amount of resources in X produces more widgets than the same amount of resources in Y.
    (c)   relative to Y, more widgets can be produced in X with fewer resources.
    (d)   All of the above.
    (e)   None of the above.

2. If, given the same amount of inputs, Canadian farmers produce 2 tons of rice per acre while Japanese farmers produce 1 ton of rice per acre, we can be certain that
    (a)   Canada should export rice to Japan.
    (b)   Canada has a comparative advantage in rice production..
    (c)   Canada has an absolute advantage in rice production..
    (d)   Japanese rice farmers must be paid twice as much as Canadian farmers..
    (e)   Both (a) and (b) are correct.

3. Comparative advantage is said to exist whenever
    (a)   one country can produce a given level of output with fewer resources compared to another country.
    (b)   a given amount of resources produces more output in one country compared to another.
    (c)   one country has an absolute advantage over another country in the production of all goods.
    (d)   different countries have different opportunity costs in production.
    (e)   two countries are of different sizes.

4. If there are two countries A and B, and two goods X and Y, and if A has a comparative advantage in the production of X, it necessarily follows that
    (a)   A has an absolute advantage in the production of X.
    (b)   B has an absolute advantage in the production of X.
    (c)   A has a comparative disadvantage in the production of Y.
    (d)   B has an absolute advantage in the production of Y.
    (e)   B has a comparative disadvantage in the production of Y.

5. In a two-country and two-good model, gains from trade would not exist if
    (a)   one country had an absolute advantage in the production of both goods.
    (b)   a given amount of resources produced more of both goods in one country.
    (c)   one country was endowed with far more resources than the other.
    (d)   the countries had the same opportunity costs in the production of both goods.
    (e)   only one country had a comparative advantage in the production of one good.

6. Which of the following statements is not true about opportunity cost?
    (a)   Equal opportunity costs for pairs of commodities between two countries lead to gains from trade.
    (b)   Opportunity costs depend on relative production costs.
    (c)   Differences in opportunity costs across countries can enhance total output of both goods through trade and specialization.

(d)   Comparative advantage can be expressed in terms of opportunity costs.

(e)   Opportunity cost can be read as the slope of a tangent to a country's production possibility curve.

7.   If production of each unit of wool in country A implies that beef production must be decreased by four units, while in country B each additional unit of beef decreases wool output by four units, the gains from trade

(a)   are maximized if country A specializes in wool production and country B in beef.

(b)   are maximized if country A specializes in beef production and country B in wool.

(c)   are maximized if country A allocates 80 percent of its resources to wool and the remainder to beef, while country B does the opposite.

(d)   are maximized if country A allocates 20 percent of its resources to wool and the remainder to beef, while country B does the opposite.

(e)   cannot be realized because opportunity costs in the two countries are the same.

8.   Gains from specialization can arise when

(a)   countries have different opportunity costs in production.

(b)   there are economies of scale in production.

(c)   experience gained via specialization lowers cost through learning by doing.

(d)   comparative advantage is either nature-given or acquired.

(e)   All of the above.

9.   Free trade within the European Community led to

(a)   each member country specializing in specific products (e.g., furniture, cars, etc.).

(b)   a large increase in product differentiation, with countries tending to specialize in subproduct lines (e.g., office furniture, household furniture, etc.).

(c)   no perceptible alteration in production patterns.

(d)   less trade among EC members.

(c)   less product diversity.

10.   Economies of scale and learning by doing are different because

(a)   one refers to an increase in variable costs and the other to a decrease.

(b)   economies of scale refer to a movement along the average cost curve, whereas learning by doing shifts the average cost curve.

(c)   economies of scale affect variable costs, but learning by doing affects only fixed costs.

(d)   learning by doing affects profits but not costs.

(e)   economies of scale affect costs, whereas learning by doing affects revenue.

11.   The gains from specialization and trade depend on the pattern of _____ advantage, not _____ advantage.

(a)   absolute, comparative.

(b)   monetary, nonmonetary.

(c)   absolute, reciprocal.

(d)   comparative, absolute.

(e)   size, cost.

12. The terms of trade
    (a) refer to the quantity of imported goods that can be obtained for each unit of an exported good.
    (b) are measured by the ratio of the price of exports to the price of imports.
    (c) determine the division of the gains from trade.
    (d) All of the above.
    (e) None of the above.

13. A rise in export prices as compared to import prices is considered a favorable change in the terms of trade since
    (a) one can export more per unit of imported goods.
    (b) employment in export industries will increase.
    (c) one can acquire more imports per unit of exports.
    (d) total exports will increase.
    (e) All of the above.

14. By trading in international markets, countries
    (a) can consume beyond their production possibility boundary.
    (b) will always produce the same commodity bundle as before trade.
    (c) can produce outside of their production possibility boundary.
    (d) must choose one of the intercepts on the production possibility boundary, indicating complete specialization.
    (e) always produce and consume the same bundle of commodities.

Questions 15 to 18 refer to the data in the following table.

Country	One unit of resource can produce Lumber (bd m)	Aluminum (kg)
Australia	4	9
Canada	9	3
Brazil	3	2

15. Considering just Australia and Canada,
    (a) Australia has an absolute advantage in lumber.
    (b) Australia has an absolute advantage in aluminum.
    (c) There are no possible gains from trade.
    (d) Canada should specialize in aluminum production.
    (e) Australia has a comparative advantage in lumber.

16. Considering just Canada and Brazil,
    (a) Brazil has an absolute advantage in lumber.
    (b) Brazil has a comparative advantage in aluminum.
    (c) Canada has an absolute advantage in only one commodity.
    (d) There are no possible gains from trade.
    (e) None of the above.

17. In Australia, the opportunity cost of 1 board meter (bd m) of lumber is
    (a) 2.25 kg of aluminum.   (b) 0.44 kg of aluminum.
    (c) 0.36 kg of aluminum.   (d) 3.60 kg of aluminum.
    (e) 3.00 kg of aluminum.

18. In Canada, the opportunity cost of 1 kilogram of aluminum is
    (a) 0.33 bd m of lumber.   (b) 2.70 bd m of lumber.
    (c) 3.0 bd m of lumber.   (d) 3.33 bd m of lumber.
    (e) 1.50 bd m of lumber.

19. According to the Hecksher-Ohlin theory,
    (a) resource-rich countries benefit the most from trade.
    (b) different opportunity costs across countries can be explained by differences in factor endowments.
    (c) different opportunity costs across countries can be explained by differences in production functions.
    (d) low wage countries gain the most from trade.
    (e) countries with similar opportunity costs can gain the most from trade.

20. For a country with one important export commodity such as coffee or oil,
    (a) a rise in the commodity's price will improve the country's terms of trade.
    (b) a fall in the commodity's price is a favorable change in its terms of trade.
    (c) its terms of trade will improve only if it is able to increase the quantity of exports.
    (d) its terms of trade will improve only if world demand for its exports is inelastic.
    (e) its terms of trade improve only if the price of imports decrease.

21. The concept of dynamic comparative advantage is best characterized by
    (a) the importance of factor endowments in determining trade patterns.
    (b) changes in a country's terms of trade due to depletion of natural resources.
    (c) acquiring new areas of specialization through investment in human capital.
    (d) changes in a country's variable costs due to economies of scale.
    (e) Both (a) and (b) are correct.

◆ EXERCISES

1. For each of the situations described determine the opportunity costs of producing each good in each country, and indicate which commodity each country should specialize its production, and trade.

(a) One unit of resources can produce:

The opportunity costs are:

	Radios	Cameras		1 Radio	1 Camera
Japan	2	4	Japan	_____	_____
Korea	3	1	Korea	_____	_____

Japan should specialize in the production of _____.
Korea should specialize in the production of _____.

(b) One unit of resources can produce:

The opportunity costs are:

	Radios	Cameras		1 Radio	1 Camera
Japan	2	4	Japan	_____	_____
Korea	1	3	Korea	_____	_____

Japan should specialize in the production of _____.
Korea should specialize in the production of _____.

(c) One unit of resources can produce:

The opportunity costs are:

	Radios	Cameras		1 Radio	1 Camera
Japan	2	4	Japan	_____	_____
Korea	1	2	Korea	_____	_____

Japan should specialize in the production of _____.
Korea should specialize in the production of _____.

(d) Which case represents reciprocal absolute advantage?

(e) Which case demonstrates that absolute advantage is not a sufficient condition for trade to occur? Explain.

(f) Which case suggests why a nation as technologically advanced as Japan can gain from trading with other countries with lower wages? Explain.

318

2. Countries A and B each currently produce both watches and dairy products. Assume that country A gives up the opportunity to produce 100 pounds of dairy products for each watch it makes, and B could produce one watch at a cost of 200 pounds of dairy products.

(a) The opportunity cost of making watches (in terms of dairy products) is lower in country _____.

(b) The opportunity cost of making dairy products (in terms of watches) is lower in country _____.

(c) Country B should specialize in and let country A produce _____.

(d) The terms of trade (the price of one product in terms of the other) would be somewhere between _____ and _____ pounds of dairy products for one watch.

3. The following table provides data on the index of merchandise export prices and the index of merchandise import prices during the 1970s in Canada.

Year	Index of export prices	Index of import prices	Terms of trade
1970	100.6	98.6	_____
1972	103.3	102.3	_____
1974	157.1	135.6	_____
1976	176.6	157.9	_____
1978	205.4	200.7	_____

(a) Using the definition of the terms of trade that involves indexes, complete the table by calculating the terms of trade to one decimal place.

(b) What does an increase in the terms of trade signify?

(c) Would you classify the change in the terms of trade during the period 1972 to 1974 as favorable to Canada? Explain.

4. The following table provides data on the productivity of a single unit of resource in producing wheat and microchips in both Canada and Japan.

| | One unit of resource produces | |
	Wheat (t)	Microchips
Canada	50	20
Japan	2	12

(a)   Which country has an absolute advantage in the production of wheat? Of microchips?

(b)   What is the opportunity cost of producing a ton of wheat in Canada? In Japan?

(c)   Which country has a comparative advantage in the production of wheat? Of microchips?

(d)   Suppose that Canada is endowed with 2 units of this all-purpose resource while Japan is endowed with 10 units. Draw each country's production possibility boundary on the following grids.

Figure 24-1

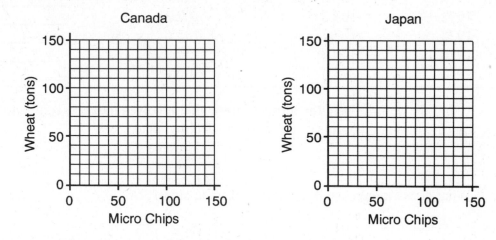

(e)   Suppose that prior to trade, each country allocated half of its resource endowment to production of each good. Indicate the production and consumption points of each country in the graphs (for simplicity, assume that these are the only two countries in the world).

(f)   What is world output of each good?

(g)   Indicate the production points of each country after trade, and determine world production levels.

320

(h) Suppose that the terms of trade are one microchip for one ton of wheat and that Canada consumes as much wheat after trade as it did before trade. Indicate the post-trade consumption points of each country and each country's imports and exports.

(i) If the terms of trade changed to two microchips for one ton of wheat, which country would benefit? Explain.

*5. The following graph depicts a country's production possibility curve between wool and lumber. Prior to trade, the country is producing and consuming at point R, which involves 10 units of wool and 10 units of lumber. Due to large increases in construction activity in this economy, the country now decides that it wishes to consume 14 units of lumber.

Figure 24-2

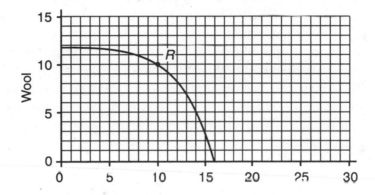

(a) How much wool must this country give up to obtain the additional four units of lumber in a no-trade environment. Explain.

(b) Suppose that the terms of trade in international markets are one unit of wool for two units of lumber. Assuming that production remains at R, how much wool would the country have to give up to obtain the additional four units of lumber if it engages in international trade? Explain.

◆ ANSWERS

Multiple-Choice Questions

1. (d) 2. (c) 3. (d) 4. (c) 5. (d) 6. (a) 7. (b) 8. (e) 9. (b) 10. (b) 11. (d) 12. (d) 13. (c)
14. (a) 15. (b) 16. (b) 17. (a) 18. (c) 19. (b) 20. (a) 21. (c)

Exercises

1.   (a)   Japan: 1 radio costs 2 cameras; 1 camera costs 1/2 radio.
    Korea: 1 radio costs 1/3 camera; 1 camera costs 3 radios.
    Japan should produce cameras. Korea should produce radios.

    (b)   Japan: 1 radio costs 2 cameras; 1 camera costs 1/2 radio.
    Korea: 1 radio costs 3 cameras; 1 camera costs 1/3 radio.
    Japan should produce radios. Korea should produce cameras.

    (c)   Japan: 1 radio costs 2 cameras; 1 camera costs 1/2 radio.
    Korea: 1 radio costs 2 cameras; 1 camera costs 1/2 radio.
    Japan should produce both and Korea should produce both. There would be no gains from trade.

    (d)   Case (a) represents reciprocal absolute advantage; Japan has an absolute advantage in cameras, and Korea has an absolute advantage in radios.

    (e)   Case (c) shows that even though Japan has an absolute advantage in producing both goods, no trade will occur because relative prices (or opportunity costs of production) are identical to those in Korea.

    (f)   Case (b) shows that even though Japanese workers are more productive in both industries (and therefore can expect to earn more than Korean workers), mutually beneficial trade can still occur if each country exports the good for which it has a comparative advantage.

2.   (a)   A.   (b)   B.
    (c)   dairy products, watches.   (d)   100, 200.

3.   (a)   102.0, 101.0, 115.9, 111.8, 102.3.

    (b)   An increase in the terms of trade means that fewer exports are required to pay for a given amount of imports.

    (c)   The terms of trade changed from 101.0 to 115.6; this was a favorable change in our terms of trade. It cost us fewer exports to buy the same imports, or for the same exports we received more imports.

4.   (a)   Canada has an absolute advantage in both goods.
    (b)   0.4, 6.0.
    (c)   Canada, Japan.
    (d)

Figure 24-3

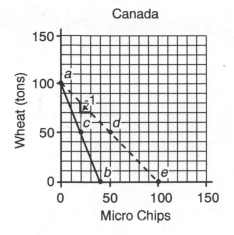

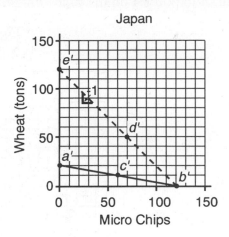

Canada's production possibility boundary is denoted *ab*, and Japan's is *a'b'*.

(e) Canada would be producing and consuming 50 tons of wheat and 20 microchips (point *c* in the diagram), and Japan would be producing and consuming 10 tons of wheat and 60 microchips (point *c'*).

(f) Assuming that these are the only countries making up the world, total output of wheat is 60 tons and world production of microchips is 80 units.

(g) Each country specializes in the commodity in which it has a comparative advantage. Thus Canada specializes completely in wheat production (see point *a*), and Japan specializes completely in microchip production (see point *b'*). World ouput is now 100 tons of wheat and 120 microchips.

(h) Terms of trade equal to one ton of wheat for one microchip mean that Canada can trade from its production point *a* to any point on its consumption possibility curve *ae* which has a slope of -1, representing the terms of trade. Similarly, Japan can trade from point *b'* to any point on its consumption possibility curve *b'e'*. Since it was assumed that Canada consumes the same amount of wheat both before and after trade, its consumption bundle is represented by point *d*, which contains 50 units of each good. Therefore, Canada is exporting 50 tons of wheat in return for imports of 50 microchips. Japan, having exported 50 microchips to Canada, has 70 remaining for its own consumption. When this is combined with its 50 tons of wheat imports, Japan consumes at point *d'*.

(i) The terms of trade lines in the graphs would become flatter with a slope of -1/2. Thus Canada's consumption possibilities would increase (the dashed line rotates outward on point *a*), while Japan's decrease (the dashed line rotates inward on point *b'*). Thus Canada would get a larger share of the gains from trade.

*5.   Five units. This requires a movement along the production possibility boundary from point *R* to point *A* on the following graph.

Figure 24-4

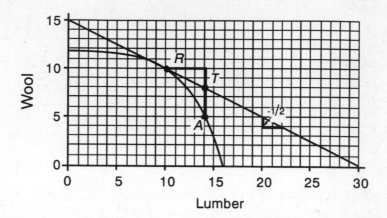

(b)   Two units. The terms of trade line has a slope of -1/2 and is tangent to the production possibility curve at *R*. Thus the economy can export two units of wool in return for imports of four units of lumber, this is represented by a movement from point *R* to point *T* on the graph.

Chapter 25

The Theory and Practice of Commercial Policy

◆ LEARNING OBJECTIVES

After studying this chapter, you should be able to:

✔ cite the benefits and costs of expanding international trade;

✔ understand how tariffs and quotas influence patterns of output and trade and affect a nation's standard of living;

✔ recognize fallacious arguments for free trade and for protection;

✔ understand trade policy remedies and procedures available in major trading countries;

✔ grasp issues under consideration in multilateral, regional, and bilateral trade negotiations;

✔ discuss the important highlights of the Free Trade Agreement and the early evidence of its impact on the Canadian economy, and;

✔ follow the debate on the North American Free Trade Agreement with the United States and Mexico.

◆ HINTS AND TIPS

You might be guided by the fact that frequent errors on examinations are attributable to:

✔ the mistaken belief that low wages necessarily imply comparative advantage;

✔ a lack of appreciation of the circumstances under which some degree of protectionism may benefit a nation.

◆ MULTIPLE-CHOICE QUESTIONS

1. Which of the following statements is *not* true of free trade?
   - (a) Free trade leads to a maximization of world output.
   - (b) Free trade maximizes world living standards.
   - (c) Free trade always makes each individual better off.
   - (d) Free trade can increase the average income in a country.
   - (e) Free trade encourages countries to specialize in production.

2. Which of the following trade practices is *not* specifically designed as a device to promote protectionism?
   - (a) Tariffs.
   - (b) Voluntary export restrictions.
   - (c) Countervailing duties.
   - (d) Import quotas.
   - (e) Costly customs procedures.

3. A central difference in the effects of a tariff and a voluntary export restriction (VER)—set at the same quantity as under the tariff—is that
   - (a) the VER yields a higher price for consumers than the tariff.
   - (b) the tariff pushes the consumer price beyond the price associated with the VER.
   - (c) government tariff revenue becomes suppliers' revenue with a VER.
   - (d) as the quantity sold decreases under the VER, the revenue of producers decreases.
   - (e) Both (a) and (c) are correct.

4. The infant industry argument for tariffs is
   - (a) only appropriate for industries where there are no economies of scale.
   - (b) an example of dynamic comparative advantage.
   - (c) theoretically valid if a new producer can sufficiently reduce average costs as output increases.
   - (d) a proposal to earmark tariff revenues to finance day care facilities.
   - (e) most applicable in developing countries because of their relative abundance of labor.

5. Which of the following national objectives is a valid argument for some degree of protectionism?
   - (a) Concentration of national resources in a few specialized products.
   - (b) Increases in average incomes.
   - (c) Diversification of a small economy in order to reduce the risk associated with cyclical fluctuations in price.
   - (d) Ability of domestic firms to operate at minimum efficient scale.
   - (e) Maximization of the national standard of living.

6. Protection against low-wage foreign labor is a fallacious protectionist argument because
   - (a) free trade benefits everyone.
   - (b) the gains from trade depend on comparative, not absolute, advantage.
   - (c) when the foreign country increases its exports to us, their wages will rise.
   - (d) the terms of trade will equalize for low- and high-wage countries.
   - (e) low-wage laborers are necessarily less productive.

7.	A large country, accounting for a significant share of world demand for an imported product, can increase its national income by
	(a)	encouraging domestic production.
	(b)	restricting domestic demand for the product, thereby decreasing its price and improving the terms of trade.
	(c)	imposing import quotas on the product.
	(d)	subsidizing imports of the good and thereby monopolize world consumption.
	(e)	negotiating voluntary export restrictions.

8.	If the objective of a government is to maximize national income, which of the following is the *least* valid reason for using tariff protection?
	(a)	To protect against unfair subsidization of foreign firms by their governments.
	(b)	To protect against unfair low wages paid to foreign labor.
	(c)	To protect newly developing industries.
	(d)	To protect against "dumping" of foreign-produced goods.
	(e)	To alter the terms of trade.

9.	Countervailing duties are attempts to maintain "a level playing ground" by
	(a)	retaliating against foreign tariffs.
	(b)	raising or lowering tariffs multilaterally.
	(c)	establishing a common tariff wall around a customs union.
	(d)	assessing tariffs that will offset foreign government subsidies.
	(e)	subsidizing exports.

10.	Strategic trade policy
	(a)	involves government assistance for key growth industries by protecting domestic markets and/or providing subsidies.
	(b)	involves erecting higher tariff and nontariff barriers across the board to protect domestic industry.
	(c)	means that the government negotiates special trade agreements with its important defense partners.
	(d)	is designed to encourage the migration of certain industries to other countries so as better to exploit domestic comparative advantage.
	(e)	attempts to encourage investment for domestic production in those markets that a country currently imports.

11.	Which of the following is *not* a fallacious protectionist argument?
	(a)	Buy Canadian, and both the money and the goods stay at home.
	(b)	Trade cannot be mutually advantageous if one of the trading partners is much larger than the other.
	(c)	Too many imports lower Canadian living standards as our money is shipped abroad.
	(d)	A foreign firm, temporarily selling in Canada at a much lower price than in its own country, threatens the Canadian industry's existence.
	(e)	A high wage country such as Canada cannot effectively compete with a low wage country such as Mexico.

12. The problem with restricting imports as a means of reducing domestic unemployment is that
    (a)   it merely redistributes unemployment from import-competing industries to our export industries when trading partners retaliate.
    (b)   Canadians would rather do without than have to buy Canadian-produced goods.
    (c)   our import-competing industries are not labor-intensive.
    (d)   our import-competing industries are always fully employed.
    (e)   Both (c) and (d) are correct.

13. Which of the following statements about nontariff barriers to trade (NTBs) is *incorrect*?
    (a)   The use of NTBs has declined worldwide since the mid 1930s.
    (b)   The misuse of antidumping and countervailing duties unilaterally constitutes an increasingly important NTB.
    (c)   Voluntary export restraints, negotiated agreements, and quotas are examples of NTBs.
    (d)   Most NTBs are ostensibly levied for trade relief purposes but end up being protectionist.
    (e)   Environmental and labor standards can be used as disguised NTB's.

14. Which of the following motivations for dumping can be of permanent benefit to the buying country?
    (a)   Predatory pricing.
    (b)   Cyclical stabilization of sales.
    (c)   Enabling foreign producers to achieve lower average costs and therefore price.
    (d)   Altering the terms of trade.
    (e)   All of the above.

15. Although the Kennedy and Tokyo rounds of GATT each reduced tariffs by about a third, it gives a misleading picture of the change in the freedom of trade because
    (a)   countries trade less than they used to.
    (b)   the use of nontariff barriers to trade has grown.
    (c)   most countries simply replaced their tariffs with import taxes.
    (d)   many countries simply imposed countervailing duties.
    (e)   very few industrialized countries are members of the GATT.

16. The "staples thesis" of Professor Innis states that
    (a)   the goods that Canada imports and exports are complementary or, in his words, "stapled together"
    (b)   it is small, inexpensive items such as staples and toothpicks that spur the Canadian export sector.
    (c)   Canadian economic growth has been tied to a sequence of exports of primary products.
    (d)   Canadian economic growth has been tied to a sequence of exports of manufactured products.
    (e)   Canadian economic growth has been hindered by trade.

17. The central trade feature of Sir John A. MacDonald's National Policy in 1878 was
    (a)   bilateral tariff reductions with the United States.
    (b)   a treaty with the United States that permitted all primary products to cross the border free of any tariff burden.

(c)   Canada's entry as a full partner in GATT.
(d)   increased tariff protection for Canadian manufacturing.
(e)   Both (c) and (d).

18.   The primary effect on Canadian industry from the GATT trade liberalization in the 1970s and 1980s has been
(a)   the total elimination of certain industries.
(b)   an increase in intra-industry trade, with firms reducing the number of product lines.
(c)   an increase in the number of industries in Canada.
(d)   large increases in imports and substantial reductions in exports.
(e)   large increases in exports and substantial reductions in imports.

19.   The countries in a free trade area
(a)   impose no tariffs on each other's goods.
(b)   each have an independent tariff structure with the rest of the world.
(c)   do not permit the free movement of labor across their borders.
(d)   do not have a common monetary policy.
(e)   All of the above.

20.   Which of the following is *not* one of the features of the Canada-United States Free Trade Agreement (FTA)?
(a)   Elimination of all tariffs within 10 years.
(b)   Elimination of countervailing duties between the two countries.
(c)   Exemption of cultural industries.
(d)   Continuance of quotas to support provincial supply management schemes.
(e)   Provision for national treatment for most service industries.

21.   The principle of national treatment that is embedded in the FTA means that Canada could, for example, introduce any product standards it likes, so long as
(a)   they apply only to Canadian-produced goods.
(b)   the standards are no more stringent than those existing in the United States.
(c)   they apply equally to Canadian- and American-produced goods sold in Canada.
(d)   they apply only to Canadian exports.
(e)   they apply only to Canadian imports.

22.   Which of the following is not an argument that was put forward by Canadian supporters of the FTA?
(a)   The FTA will help Canadian firms to more fully exploit economies of scale.
(b)   The FTA will provide Canadian firms with a more secured access to American markets.
(c)   The FTA will force a harmonization of Canadian social policies with those of the United States.
(d)   The FTA is simply a continuation of Canadian trade liberalization trend that began in 1935.
(e)   The FTA will increase the standard of living in Canada.

23.   A major effect of a tariff is to
(a)   redistribute income from consumers to domestic producers and the government.
(b)   allow consumers to benefit at the expense of domestic producers.

329

(c) discourage domestic production.

(d) encourage consumers to buy more of the good.

(e) reduce government revenues.

24. Which of the following was *not* a key issue in the Uruguay Round of GATT negotiations?

(a) Trade liberalization in services.

(b) Growth in the use of nontariff barriers to trade.

(c) Subsidization of domestic agriculture production.

(d) Copyright protection for intellectual property.

(e) Monetary policies that maintain the domestic currency at a favourable exchange rate.

25. A free trade agreement

(a) must include rules of origin.

(b) eliminates the need for customs controls on the movement of goods.

(c) allows for free cross-border movement of labor.

(d) erects a common tariff wall against nonmember countries.

(e) Both (a) and (d) are correct.

26. Which of the following is *not* true of The North American Free trade Agreement (NAFTA)?

(a) It will raise tariffs in Canada, Mexico and the United States against all other countries.

(b) A prime reason for Canada's participation is avoidance of the hub and spoke effect.

(c) It increases the difficulty for a member country to import (e.g., textiles) from a nonmember and then re-export to another member country.

(d) Includes an accession clause whereby other countries may join.

(e) It reduces barriers to trade in goods and services among member countries.

◆ EXERCISES

1. (a) The three graphs illustrate the demand and supply of an imported commodity Z in a free trade environment. Revise these graphs according to the protectionist policy outlined below each, and indicate the new price as P^* and the new quantity as Q^*.

Figure 25-1

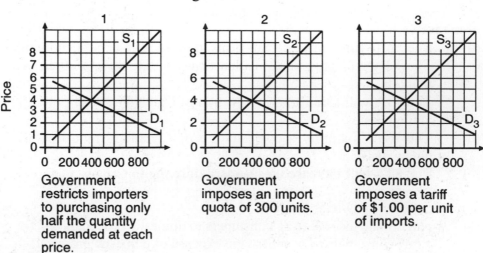

Government restricts importers to purchasing only half the quantity demanded at each price.

Government imposes an import quota of 300 units.

Government imposes a tariff of $1.00 per unit of imports.

(b)   If the demand for Z were highly inelastic, which policy would the government likely *not* choose if it wanted to maximize its restriction on the amount of the import purchased? Why?

(c)   Which policy would the government likely choose if it were concerned that protectionist policies might be inflationary? Why?

2.   Consider the market for canned tuna (assume all canned tuna is homogeneous). The foreign supply curve (S_f) is horizontal, which implies that Canada accounts for a relatively small share of the world market and any change in Canadian purchases does not affect world prices.

Figure 25-2

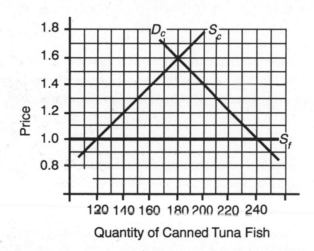

(a)   Under free trade, what is the quantity of tuna consumed in Canada, the quantity supplied by Canadian producers, and the quantity supplied by foreign producers?

(b)   If a 20 percent tariff is imposed, by how many cents does the foreign supply curve shift upward? Draw the new foreign supply curve, and calculate the consequent changes in domestic consumption, domestic production, and imports. Why is the change in imports greater than the change in domestic production?

(c)   If the government wants to ensure that domestic production rises to 160, how large a quota for imported tuna should it allow? Explain.

3. The following graph depicts the demand and supply curves for an imported good. D_C represents demand in Canada, and S_f represents foreign supply.

Figure 25-3

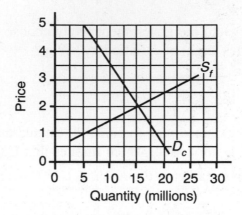

(a) What are equilibrium price and quantity and the total revenue of foreign firms?

(b) Suppose that the government imposes a specific tariff on this commodity equal to $2 per unit. What are the resulting equilibrium price Canadian consumers pay and the quantity they import? Illustrate this on the graph.

(c) What are the revenues of foreign firms and the Canadian government?

(d) Instead of the tariff, suppose that the Canadian government imposed an import quota on this good equal to 10 million units. What is the new supply curve that Canadian consumers effectively face?

(e) What would be the resulting market price and revenue of both foreign firms and the government under the quota scheme?

*4. The following graph illustrates the domestic supply of steel (S_D), the foreign supply of steel (S_F), and the domestic demand (D).

(a) Draw the total supply curve for steel and establish the overall price (P_0).

332

Figure 25-4

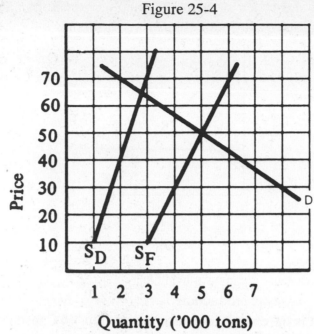

Quantity ('000 tons)

(b)   What is the level of Canadian consumption, and how much of this is due to imports and how much to domestic production?

(c)   The domestic government now levies a tariff of $20 per ton on steel from foreign suppliers. Using a broken line, draw the after-tariff supply curve for foreigners and the new total supply curve. Label the new price and quantity P_1 and Q_1, respectively.

(d)   What effect has the tariff had on imports and domestic production?

-*5.   This exercise on the efficiency gain from free trade examines the impact on consumers' and producers' surplus in moving from a no-trade situation to free trade for an imported good and then an exported good (the same analysis can be applied to the removal or reduction of tariffs). In what follows, assume that Canadian demand is a small part of world demand so that the world price P_W is independent of both Canadian demand D_C and supply S_C. Thus foreign supply is perfectly elastic at P_W. In the no-trade situation, the equilibrium price and quantity are P_E and Q_E.

(a)   In the following graph, P_W is less than P_E, so trade will result in imports of this good.

Figure 25-5

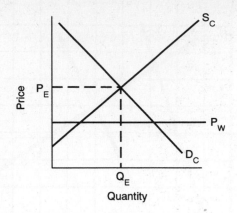

Once trade is permitted,
      (i)   label domestic consumption D_D.
      (ii)   label domestic production S_D.
      (iii)   What is the change in consumers' surplus in Canada?

      (iv)   What is the change in producers' surplus of Canadian firms?

      (v)   Is the net change in total surplus for Canada positive or negative?

(b)   In this graph, P_W is greater than P_E, so trade will result in exports of this commodity.

Figure 25-6

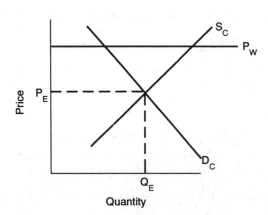

Once trade is permitted,
      (i)   label domestic consumption D_D.
      (ii)   label domestic production S_D.

(iii)   What is the change in consumers' surplus in Canada?

(iv)   What is the change in producers' surplus of Canadian firms?

(v)   Is the net change in total surplus for Canada positive or negative?

◆ ANSWERS

Multiple-Choice Questions

1. (c) 2. (c) 3. (c) 4. (c) 5. (c) 6. (b) 7. (b) 8. (b) 9. (d) 10. (a) 11. (d) 12. (a) 13. (a) 14. (c)
15. (b) 16. (c) 17. (d) 18. (b) 19. (e) 20. (b) 21. (c) 22. (c) 23. (a) 24. (e) 25. (a) 26. (a)

Exercises

1.   (a)

Figure 25-7

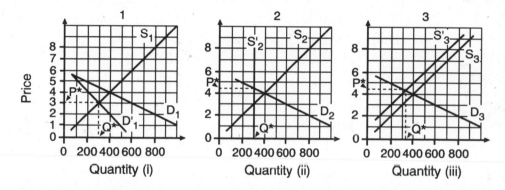

(b)   It would not choose the tariff policy. Price would rise by almost the full amount of the tariff, and there would be little change in equilibrium quantity.

(c)   Policy (i): A restriction on demand not only reduces imports but also lowers the price.

2.   (a)   Canadian production is 120, Canadian consumption is 240, and imports are 120.
    (b)   The foreign supply curve shifts upward by 20 cents. Domestic production rises by 20, domestic consumption falls by 20, and imports fall by 40. Imports fall by more than domestic production rises due to the decline in total quantity demanded.
    (c)   At a price of $1.40, domestic production rises to 160, and domestic consumption falls to 200. The government can allow imports of 40 if this is to be an equilibrium position.

3. (a) $2, 15 million units, and $30 million, respectively.
    (b) $3.50 and 10 million units, respectively.

Figure 25-8

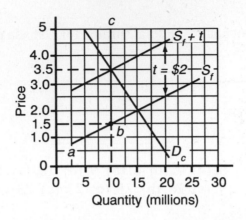

    (c) Canadian consumers pay $3.50 per unit, of which $2 goes to the government. Therefore, government tariff revenue is $20 million and that of foreign firms is $15 million.
    (d) The new effective supply curve is labeled *abc* in the graph.
    (e) The price per unit is $3.50, revenue of foreign firms equals $35 million, and, since there is no tariff, government revenue is zero.

*4. (a) and (c)

Figure 25-9

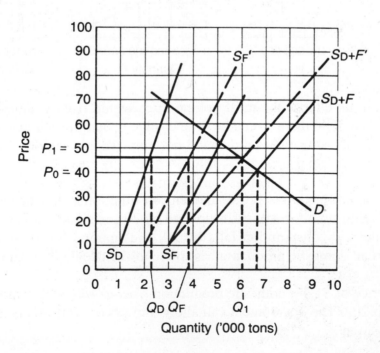

    (b) Approximately 6,500 tons are consumed, of which 4,500 are imported and 2,000 are produced domestically.

336

(d)   The tariff forces a reduction in the quantity supplied by foreign producers (i.e., imports) to Q_F and an increase in the quantity supplied by domestic producers to Q_D.

*5.   (a)   (i) and (ii)

Figure 25-10

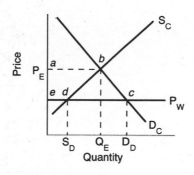

(iii)   Canadian consumers' surplus increases by area *abce*.
(iv)   Canadian producers' surplus decreases by area *abde*.
(v)   Positive. The increase in consumers' surplus outweighs the loss in producers' surplus; Canada receives a net gain in efficiency equal to area *bcd*.

(b)   (i) and (ii)

Figure 25-11

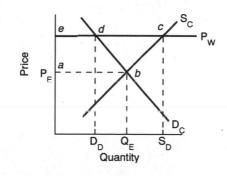

(iii)   Canadian consumers' surplus decreases by area *abde*.
(iv)   Canadian producers' surplus increases by area *abce*.
(v)   Positive. The increase in producers' surplus outweighs the loss in consumers' surplus; Canada receives a net gain in efficiency equal to area *bcd*.

NOTES

NOTES

NOTES

NOTES

NOTES

NOTES